Word Recognition and Vocabulary

Understanding Strategies

for Literacy Success

Word Recognition and Vocabulary

Understanding Strategies

for Literacy Success

Richard Sinatra
St. John's University

Christopher-Gordon Publishers, Inc.
Norwood, Massachusetts

Credits

Every effort has been made to contact copyright holders for permission to reproduce borrowed material where necessary. We apologize for any oversights and would be happy to rectify them in future printings.

Excerpt from *Stages of Reading Development* 2nd edition by CHALL/CHALL/chall. © 1996. Reprinted with permission of Wadsworth, a division of Thomson Learning: www.thomsonrights.com. Fax 800-730-2215.

Excerpt from *The Benchmark Program* reprinted by permission of Irene Gaskins, The Benchmark School, Media, PA.

Crossword Puzzle and Word Search created with Puzzlemaker on DiscoverySchool.com.

Student work used with permission.

Christopher-Gordon Publishers, Inc.
1502 Providence Highway, Suite #12
Norwood, Massachusetts 02062
800-934-8322
781-762-5577

Printed in the United State of America
10 9 8 7 6 5 4 3 2 1   07 06 05 04 03

ISBN: 1-929024-59-2
Library of Congress Catalogue Number: 2002116083

For Marco, Cosima, and Ricardo,

who helped me "skibble" this book.

Table of Contents

List of Figures and Tables ix

Acknowledgments xi

Introduction xiii

Chapter 1: Exploring the World of Words 1
  Connecting Words to the Environment 2
  Words and Their Properties 12
  The Language of Words 17
  Concept Words and Terms 26
  Word Challenge for Teachers: Word Search 26

**Chapter 2: Systems Influencing the Teaching
    of Written Words** 29
  Understanding the Alphabetic Principle 30
  The Visual and Auditory Components of Sounding Out 31
  Controlling the Words Children Learn 37
  The Constructivist View of Learning 40
  Toward a Balance of the Whole and Its Parts 44
  Upsetting the Balance 49
  Summary 50
  Concept Words and Terms 50
  Word Challenge for Teachers: Crossword Puzzle 51

Chapter 3: Pathways to Word Identification 53
  The Appeal of Phonics Instruction 54
  Phonics and Word Attack Approaches: To What Depth? 56
  Two Major Variations in Traditional Phonics 59
  The Word Family and Analogy Approach 65
  Other Approaches to the Alphabetic Principle 70
  When Spelling Occurs 78
  Summary 82
  Concept Words and Terms 85
  Word Challenge for Teachers: Tic-Tac-Toe Synonym 85

Chapter 4: How the Written Language System Works 87
  It's What's in the Head 88
  Oral and Written Language Distinctions 91
  Cues Available to Readers in Written Texts 93
  The Importance of Automatic Word Reading 101

Summary 104
Concept Words and Terms 105
Word Challenge for Teachers: The Classification
        Concept Map 105

Chapter 5: The Natural Way to Word Reading 107
Talk Language and Book Language 108
Reading Aloud: A Natural Bridge to the World of
        Print and Written Discourse 110
Getting Ready for Reading and Writing 112
Let Us Not Forget Artistic Representation 121
Building Word Reading—Naturally 123
The Language Experience Approach 125
When the Visual and Auditory Routes to Word
        Reading Are Not Enough 134
Banking One's Word Capital 139
The Retelling Strategy 141
Summary 147
Concept Words and Terms 149
Word Challenge for Teachers: The Word Structure Map 149

Chapter 6: Building a Meaning Vocabulary 151
Vocabulary Development in the Classroom Context 152
Classroom Instruction in the Understanding
        and Use of New Vocabulary 154
Developing Reading and Thinking Strategies
        for Student Transfer 170
Independent Activity Resulting in Incidental
        Vocabulary Learning 179
Summary and Conclusion 183
Concept Words and Terms 184
Word Challenge for Teachers: Semantic Feature Analysis 185

Appendixes
A: Answer Keys 187
B: Retold Books 191
C: Concept-Level Relations Taxonomy; Nine Levels 200
D: Concept-Level Relations Activities; Specific Activities 206
E: Word Parts; Prefixes, Roots, and Suffixes 214
F: Word Building Activities 219

Children's Literature Resources 225

References 225

About the Author.. 233

Index 235

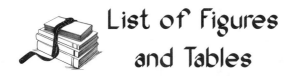 List of Figures
and Tables

Figures

Figure 1-1.   Word Formation and Operations in the
English Language System 15

Figure 1-2.   The Properties of Words 17

Figure 1-3.   Word Recognition and Vocabulary
Understanding in the Written Language 24

Figure 2-1.   The Process of Sounding Out 36

Figure 3-1.   The Process of Writing It Out 79

Figure 3-2.   Pathways to Word Identification 84

Figure 4-1.   How the Cue Systems of Written Language
Influence Readers 99

Figure 5-1.   How Reading Aloud Influences Language
Processing 112

Figure 5-2.   Labeling the Known 119

Figure 5-3.   Learning to Read the Words of the Language
Experience Story 130

Figure 5-4.   Children Scrolling Their Language Experience
or Retold Stories in a Movie Format for Their
Classmates to Read and Enjoy 131

Figure 6-1.   Ways of Developing a Meaning Vocabulary 155

Figure 6-2.   A Concept Map Showing the Major Vocabulary
Used to Describe the People and Customs of
Feudal Times, or the Middle Ages 164

Figure 6-3.   Causal Relationship of Word Reading, Word
Understanding, and Transfer of Learning 182

Figure B-1.   Accordion Book 191

Figure B-2.   Character Development Book 191

Figure B-3.   Circle Story Book 192

Figure B-4.   Create-a-Book 192

Figure B-5.   Finger Puppet Stories 193

Figure B-6.   Flip Book 194

Figure B-7.   Flip-Flop Book 195

Figure B-8.   Fold-a-Book 196

Figure B-9.   Mobile Book 196

Figure B-10.   Pop-Up Book 197

Figure B-11.   Scroll Story Books (2) 198

Figure B-12.   Shape Book 199

Figure F-1.   Pack-a-Word (Sample) 219

Figure F-2.   Pack-a-Word (Blank) 219

Figure F-3.   A Handful of Words (Sample) 220

Figure F-4.   A Handful of Words (Blank) 220

Figure F-5.   Hinge-a-Word (Sample) 221

Figure F-6.   Hinge-a-Word (Blank) 221

Figure F-7.   Unlock-the-Word 222

Figure F-8.   Leaving Words (Sample) 223

Figure F-9.   Leaving Words (Blank) 224

Tables

Table 1-1.   The Language of Words 25

Table 3-1.   A 10-Step Phonic Element Lesson, Using
                 /oo/ as in *Moon* to Illustrate 62

Table 3-2.   The 37 Phonograms 66

Table 3-3.   Pattern Boxes 67

Table 3-4.   A Letter-Pattern Approach Based on Vowel
                 Rules and the Alphabetic Principle 73

Table 3-5.   Long-Vowel Pattern Boxes 74

Table 4-1.   The Cue Systems of Written Language
                 and Their Features 94

Table 6-1.   Vocabulary Taught Through Classroom
                 Lessons Having an Experimental Base 158

Table 6-2.   How Did Dinosaurs Get Their Names? 174

Table 6-3.   Making Intelligent Guesses About Words 178

Table E-1.   Common Prefixes and Their Meanings 215

Table E-2.   Common Roots and Their Meanings 216

Table E-3.   Common Suffixes and Their Meanings 217

Table E-4.   Suffixes That Identify Parts of Speech 218

Acknowledgments

Many of the word learning beliefs and experiences I share in this book come from my literacy encounters with children, teachers, and professional colleagues. I wish to thank all those children and teachers who helped me to grow over the years as we worked on developmental and professional literacy skills. These experiences remained in my mind's eye as I wrote about different word recognition and vocabulary development strategies and activities.

I also wish to thank my colleagues, secretarial staff, and student assistants at St. John's University. They aided me greatly in the development of this book. Often, after I "bent the ears" of the literary faculty while reading excerpts from the manuscript, they offered rewarding and positive feedback. The entire production of the manuscript would not have been possible without the faithful work of our department secretary, Ann DePaulis, whose eyesight and fingers were undoubtedly tortured by the scribbling, the margin instructions, and constant revisions. Special thanks go to three of our department's graduate assistants: Kathleen Miller, for the preparation of the artwork and drawings that accompany many of the activities; Maria Amodio, for setting up the reference section; and Marie Dolce, for careful proofreading and editing suggestions. I'm also indebted to two talented undergraduate students on work-study scholarships. Kwok-Fan Chow executed all the figures and charts and designed them to fit the text specifications. Kamille James ensured that all text references were in correct manuscript and style format.

Finally, I wish to thank my wife, Camille Sinatra, who respected the quiet time when I did my "scribbling."

Introduction

This is a book about words—how they are shaped, nourished, learned, and taught, both at home and in the classroom. Having been a classroom teacher and literacy educator for more than 40 years, I am continually awed by the difference in children's abilities to learn words. To see how important words are today, even single words, one just has to look at and listen to TV commercials, where words are used to capture our attention and imagination. Many think, and rightly so, that there are many other aspects of language and literacy development beyond the mere acquisition of words. For written literacy proficiency there are such issues as comprehending, composing, predicting, confirming, and transferring to other literacy modes such as writing, artwork, and computers. At the center of all these human competencies is the ability to understand, read, and write words. It becomes a very simple issue when dealing with print resources; one has to read and understand the words so that one can "get it" and move on with logical thought processes.

In this book, I have attempted to coordinate the science of word learning with strategies and techniques in both the oral and printed languages. The science tells us that words are composed of sound "bites," letter names, understandable and movable parts, and that they have inherent meaning, which is often altered by the ever evolving culture of which words are a part. Depending on one's view of how children should learn to read and write words, one seeks support from the science and the research conducted on words for using particular word learning methodologies and techniques over others. Accordingly, I've attempted to explain the rationale for using sound-symbol or phonics approaches to word recognition, for using whole-word recognition techniques in making rapid meaning associations, and for using ways to manipulate word parts, or *morphemes*, to learn how words are formed. Also, because major distinctions occur between word learning through the oral and written languages, I explain the differences in learning words through each mode and how word recognition of familiar words involves different learning processes than print recognition of new vocabulary words.

Particular chapters focus on these distinctions in word learning and vocabulary development. Chapters 1, 2, and 4 examine the scientific, research-based, and cultural influences of word learning and how they affect success and achievement in both the oral and written languages. The reader will sense that word recognition and word reading of words already known in the oral language require different learning strategies than the mastery of words that are unfamiliar in the oral language but soon to be the new vocabulary encountered in school and in informational and literary readings. Chapter 3 presents a number of ways that sound-symbol relationships to word learning can be taught consistent with the alphabetic principle. These include, among others, examination of systematic phonics approaches, word family and analogy approaches, and inventive or creative spelling. Chapter 5 presents another means by which to achieve recognition of words in print rather than focusing on sound and letter correspondences. Chapter 5 suggests that through particular strategies and activities, word reading can be achieved naturally by using the language of talk and authors as the springboard for the language of reading and writing. Finally, Chapter 6 examines major ways that teachers can show students how to expand their meaning and reading vocabularies. The chapter presents the following three broad but mutually reinforcing components: (a) what the teacher does directly in the classroom through five comprehensive strategies to teach the meanings of new words in print situations; (b) what the teacher illustrates as transfer strategies so that students learn the reading and thinking skills to figure out new word meanings on their own; and (c) what students accomplish in and out of school during recreational, personal, and informational reading.

While discussing these various ways to learn words, I have drawn upon my own life experiences as a teacher. I present what I have actually done with children, those who were competent with reading and writing and those who found the experience troubling. I also present the strategies that practicing teachers have used in their successful work with children. In explaining these efforts, I have tried to show best practices, those that have been "tried and true" with various populations in word recognition and vocabulary acquisition achievement. Pictures show actual student work of these best practices. Procedural steps of how to accomplish "tried and true" word recognition and vocabulary development lessons are spelled out. Many figures and illustrations are included so that teachers will have practical suggestions to follow in their own word building and vocabulary development work with children. Each chapter contains a list of concept words and terms, and these are boldfaced on first reference.

At the end of each chapter, I offer an activity called "Word Challenge for Teachers" as a way to model different activity suggestions for using new words in print contexts. Each activity works in two ways. First, it provides a concrete way for you, as the reader, to have fun with the new words and concept terms introduced in the chapter. Second, each activity provides a model for you to use when you set up vocabulary enrichment activities for your own students. Answer keys are provided in Appendix A. As you use the new concept words and terms of the chapter in a particular activity, you will be able to transfer the activity format in a practical way for children to use when they are learning their own new vocabulary words.

In a sense, all adults and children are on a continuum of emerging into word reading and vocabulary understanding proficiency. Does any one person know all the words in their language, especially those words that will be found in literary and informational sources? Quite predictably, the closer a child comes to the reading experience, the more likely that new vocabulary words will enter his or her visual and mental landscape. This is due to the fact that through reading, more varied, rich, and unusual words will be encountered than through the oral language. The book presents to teachers at all levels of the teaching continuum procedures and suggestions that can be used in the classroom or at home for increasing word recognition and vocabulary development to enrich children's literary lives.

Exploring the World of Words

Focus Questions

1. Why is good old-fashioned play so important for young children, and what is the important relationship between play and talk?
2. Can you think of four major properties of words and how these properties may influence children to learn words in different ways?
3. Why are the rules of morphology—the understanding of morphemes and how morphemes are joined—so important for the teacher or parents of children who are learning new words?
4. Can you name some ways in which educators and linguists might classify words?
5. How is the reading of a word known in the oral language somewhat different from the learning and reading of a word not known in the oral language or life experiences?

Words are a fascinating subject. They are at the center of our lives. As children, students, parents, teachers, and caregivers, we use words to express our thoughts and feelings and influence the activity of others. People know and judge us by our use of words. Because of this, there is a mission entrusted to those who raise and educate children and youth during their school years. These adults help to shape and nurture both the words children learn and the means by which they can continue to learn more words.

We use words to tell about other words. In a sense, words heard and expressed in the oral language and words read and written in the printed language help to beget more words. That is the power of the process. Once the newborn child hears words and begins to respond to them, it's like sprinkling water on a germinating seed. The seed takes the water in and needs more to continue adequate growth, and as the seed matures, the intake of nourishment increases to sustain growth. Likewise, both with the oral and written languages, once the first words of talking, reading, and writing begin, there is no end to the potential nourishment and growth a child can sustain.

In this first chapter we will look at the way in which words are born, shaped, and nourished as children interact with one another and the adult community. We will discover that this topic of how and why children talk and communicate is critical to the beliefs of several renowned psychologists who have strongly influenced the climate of modern education. We will then look at the way in which words are perceived and used by those in the educational community and by those who study the nature of words. This discussion will assist both beginning and veteran teachers to help them see the overall picture of the "world of words" and to note the particular way that words and phrases are used with children as they engage in the oral and written language acquisition process. Teachers will be able to communicate this knowledge effectively with parents to help them realize the important roles they have in their children's word learning development and how the home environment they foster nourishes success with the printed forms of literacy.

Connecting Words to the Environment

We know that children are born with sensory, perceptual, and cognitive capacities that allow word understandings and language to flourish. In a sense, children are wired to listen, to talk, and to learn through talk situations. There's more, however. There's the eye traffic reaching the brain. While the neural pathways are being formed for the understanding of talk language to occur, the young child is also a very active viewer and visual explorer of his or her immediate surroundings. For instance, a child who is looking at a bird on a tree branch hears her mother say, "There's a red bird, a cardinal." As the bird flies from the tree, the child may have made the neural connection of bird-cardinal-fly (Sprenger, 1999). **Neural connection** refers to the way the neurons or nerve cells interact with each other to communicate messages within the brain. The next time the event occurs, the brain may make the connections again, only this time the connections may occur more rapidly. When neurons practice or "learn" information being transmitted through the neural network, they become more efficient in making connections, thereby making the child a more efficient or fluent learner.

How does a young child learn and continue to build his or her world of words? How does vision, listening, talking, and venturing out into the environment shape the young child's perceptual, linguistic, and cognitive life? Children's actions help them to construct what they know about the world.

The Swiss psychologist Jean Piaget believed that a young child must operate upon the immediate environment to bring about change (1963). Children learn by doing, by interacting with their local environment and by formulating **mental schema** of how the natural world operates. Through active participation with their own intelligence, children construct their own rules regarding how the environment is put together.

The immediate environment provides a field of experimentation. Children manipulate materials, such as blocks, toys, furniture, or utensils, and get visual and motor feedback about outcomes of their touching behavior. They learn how to adapt and accommodate themselves to environmental changes and mishaps, many of which may be unfortunately self-induced. For example, when a finger is inadvertently burned on a stovetop, on a barbecue grill, or by a lit candle, the child is not apt to reach out again to something that is cued or learned by the concept word *hot*. In essence, children construct mental schemata based on past experiences. According to Piaget, a schema is a mental image or pattern of action, and this mental picture becomes a way of representing and organizing all of the child's previous sensory-motor experiences. Thus, the eyes, coordinating with the hands, the feet, the ears, and the talking mouth, continually build words for experiences that are in the head.

Children's actions are channeled through vision to help them construct their logic, found in such thinking processes as classifying, ordering, and conserving. For instance, children learn that some things can be grouped and some cannot, and that some things can move when they are pushed whereas others cannot. Later they learn to see that changes of physical appearance, such as when some juice has been poured from the container to the glass, does not mean that a loss of volume has occurred. Children also learn that when a number of pieces of colored clay are merged together to make a rolled-out "snake," there is still the same amount of clay regardless of the size of the constructed creature. Other educators have noted that these insights are often independent of language and take the form of images. The collection of images becomes a mental filing cabinet of organized knowledge known as cognitive structures. Children's thinking emanates from a nonverbal core, which we might call **representational thought**. Rather rapidly, however, usually between the ages of 8 and 12 months, this thinking is aided by forthcoming language development.

At the initial level of representational thought, the learner is perceiving and interacting with the environment. This is a process of exploring, seeking out, and responding in continual interaction between the viewer and the environment. An outgrowth of this active experimentation and viewing is the formation of nonverbal, representational thought. For young children, representational thought will be expressed through such forms as body language, play, and art, whereas for older people, the physical and mental energy devoted to representational thought can be expressed through the many forms of the arts. Nonverbal, representational thought is thinking by analogy, metaphor, and symbols.

Children rapidly enlarge representational thought or mental schemata during their early years, Piaget notes. At first all four-footed animals may be called a cat, a dog, or a horse. Then, as the youngster comes into more and more visual and physical contact with each type, the schema and the word used to mean that schema take on a clearer focus. The youngster has accommodated his or her previous perceptions and adjusted to the more accepted name for each animal. Schemata, therefore, are the collective representations of all of life's experiences and form the bases of the child's conceptual filing system.

It is through such activities as observing and counting objects, sorting toys, modeling with clay, finger painting, building with blocks, playing house, and the hundreds of other visual and motor activities that children do, that they form mental schemata and learn the activity. Words can be used for objects that appear in the immediate viewing area or for those objects that appear as mental pictures in the child's mind.

Through play and social interaction, children share representational thought. During playtime, one child uses a fluff of cotton to represent a bunny because the child visualizes the connectedness of the whiteness and softness to the bunny. The child can say, "This cotton is a bunny" to another. The connectedness between the real object (cotton ball) and the representational form (the rabbit) must be in each child's experience, along with the words *cotton* and *bunny* to obtain meaning. If the second child says, "Now, this red ornament can be a cardinal," and the other youngster has experienced neither ornament nor cardinal in life or words, representational connectedness or meaning will not occur.

Forming the Foundation of Talk

Language was used in the illustration above, and in the usage of verbal labels, one child did not understand the other. "What's an ornament?" or "What's a cardinal?" the second child might ask. The concrete referents for the words were not in the second child's life experiences. This illustration serves as a caution to the teacher as well. The more that teachers plan to use new words with children who may not have experienced them in life or oral language development, the more that teachers need to construct concrete background and oral experiences for children to assimilate the new words.

Young children hear language first used in actual, immediate contexts, which Frank Smith calls **situation-dependent spoken language** (1994). Initially the object and later the mental picture or schema of the object become referents for the verbal name of the object. A mother is likely to ask, "Do you want some juice?" as a bottle or container is visually displayed before her child. The child sees and hears the connection between the object and the words used. This connection has to be mentally   woven; it has to be fabricated by the individual thinker. Connections have to be processed by the individual thinker even if adults take great pains to point out the connections they themselves have made.

Let me provide a concrete example of how words are internalized during a concrete activity. Young Marco, who will soon be 3 years old, is dropped off at my house, where I will act as caregiver until I take him to preschool for the afternoon session. Instead of saying, "Go play with your toys" or "Let's play with your toys," I say, "Let's make a display with your toys." I could have used other words, such as *parade* or *arrangement*, and any of them would have sufficed in this context. Initially, we both get on the rug, dump out the tin box of toy trucks, cars, figures, soldiers, small stuffed animals, and so forth that have been accumulating over my grandchildren's lives, and we talk through what you do in a display. You might guess what events occurred: putting the baby bear in the bulldozer's hopper, then the stegosaurus in the back of the pickup truck and the Batman figure on the hood, and on and on. We finish, then we talk through the fun experience of the display.

The next time Marco comes to visit grandpa I say, "Make a display with your toys." He says he wants me to help but I hold back, feigning that I have to do my "homework." He goes to the toy box, dumps it out on the rug, and proceeds to manipulate the cast of objects and figures. After a bit, he says, "Look Grandpa! Look at my display!"

The seed I had planted verbally took hold. The word is now his. A meaning connection of taking separate objects and materials and putting them in some kind of arrangement to form a *display* has been made in his mind. Now if his mother uses the word, as in "a display of dishware," or the preschool teachers talk of "a display of the children's drawings," an understanding should occur of what a display will look like in these contexts.

Thus, new words used appropriately in actual life contexts pay dividends for children. A new word learned is another big step in the milestone of language learning. Now let's shift to the arena of the classroom teacher. The teacher introduces a new set of meaning words centered around a topic or theme, has the children practice the words in appropriate contexts, and has them write down their definitions in their vocabulary notebooks. At the end of the unit, the children are tested on the word meanings. This is the end of a traditional teaching sequence but not necessarily the end of internalized learning. Later, in another classroom context, children begin to use those previously introduced vocabulary words in their oral language and writing. As the teacher hears and sees the words used appropriately in newer contexts, she can feel pride and satisfaction that she nourished the language process and set up situations where connections of words to appropriate contexts occurred.

Once connections are made, words, which have been used in specific situational settings, are available to be used by children as a way of imitating their thoughts or wishes in a situation. Words become a useful shortcut to acting out a meaning prompted by physical engagement in a concrete situation. Language, then, is both cued by the concrete, visual world and a cue of what that world holds. Through language, children know and talk of their past, they locate themselves in the present, and they can visualize the future in the form of mental schemata.

Words develop in children's minds from the inside out. That is, children learn the meaning of words by attaching them to meaningful situations that have become internalized in nonverbal images. Children develop what is called a **deep structure** meaning for words, according to Frank Smith. These deep structure meanings become reflected in their first utterances. Children's first talk is often composed of such phrases as "wan milk, kitty sleep, doggie goed." Because meaning is learned in wholes, the search for meaning proceeds outward from the child's inner self to become modified according to the language customs of the speaking community. By using language more and more as a tool to describe and achieve satisfaction from the world, the child receives positive reinforcement from parents, guardians, and siblings and becomes motivated to continue with talk. Because of such positive reinforcement, the child becomes more and more inclined to talk and interact with the greater language community of adults and other children.

In the early stages of listening and speaking, children produce grammatical utterances that reflect personalized, meaningful thought. The child has the underlying meaning and basic sentence structure but doesn't know how to connect words and phrases at the **surface structure**–or talk level, of language. With time and social interaction from the language community, the child's ability to produce adult talk expands. The child learns to manipulate words and phrases and to transform structures to achieve surface structure "correctness." As children become aware of word and sentence structure, they begin to generalize about the patterns and rules of language. These conventions aren't taught, they are learned. In a sense, they are reconstructed by young children as they experiment with language. Connectedness is established between language and social contexts just as connectedness was established during the nonverbal representation of *ornament* for *cardinal*.

Fresh in my mind is a language episode that I observed occurring with my second grandchild, Cosima. I didn't document the length of time this expansion took place, but it serves well to show how a young child's mind works as she internalizes language rules and patterns. At first she just pointed her hand and finger at me, indicating a desire to be recognized, and then the following utterances were made over time:

First	. . . .	[finger point]
Then	. . . .	*You*
Later	. . . .	*You nitz* (nice)
Still later	. . . .	*You is nitz.*
Still later	. . . .	*You are nice.*
And still later	. . . .	*You are a very nice grandpa.*

We can see that the meaning of the utterance remained the same; the wholeness of it just became more polished to conform to the rules of the adult language community.

During language situations, the child listens and speaks to obtain meaningful and functional interaction. Youngsters do not learn the rules of oral language production first. The learning of language comes with the use of language and with the increasing understanding of how language structures can be transformed in different ways, on different occasions, and for different people. If the youngster produces a syntactically correct utterance such as "The doggie goed," the child needs to receive feedback about the surface structure appropriateness of the response from significant others such as mom, dad, grandparents, or other siblings. The child's talk was consistent with the grammar of English, indicating that the rules of subject and verb placement in a sentence were internalized. What the child needs now is supportive feedback from the language community to achieve continued surface structure correctness. Communicative feedback to support the child's talk might be, "Yes, the doggie did go. But we also say, 'The doggie went.' Do you think you can say, 'The doggie went'? That's good. When the doggie went away, you can't see it any more. The dog went away."

There are additional dimensions to the viewing, listening, and speaking interaction as children develop. First, there is an affective, emotional side to language learning. Second, there's development of the narrative and story structure that occurs naturally in the oral language as adults and children recount events. Third, there's the book connection to story structure. All of these dimensions occur in a social context and strongly influence how children will develop linguistically, socially, and cognitively.

Social Interaction and Language Growth

The affective context occurs in natural, social situations as children experience language in situational contexts. Children's reactions to the language used during the situations are also part of the language learning process. Thus, language and social development are closely intertwined. The writings of the Russian psychologist Lev Vygotsky (1978, 1986) have contributed to a strong understanding of how language and social interaction enhance each other. Vygotsky hypothesized a **zone of proximal development** that accounted for the development of children's thinking as a consequence or an outcome of their need to communicate with others. Within the zone was a range of activities a child could accomplish with assistance and guidance from others but could not successfully accomplish on his own. When children are operating within the zone in learning situations, they can perform at their very best. What is needed for optimal performance are support mechanisms by mom, dad, older siblings, grandparents, and other significant caretakers. The support mechanisms are natural parental love, affection from others, and esteem for the child, especially in communicative situations, so that when talking and listening are occurring there's a shared, bonded interest. This is why conversing with a child and making decisions through conversing are so much more powerful for children's thinking development than one-directional messages like commands.

Planning and guiding a learner through the successive steps of the zone to a successful outcome is called **scaffolding**. In scaffolding, the older sibling, parent, relative, or teacher demonstrates or models what has to be done, guides the learner with actions and talk through the activity, points out pitfalls and offers advice, asks questions, and constantly breaks the larger task into fewer, simpler steps so that by successful completion of each "baby step," the larger task can be accomplished (and hopefully internalized).

The lesson of scaffolding can be transferred to the classroom, but the success of each stage requires reflection and understanding of the learning task. Three considerations should guide teachers in mediating student learning within the zone of proximal development, according to Dixon-Krauss (1996). First, children's learning should be augmented through social interaction; second, as children are engaged in a learning activity, teachers should be flexible and provide support based on the children's feedback; and third, according to the children's needs, teachers have to vary the amount of support from very structured to minimal. This means that in preparing lessons for students, teachers have to be mindful of creating the best conditions for learning. For instance, when students do not have the words and the background knowledge (the schemata) for the learning of new information, teachers should help students to connect and relate what they know about the topic to what they do not know. Also, the new learning must be presented in a context that is somewhat familiar to the students so that they can accommodate the new with prior conceptions of the old.

Vygotsky's concept of children's conceptual development certainly forms the foundation for many of today's current programs (May, 1998). Elementary school teachers implementing literature-based programs, emergent literacy programs, or programs based on the whole-language philosophy in their classrooms should be aware that Vygotsky's ideas form the underlying construct of much of their teaching procedures.

Tanya Gallagher (1993) notes that peers play an important role in language development because they provide opportunities to practice language skills, they act as role models for the appropriateness or inappropriateness of particular utterances, and they provide feedback. She adds that particular factors relate peer acceptance with language facility, such as the ability of children to: adjust their messages to tune in with their listener's needs; begin conversation; ask questions appropriately; add to ongoing conversations; verbalize one's intentions in a clear way; talk to all participants in a group situation; and be positive rather than negative when commenting on a topic.

Development of the Narrative

Representational play, also called **pretend play**, is very beneficial to the social, affective, and linguistic development of playmates as they talk to one another in the context of the play. Pretend play, the thinking of metaphor and representation, occurs when children transform actions like pushing a wooden block into words, such as "the train is moving." By playing and collaborating with others in pretend play, children add more language and story structure to their internally conceived stories. Thus, pretend play lays a foundation for the **narrative**. Children have objects or characters doing something (the plot) so that something else (the resolution or outcome) happens.

The structure of the oral narrative also develops through talk in the home or in the community. Children and parents talk about experiences they have had, and the ability to sequentially order events becomes more and more developed. In some cultures, the structure of the narrative is shaped as traditional stories, and tales are told orally to each new generation. In many cases, the development of the narrative or story structure forms more readily when the parent, guardian, or older sibling begins to read to the child. Now in this one great act, viewing, listening, speaking, affective engagement, and social bonding come together as the child watches the pages of the storybook turn. As children hear their favorite stories read aloud, their thinking and expectations become that of the story. They hear words, they begin to take note of word shapes, and their attention is guided by the pictures and printed words that are read aloud. They are encouraged to sit in an acceptable way so that they can listen attentively and communicate when they want to ask a question or react to a story part. They note that parents, grandparents, guardians, and brothers and sisters try to read to them during a "quiet time." Finally, a major by-product of this home reading is that children internalize the structure of the narrative. Much more will be said about the discourse style of the narrative and its importance in literacy development in later sections of this book.

The child who succeeds early in reading is often reared in a language-enriched, emotionally supportive environment. David Elkind (1975) wrote many years ago that children who succeed with early reading come from homes in which immersion in the oral and written language is rich, in which parents frequently read to their children, and in which social motivation to please adults who model and reward reading behavior is important. Research has also pointed out that the great majority of early readers are children born to parents who like to read and write themselves and who share their love of reading and writing with their children (May, 1998). Furthermore, they allow their children's scribble to represent written communication, and they allow children's pretend reading to occur without correcting them needlessly. Frank Smith (1999) adds that when the conditions of print materials and people relationships are right, children will be motivated to read early.

Young children's speaking or expressive language facility (the oral language), and their listening or receptive language facility (the aural language), develops and is reinforced by encounters in the home, community, and school. As children learn to speak more and graduate through developmental phases such as single-word utterances to phrases to more complete and complex statements, their fluency increases, notes Margaret Hunsberger (1994). Fluency, like other language features, is developmental and becomes a real benefit to children early in their lives. Early oral language fluency serves as a factor of success for later school and public accomplishments. It is a major contributor to success in beginning reading and writing development, and emergent literacy instruction is fundamentally built upon the competence and development of children's oral language. A number of educators and researchers have confirmed that those children who have the opportunity to use language in scaffolding interactions with the speaking community and are provided with rich and various forms of language will develop a greater facility with the forms and functions of language than children who have more limited opportunities (Wishon, Crabtree, & Jones, 1998).

Thus, it becomes quite important for the teacher, particularly for the teacher of young children, to aid and assist children to grow in oral language fluency in the school setting. Furthermore, the teacher should encourage parents to continue helping their children to gain in aural and oral language development and should provide suggestions for doing so. Listed below are some suggestions for teachers to use in classroom contexts and to pass on to parents as they engage with their children in life activities.

- Make the child a conversational partner, not just a listener. Try to elicit sentences using new words that are being used in novel activities in the classroom or out-of-school settings. When parents shop, travel, drive, or go to events with their children, they are providing potentially novel situations to which new words can be attached.

- Be aware that language reflects thinking. Help children put their thoughts into comprehensible sentences. Say their sentences back to them in correct English so they can hear the appropriate syntax.

- If the child experiments with a new word in a sentence and it doesn't come out quite right, show respect and model or scaffold the appropriate utterance. Remember that risk taking and experimentation with language in either the oral or printed form is a means by which children match their hypotheses with usage.

- Provide different situational contexts in which a child has to use language to accomplish something and/or to figure out a problem. "Tell me what you're trying to do," the teacher or parent might say.
- Provide opportunities for the child to talk and hear talk in social and collaborative interactions, such as when small groups or pairs are preparing classroom or home materials for special holidays or events.
- Use stories and books as springboards for talk. More often than not, children do not like it when you interrupt your oral reading of a story with questions to engage them in talk. This is understandable, as their minds are involved in the magical fabric of the author's tale. However, with a story that is being read for the first time, you might be able to space the story out with conversation and engage them in talk about characters, plot, and outcomes.

Words and Their Properties

What are words? We would probably say that they are the smallest part of the language we use to convey meaning. *Up* and *down* and *yes* and *no* have pretty clear, singular meanings and are heard and spoken quite early in life. However, words are used in larger meaningful structures called sentences, and sentences shape the meanings of words because of the way a word can be used in any particular sentence. We call this the *contextual* use of a word, and "using the context" becomes a very important aspect, if not the critical aspect, of the reading comprehension process. The larger context of a paragraph, a story, or a selection, as well as the culture itself, also shapes the meaning of a word.

Thus, word meanings are not fixed. Words will change their meaning as word users shift their views of how any particular word is used in a particular context. Think of the word *web*. When we were young, our perspective and mental dictionary meaning for this word was the silky network of the spider. Now educators' perspective of the word might be more apt to be in the context of semantic or cognitive mapping, as in the "webbing" of ideas or in the context of a network of computers linked by electrical wires in a worldwide system called a "web." As meanings for some words are becoming reshaped by cultural contexts, other words are dropping out of popular usage altogether, to be replaced by a newer counterpart, indicates Anita Barry (2002). Have you heard the words *trousers, breeches, icebox,* and *phonograph* recently?

While working on this chapter, I heard a word for the first time. I don't know whether the commentator coined the word himself or if it has been used by others in the financial community, but it serves well to illustrate the wonderful elasticity of our language. The context was the collapse of the Enron Corporation and the waves of financial calamity heaped upon its employees and investors. The commentator appearing on a TV news show stated, "People who wish to invest in the stock market at the present time are suffering from Enronitis." Notice how the suffix word part *-itis* was merged to the proper name of a corporation in the context of the verb *suffering*. The suffix *-itis* means "the inflammation of, the infection or irritation of," as in the maladies of *arthritis* or *bronchitis*. Thus the meaning of *Enronitis* becomes clear and is compounded by each individual's closeness to the collapse—whether a relative or friend was involved or whether stocks or mutual funds were heavily invested.

Words, then, act as names or labels for representations of life's experiences. When a learner has a label for a new topic or experience, his or her perception of that experience enlarges, and concept understanding becomes enriched. Think of any new experience that a young child encounters, such as learning to ski, or the first trip to a zoo, an aquarium or a planetarium. As youngsters become involved in the activity, and adults or teachers use the concept words associated with that activity, youngsters acquire new words, new labels for objects and happenings.

One major feature or property of words is that they contain meaning. We noted that children's first words were learned as wholes and connected to events in the nearby environment. Words continue to build, and their meanings become precise in some cases and become attached to other usages as meaning connections expand. Soon—and undoubtedly schooling helps here—a person's mental dictionary, or **mental lexicon**, realizes that words belong in different classes or categories depending on how they are used in sentences. Some words name things, persons, and places (we call these nouns), some words tell actions (verbs), other words tell about or describe things (adjectives), and still others are words that connect ideas (conjunctions, prepositions). Now the speakers probably will not know the names of the **syntactic category** or **syntactic class** of the words in particular sentences, but they have that knowledge building in their heads connected to the words' meanings. Otherwise, the speaker would not be able to form grammatically correct sentences, such as, "I love you, Mom" in which "love" is used as a verb, and "Mom, you are the love of all our family" in which love becomes a noun (Fromkin & Rodman, 1998).

Each word also has a sound or phonological representation, and the physical sound of each word is called up by the speaker to identify the word that he or she wishes to use. Words are pronounced in wholes to name their meaning intent, but also within words are syllables and sound parts called **phonemes**, which when joined together serve to produce the physical form of the whole word in the oral language.

As speakers of a language are brought to the written representation of the language that occurs in reading, the spelling of words, or their **orthographic representation**, becomes learned behavior. Both the sound and spelling features of words allow for the recognition of one set of features, to cue the recognition of other features, according to James Coady (1994a). This means that when a person needs to "call up" any particular word in the mind to pronounce it, spell it, define it, or use it correctly in a sentence, the person uses the most efficient of the features.

Another type of mental access to words begins early in life and becomes more internalized over time. Success with this access, we will see later, is highly related to acquisition of a large vocabulary and competency with advanced levels of reading. This access is known as the understanding and analysis of word parts called **morphemes**. The rules learned in the head over time for joining the parts or elements of words to make more words is known as **morphology**. In the school setting, these structural parts of words that alter meaning and syntactic category are called by such terms as *inflectional endings, structural elements, affixes, prefixes, suffixes*, and *roots*. Children begin to use some of these word-part structures as early as 18 months to 2 years old, according to Eve Clark (1998). They use inflectional endings such as an -*s* to pluralize a noun and an -*ed* to denote past tense even earlier. They begin to use roots and stems in complex words and manipulate affixes, either suffixes or prefixes, onto new word formations. Clark maintains that such analysis of word parts is a necessary prerequisite for new word formation.

Interestingly, a word composed of a single morpheme is both a word and a morpheme (e.g., *pack*), and a morpheme composed of a single word with connected structural parts, the affixes that are bound to any one word, is also a word (e.g., *repackage*). What might distinguish the essential quality of morphemes, as noted by Andrew Spencer (1996), is that they provide meaning or a function to the word of which they are a component, and they themselves cannot be broken down into smaller morphemes. Take the prefixes *semi-* (meaning "half") and *ante-* (meaning "before"). They can be broken down into phonemes but the smallest unit of meaning remains the prefix, which is attachable to a central morpheme, also known as a word. One way to designate a morpheme that is also a single standing word containing its own meaning is to call it a **free morpheme** (e.g., *script*). A morpheme that is attachable to a free morpheme to contribute additional meaning or to provide a grammatical relationship is known as a **bound morpheme** (e.g., *antedate*) (Spencer, 1996).

Figure 1-1 provides an overview of the two types of mental processes that occur for users of the language and attempts to clarify the distinctions between morphemes and the rules of morphology. On the left side, words as free morphemes have been collected and sorted and are available for verbal production inside the head of each and every user of the language. The person doesn't know the exact categorical names of these meaning-bearing and function words but is able to use them quite functionally in conversation and possibly in writing at an early age.

Figure 1-1. Word Formation and Operations in the English Language System

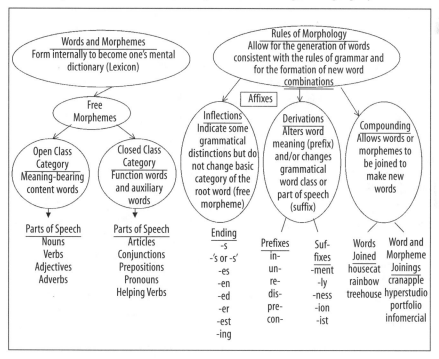

On the right side, the rules of word generation and the rules consistent with the grammatical system have been occurring at the same time in the person's head. Two types of affixes, also known as the bound morphemes, are categorized as inflections or derivations. An **inflection**, rare in the English language system, does not change the basic category of the root word, but it does provide some grammatical information such as pluralizing or indicating past tense (Barry, 2002). For instance, an *-s* or *-es* added to a root word or free morpheme such as *dog* or *bus* would mean that there is more than one item being identified. However, the basic category of the root word is still a noun. The inflectional endings *-ed* and *-en* become attached to verb roots when past tense needs to be indicated ("I *visited* that museum last year") or if a past participle is required ("I have *spoken* of her before"). The most common inflectional suffixes in English are shown in the figure.

A **derivation**, on the other hand, can alter a word's meaning, as often occurs when a prefix is added to the free morpheme or root word (e.g., *dis-agree*) and can change the syntactic category, such as when the verb *state* becomes a noun, as in *statement*. Such use of derivational operations usually results in the formation of a word of a different syntactic class from that of the root, but it can also add additional elements of meaning. For example, addition of the suffixes *-or* and *-ation* changes verbs into nouns; yet with *-or* and *-er*, a meaning follows of an agent ("one who") as in *creator*, and with *-ation* an abstract noun of *creation* is formed (Spencer, 1996). The power of derivations is that morphemes can be linked or connected to other morphemes to enrich the power of words within a language.

Compounding is basically the joining of two words to make one word, although an upper limit of the number of words to be combined would be difficult to state, according to Victoria Fromkin and Robert Rodman (1998). Look at such compounds as *man about town*, *mother-in-law*, and *jack-of-all-trades*. Moreover, the meaning of a compound word is not necessarily the sum of the meanings of its word parts. For instance, in our field we use the compound words *chalkboard* or *blackboard* almost on a daily basis. Yet the board that is written on may not be the color *black*, and more often than not, felt-tip pens are used instead of chalk.

Although the parts in most compounds are usually considered words, it is possible to find compounds that can be decomposed into one independently attested word plus another morpheme that is not considered an affix and is not an independently attested word, according to Nigel Fabb (1998). He provides such examples as *cranberry* and *ironmonger*. I have provided some other examples in Figure 1-1 under the heading "Word and Morpheme Joinings." Is *portfolio* the joining of two words, or is it the joining of a root part *port*, meaning to carry, with the word *folio*, which means a sheet of paper or a somewhat large book? Such is the form of words, that they can constantly evolve and join with other words. Fromkin and Rodman (1998) note that compounding is a common and frequent process for increasing the vocabulary of a language.

Through an understanding of these word parts, shown in Figure 1-1 under "Rules of Morphology," a person makes mental connections to the various structural parts that convey meaning so that new words can be understood and even created. For instance, once a person understands the meaning and position of the word part *re-*, the person can successfully understand and make new words with *re-* in the initial position, meaning "to occur or happen again."

Figure 1-2 provides an overview of the four major properties that are inherent in words. These inherent features in words—the meaning or grammar aspect, the sound, the spelling, and the rules governing structural parts—have caused educators to deeply consider how printed words are introduced and taught to children through the grades. I hope that this discussion of morphemes and morphology has not been too taxing for the reader. However, we cannot enter the arena of word understanding and vocabulary growth without understanding the power resident in the language system itself.

Figure 1-2. The Properties of Words

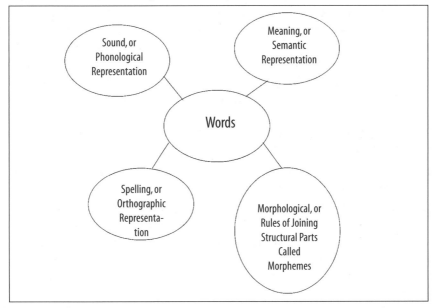

The Language of Words

Educators, researchers, and linguists have used different terms and phrases to explain word concepts. In a sense they have attempted to give meaning to the world of words encountered in the classroom by using terms and phrases to designate certain kinds of words. The terms and phrases also reflect conditions of the four properties of words discussed above. I have tried to give the most agreed upon definition provided by previous educators and researchers who have worked with words through the years. What follows is a discussion of the "language of words."

A **familiar word** is recognized and understood by a person in either the oral or written language. The person knows the meaning of the word or can use the word appropriately in an oral or written context without being able to explicitly define the word. A familiar word is contrasted with an **unknown word**.

A **high-frequency word** is frequently used and is necessary in the language system to transmit basic meaning and permit ideas and sentence elements to be joined together. Over the years, researchers have studied the frequency counts of printed words in various types and genres of reading material. By studying word counts, researchers can determine what the most frequently used words are in child and adult reading materials. For instance, we could predict that the words *the* and *a* will be two of the most frequently used words in English because the language system is basically composed of these two articles. The frequency of words exists on a continuum of high-frequency words to rare words.

Word lists were amassed by researchers as they recorded how frequently particular words occurred in written texts. In 1944, Edward Thorndike and Irving Lorge published *The Teacher's Word Book of 30,000 Words*, and this compendium of words became one of the most widely used books for vocabulary research. Soon, computer-based analysis allowed for more words to be studied. In 1967, Henry Kucera and W. Nelson Francis accomplished a computational analysis of one million words, and in 1971, J. B. Carroll, P. Davies, and Barry Richman analyzed the frequency count of more than five million words. These authors studied the textbooks and recommended readings of students from grades 3 to 9. In the texts of 17 different subject areas, including mathematics, literature, social studies, science, and music, the authors found highly frequent words such as *receive*, which occurred in most of the content readings, and moderately frequent words such as *reciprocal*, which occurred 67 times in the material.

Some very interesting statistics emerged from the Carroll et al. study that somewhat confirmed and reinforced what educators had known about words. Ten of the words studied occur 24% of the time in running text; 100 words occur with 49% frequency; 2,000 words occur with 81% frequency; 3,000 words occur with 85% frequency; and 5,000 words occur with 89% frequency in consecutive text. As predicted, *the* is the most frequently used word. The 10th most frequently used word is *it*.

Some educators and researchers analyzed word frequency counts in children's reading materials across age and grade levels to arrive at a **core vocabulary**. They published word lists of the core vocabulary, and these became known as **sight word lists.** The most famous of these lists, produced from the 1930s to the 1970s, is undoubtedly the *Dolch 220 Basic Sight Words*, published in an article by Edward Dolch in 1936. It was commonly believed that readers who mastered the Dolch list would be able to meaningfully read approximately 70% of the words used in a typical first-grade reader (Robinson & McKenna, 1994). A list targeted for students experiencing reading difficulties was published by Fry in 1975, and a more recent list of 240 words, called **instant words**, was compiled from more than a thousand 500-word samples taken from books covering 12 subject areas from grades 3 through 9 (Fry, Kress, & Fountoukidis, 1993). The instant words or Fry List is somewhat consistent with the Dolch 220 words as far as the first 100 words are concerned, but the 1993 list should be considered a new list of high-frequency words (May, 1998).

An important list that was highly predictive of the readability levels of reading materials from fourth grade to college level was compiled by Edgar Dale and Jeanne Chall in 1948. This list of 3,000 words formed the core vocabulary of their widely used readability formula. The authors maintained that the 3,000-word list contained the most basic and necessary words needed by children in fourth grade. Chall (1996) equated mastery of these familiar words with that of a fourth-grade reading level. Words learned after mastery of the list would be less familiar or more specialized, technical, or literary, and would advance the reader into the higher stages of reading.

A **function word** is a "little" English word that allows sentence structure to operate and that links the meaning-bearing content words to one another. In the sentence preceding this one, the reader will notice four function words: *that, to, and,* and *the*. These words connect sentence ideas with each other, and if they were omitted the sentence meaning would be somewhat incomprehensible. The reader would undoubtedly find many function words in a grammar book in the "parts of speech" section, particularly the section that discussed and listed prepositions, conjunctions, articles, pronouns, and adverbial words of degree (such as *most, yet,* and *still*). Because many of these words are irregular in spelling and pronunciation, they may be difficult for beginning readers to read and conceptualize if taught out of context (Leu & Kinzer, 1999).

Though relatively few in number compared to other words, function words are extremely important because they help speakers and writers to express specific relationships between ideas. In other words, we wouldn't have understandable sentences without function words.

In 1981 I conducted a small but revealing study of function words. Function words appearing on five widely used high-frequency lists (cited above) were compared with those actually listed as function words in a curriculum guide for second language learners (Sinatra, 1981). I wished to determine what function words listed separately in the curriculum guide for second language learners as being critically important for the understanding of English vocabulary would also appear on the five high-frequency word lists. The words on all six lists were further categorized into three major idea relationships: words that connected ideas sequentially (e.g., *first, now, and, then*), words that connected spatial relationships (e.g., *between, over, under, around*), and words that compared and contrasted ideas (e.g., *most, less, also, but, still, yet*). When the words were analyzed on all six lists, some words appeared all six times, some five, some four, and on down to those appearing on only one list. There were 61 occurrences of words appearing on the six lists at least three or more times. The words *and, or, because, if, of, about, over, under, before,* and *first* appeared on all six lists. The reading of function words would appear to have a high degree of importance for both native speakers of English and English language learners.

We are arriving at a conclusion about the labels used by educators for words. The formula for this conclusion looks something like this:

Function Words = High-Frequency Words = Words on Basic Sight Word Lists

I hope that the reader can recognize the significance of the various names given to the same class of word. Later we will consider the importance of these words for early and fluent reading success.

A **content word**, or meaning-bearing word, names, labels, or symbolizes a thing, an action, and/or a quality. The parts of speech to which content words belong are nouns, verbs, adjectives, and some adverbs. A language has many content words to accommodate the richness and character of a language's people as they describe and define themselves and their actions. Whereas function words provide the "glue" between ideas expressed through content words, the latter are constantly evolving. Whereas function words may be described as a "closed class" of words, meaning that only a few hundred exist in our language, content words are an "open class" of words. That is, meaning-bearing words are not bound or closed, and new ones can be invented (Rayner & Pollatsek, 1994). As a culture advances and words are required to describe what people do, content words become added to our daily vocabularies. For example, in the past, when word frequency studies were conducted, the terms *Internet, World Wide Web*, and *servers* were either not in use or not used as they are in the digital age. Now if a sentence is generated, such as "The Internet and the World Wide Web are supported by servers," we can see how the function words *the, and*, and *by*—prevalent in the language for eons—help the recently coined content words to stick together.

A **sight word** is part of an individual reader's known vocabulary. It is immediately recognized in print as soon as a reader sees the word. Because such words are recognized instantaneously, they do not require analysis with various strategies. The time factor for immediate recognition of the word has been acknowledged to be within 1 second (Leslie & Caldwell, 2001) or even a fraction of a second (Rayner & Pollatsek, 1994). Each reader adds words to his or her sight vocabulary as soon as they are learned in long-term memory. The words come from personal readings of a favorite topic, from content topics and themes covered in school, and from being observant and curious about words. The more interest and motivation there is to read about a topic, the more likely it is that words will be learned rapidly and securely.

An individual reader's sight words are not to be confused with a published list of basic sight words. Many educators, even veteran teachers, make the erroneous assumption that sight words are only those words listed on the well-known sight word lists. We know the reason for this. Basic sight word lists contain words of high frequency usage in the printed language, and these same words are quite necessary to join ideas within sentence parts and between sentences. Thus, due to the very nature of the reading materials they are initially offered, beginning readers are exposed to high-frequency words. This initial repeated exposure predisposes them to learn to read many words that are found on basic sight word lists.

However, some children do not efficiently learn all of their initial words. For instance, they might read *of* as *from, but* as *by*, and *is* as *so*. If the practice of miscalling basic words persists, these children might experience more confusion and more misnaming of words as additional words are encountered in classroom offerings. It is wise to ensure that each individual child is quite secure and accurate in the beginning words they are asked to learn before new words are added to their "diet."

A number of terms have been used by educators to refer to the strategies of working out, or **sounding out**, words that are not immediately recognizable in print. These terms are known as *word analysis, word attack skills, word mediation, decoding, breaking the code, phonetic analysis*, and using *sound-symbol relationships*. To these more global terms have been added the specifics of *phonics, phonological* or *phonemic awareness, alphabetic understanding*, and *word families* (Chall, 1992; Johnston, 1999). In the classroom, these words and phrases can be reduced to the teacher's exhortation to "sound it out." What happens in a reader's mind is that the reader has to associate the printed letters of the alphabet with the speech sounds they represent in order to achieve a word's identity in the oral language. Of course, the single word *phonics* is the one that captures the general public's attention and is a term that has become associated with a method of reading based on using sound-symbol associations to unlock the identity of words. There will be more devoted to the various ways to accomplish sounding out in a later chapter.

A **new reading word** is one that the reader has learned to recognize and now reads without hesitation and without application of word attack skills or sounding out. The new word may have been taught through a phonics-oriented approach. Because so many confuse the idea of sight vocabulary with that of basic sight words appearing on high-frequency word lists, I have made a separate distinction for a new reading word. Generally the word is already familiar to the reader in the oral language, but the reader has not met the word in print. There are two essential conditions here. First, the reader must encounter the word in print, so that when it is recognized the match is made with the same word in the spoken language, and understanding occurs. Second, the reader must have enough encounters with the word so that it is read instantaneously, meaning all at a time, and not confused with another word that may look the same. This is called **instantaneous word recognition**, and it means that the word is consistently recognized with accuracy, has been committed to long-term memory, and has become another word added to the reader's sight vocabulary.

A **vocabulary word** is not familiar in the oral language or the printed language for any given learner. This is a very difficult and befuddling category for teachers because they can't possibly know the range of vocabularies and experiences of each child in the classroom. Recall from the earlier discussion in this chapter that experience and vocabulary development are closely connected. It has been estimated that young children enter school with a spoken vocabulary range of well under 10,000 words to more than 20,000 words. Because of the unique partnership of words to experience, the teacher doesn't know what child has had what experiences, and if several children have had the same experiences, what words were learned during the context of those experiences. As children become fluent readers and read outside school because they like it, reading becomes part of their daily experience. Both theorists and researchers have maintained that the majority of children's vocabulary growth occurs through language exposure (and this includes plain old book reading) rather than through direct teaching (Cunningham & Stanovich, 1998).

A **concept word** is a vocabulary word and a new reading word that is associated with the learning of a new concept or topic. Students have little or no background experience with the topic or frame of reference with which this word is associated. For instance, when the topic of photosynthesis is initially encountered, students may not even be aware that green-plant leaves make their own food through the action of sunlight, water, and carbon dioxide. As they become familiar with the experience of the photosynthesis cycle by studying figures and charts, by teacher discussion and readings, by analysis of a green-plant leaf, and by viewing slides, filmstrips, and movies, students grow in conceptual understanding of all the terms and characteristics of the process. Thus, when they hear or read the word *photosynthesis*, they will associate the other new words learned and picture the relationship of the components of the process, such as *chlorophyll*, *chloroplant*, *carbon dioxide*, and *oxygen*.

Thus the concept word embraces all the parts of a concept. Many words, such as *mammals*, *insect*, *migration*, *pioneer*, and *Internet* belong in this category. It is wise for the teacher to spend time with such concept words and establish ways for students to use and take ownership of the words. One such economical and conceptually wise way is to present a concept map, which shows the relationship of the concept word with its associated terms. Such concept maps will be illustrated in the last chapter of this book.

Figure 1-3 illustrates the fine distinction that occurs when learners face words in the written language. The left side of the figure indicates that there are many words that are known in the oral language and others that the child may have encountered in life experiences. Mental constructs or schemata have formed for these word meanings and how the words are used grammatically. Now the strategy is to develop word recognition or word reading of these same words. Whether to accomplish this transfer of oral language proficiency to print proficiency in a natural way or through a sound-symbol approach has "rocked the boat" of literacy practice for years.

The right side of the figure shows that there are other words not yet met in the oral language or through life experiences, and consequently the learner doesn't know what these words mean or how to use them appropriately in context. We simply call this *vocabulary building* in the school setting, and schools in our modern culture are probably one of the last outposts in which new words arise in a number of different discipline contexts. These two streams of words—those familiar in meaning and those unfamiliar in meaning—and how to bring them to children in different contexts through the grades form the basis of the remaining chapters of this book.

**Figure 1-3. Word Recognition and Vocabulary
Understanding in the Written Language**

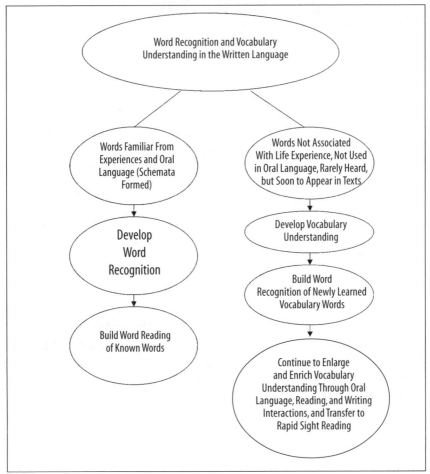

Using the context, *context clues*, and *context cues* are phrases used by educators and classroom teachers when they encourage children to figure out a word's meaning from a particular sentence or contiguous sentences of a larger text. To figure out a new word from the context means that the reader has to know how sentences work and how parts of sentences (called *phrases* and *clauses*) can be arranged in standard English to make written communication understandable. This ability is related to one's understanding of grammar or syntax and how grammar can help to signal the meaning of an unknown word. Suggestions for teachers on how to help children use the context will be presented in chapter 6.

Table 1-1 summarizes the language of words.

Table 1-1. The Language of Words

A phrase often used by educators to define Certain types of words	General Meaning
Familiar words	Words known and understood in either the oral or written language.
High-frequency words	Words frequently used in the language. Word counts were made of children's and adults' reading materials to determine most familiar or high-frequency words to rare words.
Sight word lists	Lists of the most frequently used words in print; consequently, suggesting to practitioners what words would be most productive for readers to learn first.
Function words	Often those "little words" in English that allow sentence elements to function and that link the meaning-bearing content words to one another. Articles, prepositions, and conjunctions are types of function words.
Content words	Words used to name things, actions, and qualities. They make up the vast majority of words in the language. Nouns, verbs, adjectives, and many adverbs are in this grouping.
Sight words, or a reader's sight word vocabulary	Words immediately recognized in print as familiar words when the reader's eyes transmit the words to the brain.
Word analysis, word attack, word identification, or "breaking the code"	Terms used to describe a process that often occurs when a reader encounters unfamiliar words in print. Words that are not readily recognizable in print may need to be sounded out, worked out, or analyzed by sound-symbol associations in order to obtain the word's spoken identity. This is where the terms *phonics*, *word families*, *phonograms*, and *analogy phonics* are used.
New reading words, or words recognized in print	Words that the reader can learn or has just learned to read with one or a few repetitions. This often occurs with words familiar to the reader in the oral language, but the words are just becoming mastered by the reader in print contexts. This category becomes rapidly aligned with that of the reader's sight word vocabulary, and the process is generally known as *word recognition*.
Vocabulary words	Words that are neither familiar to the reader in the oral language nor familiar to the reader in print. Because these words aren't known as spoken words, the reader may often mispronounce them when encountered in print. Through the act of reading itself, readers can learn the meaning of new words even though they may not pronounce them correctly.
Concept words	Words that embrace a concept. They become powerful organizers and categorizers in the learner's lexicon system. The word *migration* doesn't just mean "move"; it opens up a way of telling about what may happen or what happens to people or animals under certain circumstances.
Context-based words	Words encountered in context whose meaning is unknown. However, because of context relationships, the reader skillfully works out the word's meaning even if the reader can't say the word correctly in the oral language.

Concept Words and Terms

bound morpheme
compounding
concept word
content word
core vocabulary
deep structure
derivation
familiar word
free morpheme
function word
high-frequency word
inflection
instant word
instantaneous word
  recognition
mental lexicon
mental schema
morpheme
morphology
narrative

neural connection
new reading word
orthographic representation
phoneme
pretend play
representational play
representational thought
scaffolding
sight word
sight word list
situation-dependent spoken language
sounding out
surface structure
syntactic category
syntactic class
unknown word
using the context
vocabulary word
zone of proximal development

Word Challenge for Teachers: Word Search

This first word challenge is in the format of a traditional word search. Because I have provided clues to generate the different vocabulary words and phrases, you are required to read the context and find the equivalent meaning. This word search format is like a matching column activity in which the new word or phrase is in one column and the meaning phrase or sentence is found in a second column. The student connects the two parts from each column.

To accomplish this word search activity on your own, you could go to www.puzzlemaker.com. Go through the provided list and click on the bottom item that says "create." After you write in the title of your word search name, you then enter the words you want to use in your search. Just follow the provided instructions.

After you try the activity, you can turn to Appendix A of the book to find the answers. I hope you did well on your own and didn't peek first!

```
F  A  D  H  O  G  P  O  A  H  L  E  S  M  I
Y  C  M  U  L  P  F  F  Z  Q  L  R  I  E  R
I  Q  O  E  E  O  G  H  X  Z  I  U  G  N  L
J  V  X  Q  H  F  C  X  N  L  C  T  H  T  E
I  N  F  L  E  C  T  I  O  N  S  C  T  A  V
W  U  Z  N  X  H  S  D  S  W  B  U  W  L  E
A  K  P  K  N  Q  G  L  T  W  S  R  O  L  L
V  X  E  U  Z  Q  R  K  A  D  L  T  R  E  E
N  J  X  M  T  Y  L  X  K  T  I  S  D  X  C
S  E  M  E  H  P  R  O  M  N  N  P  S  I  A
F  R  E  E  M  O  R  P  H  E  M  E  S  C  F
C  O  M  P  O  U  N  D  I  N  G  E  M  O  R
D  R  O  W  T  P  E  C  N  O  C  D  K  N  U
B  B  K  X  N  C  H  P  T  X  W  F  A  U  S
D  S  E  U  L  C  T  X  E  T  N  O  C  P  N
```

2
Systems Influencing the Teaching of Written Words

Focus Questions

1. How might your understanding of the alphabetic principle influence how you approach the teaching of letters and sounds?

2. What are the implications for the reading and spelling of English words if a limited number of vowel letters are available to produce a number of vowel sounds?

3. How is phonemic awareness different than phonics?

4. What is meant by the practice of vocabulary control in children's reading materials, and how has this practice been accomplished through the years?

5. Why would a "whole-part-to-whole" instructional framework be a way to achieve a balance in literacy instruction, and how might this framework provide a compromise position for both the holistic and skills-oriented advocates in word learning?

In the first chapter we noted that words have inherent features and that they are used in larger meaningful contexts of sentences and conversation. These larger contexts also shape and flavor word meanings. There is one major feature that exists in the written language that is not necessary for word generation or production in the oral language. That feature is spelling, or the orthographic representation of the word. Just as an oral word's sound representation is composed of smaller sound units called phonemes, the written word is composed of smaller visual symbols called **graphemes**. Most of the time we use the more universal word **letters** to mean the grapheme units.

What happens when the transfer occurs from the sound equivalents of words to the letter representations of words? Another way of saying this that is more appropriate to the classroom would be, "How do children see letters and written words and produce the names of words as they are called in the oral language?" This is, in essence, the sounding out condition of word learning.

Understanding the Alphabetic Principle

Let's see if we can capture the sense of what it means to decode or sound out, and the principles of language upon which this processing appears to rest. The English language is based on an alphabetic system or principle, meaning that letters (written symbols, graphemes) represent sounds (phonological representations, phonemes). The strength of the **alphabetic principle** is that a productive writing system is created whereby from a small set of reusable letters an extremely large number of words and morpheme-bearing meanings can be produced (Rayner & Pollatsek, 1994).

The ability to understand that the 26 letters of the Roman alphabet make up the visual components of words is an important one for early literacy success. Also important is visual recognition of the different features that make up the letters. For instance, a vertical line or stroke makes the letter *l*, but adding a little horizontal stroke or "hat" makes the letter *t*. Some letters have directionality or spatial orientation features, such as the letters *d* and *b* and *p* and *q*. It is good practice to encourage young children to write so that they use their visual discrimination skills to look at and study the visual orientation of the letters as they attempt to write them. Young children's early writing experiences will undoubtedly appear as scribble to adults; then as strokes, lines, and circles that may contain some of the features of letters; and finally, as **creative** or invented **spelling**, which reveals children's approximation of letters to sounds.

The issue therefore appears to be a simple one. There are 26 letters in our alphabet. If teachers concentrate their efforts on helping children learn the letters, then children will succeed early on with reading. Common sense and even numerous research studies have shown that knowledge of letter names in kindergarten and first grade is a strong predictor of early reading achievement (Kameenui & Carnine, 1998). Nevertheless, the issue with the English language is not that simple. Although there are 26 alphabet letters, there are about 40 distinct sounds, or phonemes, in speech. To represent the sounds in speech with the letters of the alphabet means that some letters serve twofold functions. Furthermore, some letters represent more than one sound, and some sounds are represented by more than one letter.

A further complication arises in establishing a clear one-to-one letter-sound correspondence. Some sounds are not represented by a single letter, but by a combination of letters, such as *oi, oy, ew, ch,* and *th.* These combinations give rise to the concept of *spelling units,* which are distinct combinations of letters and sounds. Citing the 1967 and 1970 research of Richard Venezky, Frank Smith (1994) notes that in a computer analysis of more than 20,000 words, 52 major spelling units evolved—32 for consonants and 20 for vowels. So now we have the alphabet clearly doubled in duty.

There's even more to confound the issue of sound-symbol relationships. Additional research conducted by Berdiansky, Cronnell, and Koehler in 1969 was performed on 6,092 one- and two-syllable words in the understanding vocabularies of children from 6 to 9 years old to see if a clear set of phonics rules could be established for the English language (cited in Smith, 1994). Although the researchers found that analysis of their words produced 211 different spelling-sound relationships, they excluded 45 correspondences because they did not occur at least 10 times in the 6,000 or more words analyzed. That left 166 sets by which clear sound-symbol rules would apply. Of the 166 spelling-sound correspondences, 60 rules were established for consonants, 73 for the primary, single-letter vowels (*a, e, i o, u, y*), and 33 for complex vowels, meaning a vowel-letter combination that produces its own sound (such as *ei* in *eight*). Thus, in the potential world of phonics instruction alone, there are 166 rules of **grapheme-phoneme correspondence** suggesting that 166 distinct lessons could be generated to ensure that *all* children are beneficiaries of *all* the rules.

The Visual and Auditory Components of Sounding Out

Implicit with all the terms used for sounding out words is the understanding that there are visual and auditory components involved in the process. Although the alphabetic system has produced 26 letters that allow us to make an infinite number of words that we can understand, the same system can result in difficulties for beginning readers (and those who experience spelling problems throughout their lives) in learning to read many of the words they already understand. One reason for children's difficulty is that the phoneme is an abstraction rather than a natural physical aspect of speech. The second reason for the problem is the limited number of English vowel letters that do double and triple duty in the generation of vowel sounds (Rayner & Pollatsek, 1994). Phonemes are considered to be abstractions because their sound equivalents don't exist by themselves. Phonemes require sounds before and after them to be accurately represented as sounds in speech. For instance, the phoneme /b/ is governed in pronunciation by the vowels and additional sounds that follow it, such as with the words *boy, bat, butter*.

Auditory Factors of Word Identification

The most important auditory aspect related to word identification has been called **phonological awareness**, or **phonemic awareness**. This refers to the sound representation for a word and can be assessed by asking children to segment or blend (Fox, 2000). To segment, the child is requested to break down a spoken word into its component phonemes and to do tasks like saying the components individually, counting the phonemes, or rearranging them. To blend means to combine individual phonemes to produce a word, such as with /c/ /a/ /t/ to make *cat*.

This awareness of sounds has been developing in children as they use the oral language in their everyday lives. They come to school with an intuitive, implicit insight that spoken words are composed of smaller elements or parts that we call syllables and phonemes (May, 1998). Phonemic awareness is the ability to think analytically about words, to be able to manipulate the sounds and rhyme schemes of words (Fox, 2000). Phonemic awareness activities focus on playing with the syllables and phonemes that make up spoken words, such as clapping to distinguish syllables, thinking of other words that rhyme with a certain word, like *cat*, adding the phoneme /d/ in front of a letter cluster like *ad* to make a familiar word, and raising one's finger or hand when rhyming words are heard.

I have been playing a fun game with my grandchildren for the past few years as their language has become more precise in pronunciation. Remember those words your children have difficulty pronouncing correctly; we adults often call their verbal mishaps "baby talk." I have been capitalizing on these so-called mishaps as a way to sharpen their phonemic awareness. The play goes something like this: I say, "When Ricardo was little, he used to say *ight* for *light* and *ady* for *lady*. What sound did he leave out?" I watch as the others put the sound *l* on their lips and yell out the correct sound. Then I say, "What words did he mean?" They say the words *lady* and *light*. Then I say, "Can you name other words that begin with the *l* sound?"

Then we go to the second oldest child. She initially had diffi- culty with the hard /c/ and /g/ phonemes. *Cat* was *tat*, *coat* was *doat*, and her nickname, *Cookie*, was *Dookie*. For a long while I was *cramp pa*. (Maybe I still am). Anyway, we play the same type of ex- ercise, isolating the incorrect phoneme to substitute the correct one. Of course, they are also curious to know about the words my own children, including their mother, had difficulty pronouncing. What is most interesting to observe during their play is the way they at- tentively listen to the words and mouth the phonemes. Sometimes they first repeat the incorrect and then say the correct, probably in an effort to distinguish the two.

The phonemic awareness play discussed above is not too far removed from one of the activities recommended by Hallie Kay Yopp and Ruth Helen Yopp (2000) for building sensitivity to the sounds of speech for young children. Using the charming book *The Hungry Thing* (Slepian & Seidler, 1967), children have to predict and guess what to feed the hungry creature and then their fellow classmates. Children have to make the appropriately correct sound substitu- tions for such silly statements as, "The Hungry Thing wants *feet* loaf" (*meatloaf*), "I have *mogurt* for lunch today" (*yogurt*), "I have a piece of *nizza* for my lunch" (*pizza*), and "We have *napes* to eat" (*grapes*).

Two good articles in the literature that would assist teachers with additional instructional strategies and means of assessing pho- nemic awareness are offered by David Chard and Shirley Dickson (1999) and Hallie Kay Yopp and Ruth Helen Yopp (2000). Chard and Dickson discuss guidelines for assessing children's phonologi- cal awareness and provide a description of a number of published instruments that measure kindergartners and first graders' abilities in phonemic awareness. The Yopps present a nice way to conduct phonemic awareness instruction through four major types of ac- tivities: those that focus on (a) rhyme, (b) syllable manipulation, (c) onset-rime manipulation, and (d) phoneme manipulation. They have also connected the use of some well-known children's literature with the activity's aim. For instance, *Tikki Tikki Tembo* (Mosel, 1989), is read and enjoyed as children clap their hands to account for the number of syllables in the Chinese brothers' names. Books that have a rhyme pattern can help young children with various types of sound ma- nipulations such as the matching, subtraction, and blending of sounds. Books of rhyme can also be used with children during reading expe- riences to help them see grapheme and phoneme connections.

However, spoken words can be broken down into larger sound units than just the individual phonemes; they can also be analyzed into syllables or into units called onsets and rimes, according to Rebecca Treiman (1983, 1985). An **onset** is any consonant or consonant cluster before a vowel in a syllable, and a **rime** is the sound of the vowel and consonant component after the vowel in the syllable as in *-at* or *-ot*, and *-our*. Of course, many words are just one syllable, and they contain a basic spelling pattern or rhyming pattern in the oral language. Thus in the word *blame*, we have the onset *bl* and the rime *ame*. Teachers often have children compose a poem or story using different rhyming patterns such as that contained in the *ame* rime—for example, *blame, tame, same, name, flame, came*. Much more will be said of onsets and rimes in the next chapter and how teachers might capitalize on their use in developing word attack behavior.

Visual Factors of Word Identification

Visual factors related to word identification include letter or alphabet recognition, letter discrimination, left-to-right orientation in word and text order, and an understanding of the word concept in print—that words in print are separated by space boundaries and that each contains its own meaning representation. Alphabet recognition, in itself, reinforces the alphabetic principle because many letters have distinct, corresponding phonemic sounds, such as *b*, *d*, or *m*.

Have you ever noticed a common behavior when young children and children experiencing reading difficulties are asked to read? You'll see some track each word with their finger as they move across the line. These children have a sense of words, and they touch the printed page to ensure that their eyes capture each word in sequence because they are so intent on obtaining meaning. Others will touch the words and read aloud, move their lips, or do some reading silently and some orally. Again, these children are regulating themselves to gain each word in sequence so that they can adequately understand. Still others stop at a word with their finger on it, go back to read other words, trace letters with their fingers, or work their lips to sound out or produce the correct name of the word. These are all necessary thinking behaviors for these children at this time in their reading careers. The children are visually engaged in the world of print and need accommodating, reinforcing behaviors to help them learn both the words and the printed word concept.

The Auditory and Visual Connection

The condition of matching phonemes with graphemes is called **phonics**. Although phonics, phonological awareness, and phonemic awareness appear to be the same, researchers and authors point out that they are not, even though they develop reciprocally in children (Vanderuelden & Siegel, 1995). Instruction in phonemic awareness in classroom settings necessitates teaching children to manipulate the phonemes in spoken words and syllables, according to the National Reading Panel (2000). Phonemic awareness activities should not be confused with phonics instruction, although this overlap may occur when children are asked to blend or segment the sounds in words when letters are used as well.

Awareness of how phonics works is a bit more serious for reading and writing development. When children demonstrate their use of phonics, they make letter-sound associations to work out unfamiliar words they encounter during reading or to conjure up the correct spelling during writing.

Thus, with words, there's a lot more than meets the eye, although it is the eye that is confronted with printed words as they appear in reading, and it is the mind's eye that has to recall the visual form of the word to reproduce it for spelling. The relative importance afforded to either the visual or auditory aspect of reading words has resulted in a sort of tug-of-war between whole-word and phonics enthusiasts, with the teacher bystander often befuddled by the tugging exertion. The reflective teacher needs to consider which side of the rope to tug on more forcefully when certain conditions of reading and writing apply. The teacher should consider how much time and energy to devote to phonics instruction dependent on children's understanding of the alphabetic principle and their ability to use this understanding during reading and writing.

In summary, the sounding out condition of reading rests on the alphabetic principle. The positive aspect of having a limited set of alphabet characters is that new words can be added to the written language as long as the letters representing the words can be read by others. The negative aspect of the English alphabetic system is the difficulty and confusion created for beginning readers of English due to the nature of the phoneme abstraction and vowel letter-sound correspondences. The teacher should consider the aspects of the 166 spelling-sound rules that apply regularly in English, remembering that 45 sound-spelling correspondences were excluded because they didn't reach strict standards (but they're still there!) and that 106 correspondences in spelling-sound relationships occur with vowels.

Figure 2-1 presents a schematic view of what generally occurs during the decoding process. The reader can note that two major mind components are involved somewhat simultaneously, although the "eyes have it" initially. It is the eyes that perceive the letters, calling into activation the phoneme equivalents (if the word is not recognized immediately at sight). Then, once the process is initiated, it moves through the next phase until the learner recognizes the word as a known word in the oral language or as an unknown word, prompting other strategies to occur.

Figure 2-1. The Process of Sounding Out

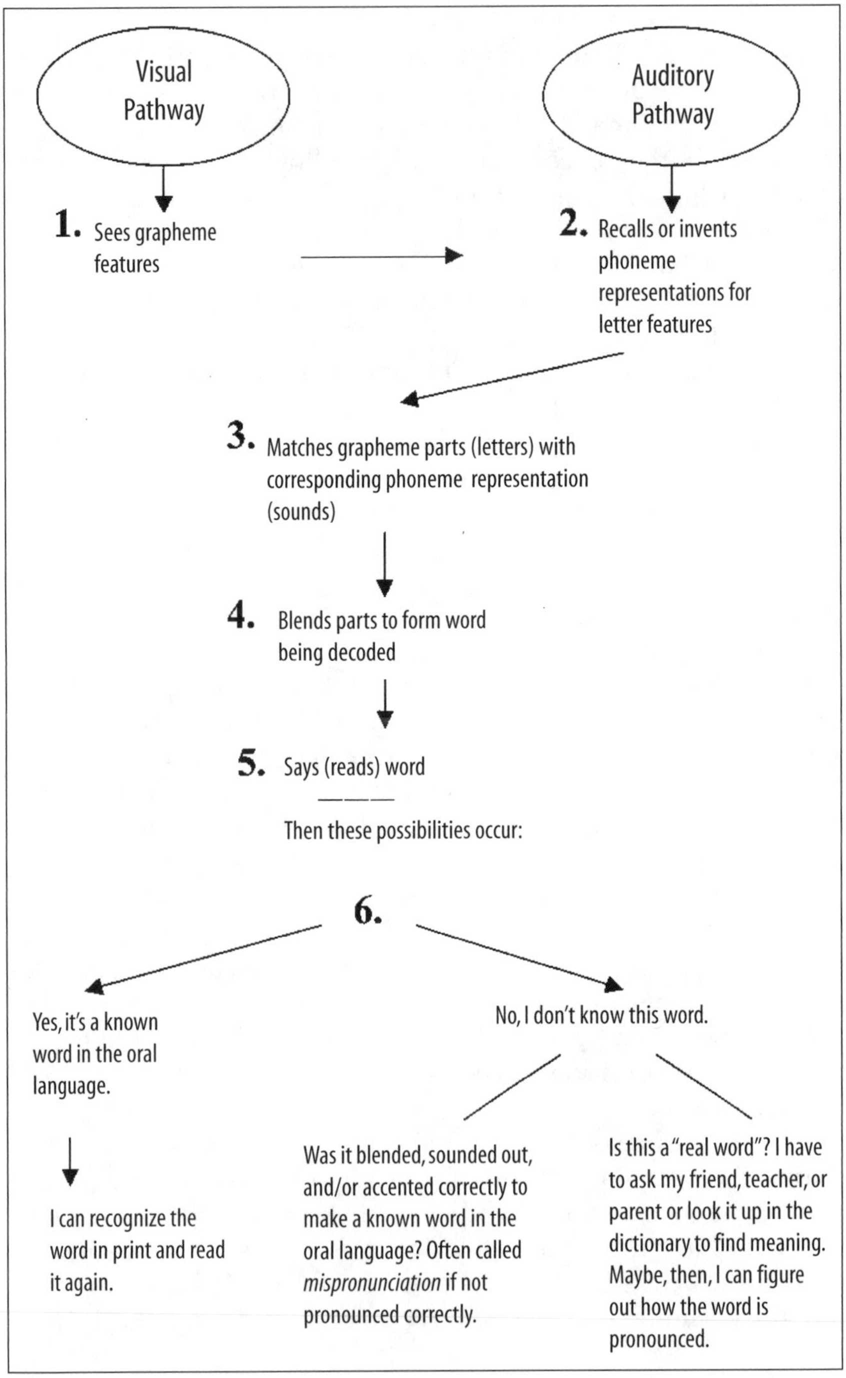

Visual Pathway

Auditory Pathway

1. Sees grapheme features

2. Recalls or invents phoneme representations for letter features

3. Matches grapheme parts (letters) with corresponding phoneme representation (sounds)

4. Blends parts to form word being decoded

5. Says (reads) word

Then these possibilities occur:

6.

Yes, it's a known word in the oral language.

No, I don't know this word.

I can recognize the word in print and read it again.

Was it blended, sounded out, and/or accented correctly to make a known word in the oral language? Often called *mispronunciation* if not pronounced correctly.

Is this a "real word"? I have to ask my friend, teacher, or parent or look it up in the dictionary to find meaning. Maybe, then, I can figure out how the word is pronounced.

We need to take note of two considerations regarding the sounding out process. First, reading, particularly the reading of words at this level of proficiency, can neither be purely auditory nor purely visual, as some might claim. The decoding process by its very nature requires a match, and the matching up of sound to symbol necessitates that the visual and auditory pathways work in harmony. Second, the whole process is superfluous if the reader knows the word by sight. For those tens, hundreds, or thousands of words embedded in the reader's sight vocabulary, there is no need for activation of the auditory pathway because the eyes can already respond accurately to the words. So instead of seeing grapheme features, noted in phase 1 on Figure 2-1, the reader sees the whole word, including its length, its shape, and the grapheme features within it, and rapidly moves on to the next word. Aha! You might be thinking at this point, "What about the child who reads *little* for *letter*, *horse* for *house*, or *committee* for *community*, etc. Shouldn't he be encouraged to be more attentive to sounding out words, to practice more phonics, and to slow down his reading to be more accurate?" Much more will be said of this mental processing in chapter 4.

Controlling the Words Children Learn

The early frequency studies and the establishment of core vocabularies, or sight word lists, have generated four important implications regarding words, according to James Coady (1994b):

1. The reader can determine that, on any given page of text, relatively few different words make up a large proportion of the words on that page. Also, while almost 50% of all text in written English is made up of 100 words, these words conform to highly regular spelling-sound principles more than two-thirds of the time (May, 1998). This means that about one-third of the most highly frequent words would be difficult to read with understanding like the words *the* and *you* if "sounding out" were the only strategy used. The word *the*, the number one most frequent word in print, does not conform to the same rules of pronunciation as *he, she,* and *we*.

2   If the reader knows 5,000 words as familiar words in reading (i.e., has them solidly in her sight word recognition), the reader can fluently process about 89% of the words on any given page.

3. Highly frequent words occur over a wide range of reading materials, whereas highly infrequent words, which are often technical or specialized words, occur within a narrow,

specific context. For instance, to read 99% of the words in a more complicated text, the reader would face about 44,000 words. The gap in the percentage of words frequently recorded in print, between 89% and 99%, is quite large.

4. Coady points out that whereas high-frequency words usually have few syllables, about two-thirds of the low-frequency words found in the English language come from Latin, Greek, or French and are multisyllabic with those identifiable parts called morphemes.

There is another idea associated with the study of the frequency counts of English words. The publication of Thorndike and Lorge's *The Teacher's Word Book of 30,000 Words* in 1944 is believed to have set the stage for all the readability research that has been conducted to the present (Estes, 1994). **Readability** refers to the ways in which the reader might predictably understand the ideas and information in any given text; these include such factors as the clarity of text presentation, the style of writing, and the words used by the author. Every readability formula since 1944 has been based on the notions of sentence length and word count with the assumption being that reading ease or difficulty depends on the length of sentences and the percentage of familiar words in the text. The premise of the **readability formula** is that long sentences and little-known words make for difficult reading, and short sentences with simple, high-frequency words make for easy reading.

However, over the years, the concept of readability has shifted to consider other factors besides familiar words and sentence length. Essays regarding past, present, and future issues in readability were featured in an International Reading Association publication (Zakaluk & Samuels, 1988). Questions were raised about the use of various readability formulas to judge the merit and value of children's reading materials. What about learner interest and the intent of the author? Where would Ernest Hemingway rate on a readability scale? This is one author whose works are widely read in high school and college and who writes in a simple, crisp style. The reader may therefore see the value of the information about words gained from the word frequency studies but may question the validity of using readability scales or formulas to judge whether to offer literary works or quality literature to children.

Let's take a reflective pause to note the influence of the high-frequency word-count studies on education, particularly on the books children read in their classrooms. What developed was a writing style and a word foundation for the materials published for children in the different grades. Textbook authors looked at the words that were most representative of the vocabularies of children at particular age or grade levels. They evolved a concept of **controlled vocabulary**, which refers to the choice and use of a limited number of words in a printed text for children. Introduced in the 1930s, the concept of controlled vocabulary has had important implications for reading instruction up to the present (Robinson & McKenna, 1994). The most common procedure for word selection to control vocabulary was to choose the most frequent words for the first book children would read in school, followed by a group of the next most frequent words, to a choice of the least frequent words for upper-grade reading materials.

The Basal Reader Systems Approach

The name of such styled books to be used by children was **basal readers.** The basal reader concept was grounded in a belief of control by textbook authors to write in a helpful way for children (or so they believed). If children were first exposed to the most frequent words in their classroom reading materials, the logic went, they would have a strong base from which to launch into successful reading of other materials. Thus, in basal reading series published for the classroom the most frequent words were selected, and these words were then reinforced by repeated use in the same book. The premise is that the more often a young reader faces a controlled or limited number of new words, the more success he or she will have in adding these words to sight word proficiency. Another premise is that in reading the most frequently used words in their school texts, children would also be familiar with these words in the oral language. Therefore, word understanding would not be difficult for children, and comprehension of the written selection would be facilitated if word meaning was already known.

The basal reading system was a dominant literacy force in the elementary and middle school language arts curriculum throughout the 20th century and will probably continue to be so well into the 21st century (Reutzel & Cooter, 1999). The basic controlling feature of the traditional basal reader was on the words that would make up a reader's vocabulary. The lower the level of the reader, the more that high-frequency words and words in regular spelling patterns would be used. The words were practiced again in skill books and appeared liberally on tests. There were usually two readers produced for each half-year up to the fourth-grade level. From fourth grade to sixth or eighth grade there was generally one reader for the entire year, but it was still enhanced by all the other aides for each reader. Because vocabulary control, with just so many new words introduced at each level and in each story, was the prevailing view governing what should make up the reading content, the publishing companies capitalized on sales by producing "bridge books" to be used between levels. If a child did poorly on the word and vocabulary tests accompanying a particular basal level, then the child could be assigned a bridge book, which repeated the words of the basal book in a different context.

By 1986, research indicated that in American primary classrooms, basal readers were used 92%–98% of the time in daily reading instruction (Flood & Lapp, 1986). At about the same time, the National Council of Teachers of English began a study to examine the basal system, the philosophical premises that controlled its makeup, and the effect it had on learners (May, 1998). In 1988, the findings showed that all basal books used the control of vocabulary as the major means to sequence their texts, resulting in an effect of more concern with the words used than with the quality of the tales (Goodman, Shannon, Freeman, & Murphy, 1988).

A sharp backlash occurred in the early 1980s to the basal-reader approach in the classroom. The backlash was grounded in the works of some psychologists, such as Jean Piaget and Lev Vygotsky, and the writings about literacy learning expressed by Frank Smith, James Moffet, Ken and Yetta Goodman, Marie Clay, and others. The new movement had such names as "whole language," "literature-based instruction," and "emergent literacy." The types of criticism raised by educators against the use of controlled vocabulary as a basis for children's reading material are echoed in these names and in the concept of constructivism.

The Constructivist View of Learning

According to **constructivism**, learners are actively involved in their own learning because they construct their own understandings from information presented. Learning, then, is not simply a matter of passively absorbing information from someone else, such as by listening to a teacher lecturing, or copying notes taken by someone else. The learner needs to be actively engaged in the learning task in order to connect ideas in a manner that makes sense. In essence, in a learning task of new information or concepts, the student adds on or accommodates the new ideas with stored mental constructs of previous learnings. Because learners are different in their stored mental constructs, the new knowledge that one constructs might be quite different from that of another. Realizing this, skillful teachers in a constructivist classroom scaffold lessons involving new ideas and information with new vocabulary and concept words in incremental steps, being aware of each student's engagement during each step. Teachers can thus feel positive that they are shaping the lesson in the way they wish students' literacy and content development to occur.

Furthermore, students should not be controlled or limited in the initial word learnings offered in printed texts and materials. If reading is regarded as a natural extension of oral and aural language learning, children can be exposed to the writings of good authors, because these authors are writing to children to capture their minds and interest. Children can also learn to read the words of those authors if teachers just show them how to do it. Many literacy authors think that it takes the same amount of energy to learn the word *astronaut* as it does *at* or *hippopotamus* as it does *hat*.

Another key aspect of constructivism is a social one: Classroom interaction does not just involve a teacher and learners in a didactic format. Learning is influenced by the social context and the society of peoples influencing the learning task. Thus, in a constructivist classroom there is a great deal of social interaction between students and between students and the teacher. The social arena could be extended to many teachers if it were increased to bring in school and local community mentors and leaders. The teacher encourages students to interact with one another in reading and writing situations and establishes classroom procedures for doing so, such as paired or "buddy" reading, peer conferencing, learning centers, cooperative learning groups, and workshop groups. When students are connected with other students, the opportunity to expand the scaffolding, guidance model increases. Students are assisting other students in learning situations, and such support greatly aids those students who need more reinforcement with reading and writing.

Constructivism has found its way into many current educational practices. Some of the names used for these practices have a negative association for some in the educational community, and some practices may have just involved a relabeling of the familiar, according to James Moffet (1994). Be that as it may, "whole language," "emergent literacy," "process writing" or "the writing process," "literature-based instruction," "thematic unit instruction," "invented" or "creative" spelling, "peer conferencing," and "readers-writers workshop" are all siblings of constructivist thinking. These philosophies of language learning and classroom practices received their names, in part, because they were conceived as being contrary to popular, skill-based, packaged programs. For instance, James Moffett (1998) maintained that worry over grammar instruction had blocked serious improvement in written literacy education for generations. The analysis of parts of speech and the dissection of sentence parts had substituted for real writing and had taken up time and resources desperately needed for actual language activities. So what's the contrary view to grammar introspection? It is the "writing process."

Likewise, a shift occurred in the belief that young children could naturally emerge into written literacy rather than follow a sequence of preordained stages. Thus, from "reading readiness" and the famous stage models of reading proposed by Jeanne Chall (1996) came the constructivist view of "emergent literacy." The phrase **whole language** came into being as a way to conceptualize a reader's or writer's whole text or literary piece rather than a fragmented, often stylized segment of the piece. Whole-language enthusiasts wanted actual children's authors to be read by children, rather than selections produced by textbook companies who have a different mindset regarding the selection of words for children. Because readers actively interact with texts in the constructivist view, whole-language advocates believe that the actual language, word choice, and style of the author should be the model for children's reading. Thus, whole language represented a contrary view to skills-based, piecemeal instruction occurring out of the context of reading intact textual or literary pieces.

Unfortunately, the name *whole language* has left many educators uncomfortable with the constructivist view. This is unfortunate for a number of reasons. First, many did not realize that whole language was not a distinct program. It was not a ready-to-install package. It was basically a philosophy of instruction regarding all facets of literacy, based on the underpinnings of constructivism. Second, it is probably the older sibling of all the other named practices that have constructivist views, such as literature-based instruction, workshops, and so on. Probably all the other terms could be placed under the whole-language umbrella. Third, to succeed, a whole-language instructional philosophy needs intensive teacher training in the school or district that wishes to use it. Teachers must understand the underlying constructivist concepts and, most important, be practitioners of strategies that allow them to do implicit teaching based on the scaffolding principle.

Finally, as Frank Smith (1999) has noted, whole language has become the "red herring," the strategic ploy used by the phonics enthusiasts to advance their position. Others have characterized the rhetoric of the "return to systematic phonics" as one that has a strong moralistic tone, such as might be equated with "return to family values" (Pearson & Raphael, 1999). We will see that phonic elements can be analyzed, broken down into quite a number of programmed instructional parts. Thus, virtually anyone can make phonics lessons for children once they understand the relationship of sounds and letters and how they work in English. Thus, phonics believers establish a methodology—lessons regarding phonic elements that are packaged and sequenced. Whole-language believers don't have a package and a sequence; they have a belief that what's in learners' heads is a guiding influence on how they construct meaning when they read and write. In this regard, emergent-literacy teachers do help young children construct their phonics skills. They structure their learning environments so that young children become engaged with letters and sounds as they accomplish activities making them construct meaning with letters and sounds.

The Rise of Anthologies

By the early 1990s, a shift occurred from teaching the words of commercially prepared, controlled reading resources to the real language used by original authors. Most, if not all, of the major publishing companies of basal reading series now focus on authentic children's literature and other genre forms, such as poems, plays, and informational readings as the basis of children's reading. Many conceive of the modern reader as a **literature anthology** in which whole selections or excerpts from high-quality children's literature will be found. For instance, from A. A. Milne's collection of stories on Winnie the Pooh, one such vignette may find its way into a new literature-based basal as a complete story.

One has to keep in mind the point of view of the reading series. There are still basal series in the nation's classrooms that are based on the traditional philosophy of vocabulary control, and there are reading series that follow a phonics and/or a spelling pattern orientation. In these, the materials children read are based on the words that have the sound-symbol relationships that are being taught. So when one uses the word *basal* to describe a published reading series, one has to think of the philosophical orientation of that series and mentally place it in the traditional word-centered camp or the literature-based camp. Likewise, when one reads the literature and authors use the word *basal*, one needs to read carefully to see the author's reference point.

The publishing companies are still in control of the reading series market, although the consensus is that they're doing a better job of it with literary infusion (Burns, Roe, & Ross, 1999; May, 1998). They are still producing teacher's manuals, which are especially useful to beginning teachers by providing suggestions and economizing preparation time. There are still individual student workbooks, which may be renamed "practice books," and there remains the checkup procedure of informal assessments through checklists, tests, and suggestions for portfolio collections. However, the more recent resource additions—such as the focus on thematic units (usually five to seven per reader), the inclusion of trade books related to the theme, and the availability of manipulatives, audiotapes, and multimedia software—are very appealing to the average grade-level teacher.

Toward a Balance of the Whole and Its Parts

Since around the mid-1990s, another pendulum shift has occurred in the teaching of printed literacy. This shift has been called **balanced literacy instruction**, and it was undoubtedly fueled by the tug-of-war between phonics and whole language enthusiasts. Indeed, a balance was conceived to exist between the two camps, indicated Ellen McIntyre and Michael Pressley (1996), and the debate centered on how best to teach grapheme-phoneme relationships in beginning reading instruction (Moustafa & Maldonado-Colon, 1999). A major debate question regarding the nature of word learning centered on the following question: Are letter-sound correspondences to be taught within whole contexts, such as those arising from stories and literary works, or are they to be taught explicitly, as had been traditionally done in a specific-skills, systematic approach?

Whole-Part-Whole Instruction

There is an instructional framework that provides a strong way to achieve balance in the classroom, particularly in regard to balancing skills instruction with whole reading and writing experiences. According to both Dorothy Fowler (1998) and Dorothy Strickland (1998), **whole-part-whole instruction** is a way to achieve a balance in literacy instruction, particularly in regard to the weight given to phonics skills instruction and that given to a whole-language, or holistic, orientation. Literacy has a number of processing and representation modes, and the whole-part-whole framework allows the teacher to capitalize on students' active involvement in these modes while providing for various classroom grouping patterns.

In the initial "whole," the entire class is together in one group, and the students generally participate in an entire reading, listening, discussing, and/or viewing event. During the "part," either individually or in groups, they participate in some directed skill work that has emerged or is grounded in context of the "whole." Here is where the teacher can engage students in the various kinds of word study activities that will be presented in chapters 3, 5, and 6. Based on the words used in a particular reading selection, teachers can have students focus on a grapheme-phoneme relationship, practice with the new and unique words used by the author, or get involved in word play by manipulating the prefix, suffix, and root parts to form real and unusual words. With the second "whole," students practice the skill or the new words they learned by using another literacy mode such as writing, artwork, or computer representation. They then often share their work with the whole group.

As whole-part-whole instruction provides a balanced conceptual framework for planning skills instruction, it addresses learners' needs in that it (a) provides for meaningful understanding of whole texts such as literature, basalized stories, information books, poems, and experience stories; (b) allows for in-depth work on language parts with specific skill work; and (c) includes planned practice about the parts of language in meaningful contexts, usually with additional reading and writing activities (Strickland, 1998).

The whole-part-whole instructional framework can be seen as operating as a balance between "wholes" and "parts" in two successful classroom practices of today: Reading Recovery and Reading-Writing Workshops.

Reading Recovery

Reading Recovery is a highly individualized program aimed at one level of student, the beginner who is having difficulty learning how to read and write. Its purpose is to catch children, or "recover" them, before they fail to achieve success with early reading. The program was introduced in New Zealand during the early 1970s by psychologist and educator Marie Clay (1985) with first graders who had received a full year of formal reading instruction in kindergarten in that country.

Reading Recovery, as adapted in the United States and Canada, provides individualized daily literacy instruction to those first graders most at risk for reading and writing success. The young child receives a 30-minute, routinized session with a trained Reading Recovery teacher. The child remains in the tutoring sessions for a number of weeks and is discontinued in the program when he or she attains an average level of reading as compared with other first graders and is believed to be capable of functioning on an average level in ensuing grades (Pinnell, Lyons, & Jones, 1996). The daily individualized session occurs as a supplement to the child's regular first-grade instruction in reading. First-grade children are identified and selected to participate in Reading Recovery through the use of norm-referenced and/or criterion-referenced tests and the judgments of individual teachers. However, Reading Recovery teachers tend to use the assessment criteria originally developed by Marie Clay as part of her total program. The six observational assessments that focus directly on word achievement include the following:

1.   Letter knowledge
2.   A word list to be read
3.   Concept understanding of print
4.   The measurement of letter-sound relationships
5.   The writing of words
6.   The recording of how a child reads an actual text, called a **running record**

The 30-minute lesson framework developed by Clay was based on observations made in classrooms and one-to-one clinical settings and was tailored to achieve an accelerated, efficient use of instructional time so that the child could interact with reading and writing activities with as much engaged time as possible (DeFord, Lyons, & Pinnell, 1995). Each lesson had four components that became a daily, predictable routine for the child allowing the student to know what to expect each day. The lesson components contain many of the good instructional practices to use with emergent readers and writers presented in this book. These include the significance of book reading so that a bond is established among the adult, the child, and the book; the importance of smooth, early fluency in connected reading; and the importance of focusing on the features of words to improve word recognition and writing.

The lesson begins with reading previously read stories and books that the child might choose. Here is where the child enjoys a favorite experience and begins the lesson with a high degree of success. The goal is to practice and achieve fluency with smooth, coordinated reading, with full understanding and enjoyment of the reading experience.

The second segment of the lesson repeats the objective of the first, to practice reading previously introduced material. In this case, the child rereads the text of the day before. The teacher now observes how the child reads and records each word inaccuracy, or **miscue**, that the child makes. The Reading Recovery teacher asks appropriate questions about the **miscued text** and may redirect the child to the text in efforts to improve the child's word-reading proficiency.

After the more global or holistic reading of connected text, the child is directed to focus on parts. Here is where the child becomes engaged in the writing process in order to focus on the components and features of words. Early on, the child may say the sentences that he or she wishes to be written Then the teacher writes them, rereads them for the child, and asks the child to rewrite them. After connecting the sounds of words with their letters, the teacher writes a sentence strip and cuts it up into individual words. The child rereads the words and puts them back in order to make the correct sentence. The word cards may then be taken home by the child for further practice and reinforcement (Rasinski & Padak, 2000). This third component of the Reading Recovery lesson framework contains many good instructional practices for emergent readers and writers, including inventive or creative spelling and the language experience approach, which will be presented in a later chapter.

The lesson concludes with the introduction of a new book or reading selection that is predicted to be just a bit more difficult than the preceding reading selections. The teacher guides the child through the reading. Initially the teacher may discuss the book and engage the child in a "picture walk" through the book. As the child examines and discusses the pictures, he uses the oral language to become engaged with the characters and plot events. Through "talk" and the shared view and reading interaction, the teacher may capitalize on the language used by the child. For instance, he may say a word to describe an event in a picture, but the author may have used a different word. The teacher can reinforce the child's talk by introducing the author's word or words as an alternative, seeking acknowledgement from the child. Therefore, when he actually reads the book during the day's lesson and the following day during the second segment of that lesson, he can predict the words actually written by the author.

Supporters of the Reading Recovery intervention approach for first graders are very keen on the process and methodology. Overall research on Reading Recovery indicates that it is a more effective program in advancing children to average reading levels than other programs seeking to correct reading difficulties (Pinnell, 1994; Rasinski & Padak, 2000).

Workshops

The intent of the workshop structure is to maximize individual student engagement with literacy, particularly with the actual thinking processes necessary for effective use of many words during the reading and writing process. There are two kinds of workshop frameworks, the **writing workshop** and the **reading workshop**, each with a slightly different but complementary focus. In reading workshop, students often write in response to literature, and in writing workshop, students may read in order to obtain ideas of what to write about or to learn aspects of the writer's craft or of written conventions.

A key aspect of both reading and writing workshops is that students take charge of what they do with their time, are able to make choices about what they read and write, and are encouraged to take risks in their written expression. These are all aspects of the constructivist influence. The focus of the workshop structure is on the processes of reading and writing. That is, students discover what readers actually do while reading. They reflect on what they read and what writers do with words to accomplish a publishable, highly readable piece.

According to Elinor Ross (1996) the basic procedures of the workshop structure are as follows:

- A minilesson deals with some aspect of the reading or writing process, such as how to start a written piece with the best word choices to grab the interest of the audience (often referred to as a "good lead"), or on the presentation of a particular literary genre and how to show an appreciation for that style of writing.

- An informal check of each child's progress and intent during the workshop time is often referred to as "a status-of-the-class report." This is accomplished by the teacher recording what each student has done and will be doing as each child's name is called.

- Quiet, individualized reading or writing time, running anywhere from 15 to 30 minutes, comes next, in which students read a literary or informational piece of their choice or are writing and reflecting upon a self-selected topic.

- While students are engaged in individualized reading or writing work, the teacher circulates within the group and conducts individual conferences with students regarding the status of their work in progress. The teacher can appraise and assist with content, understanding, and suggestions for revision.

- Finally, there is whole-group "share time," in which students may tell about what they read, read lines from their book or comments from their response journal, or read excerpts from their in-progress paper in an effort to elicit feedback from the larger group.

Nancy Atwell (1998) cautions that inflexibility and adherence to workshop rules can limit student and teacher interaction during the workshop process. Earlier she suggested that minilessons should run from 5 to 7 minutes, but through actual teaching practice found that minilessons can take up to half an hour. This happens, for instance, when the teacher demonstrates to the whole class how he or she operates as a writer, when students critique a written piece, or when computer use is integrated into the writing process.

Regie Routman (2000) suggests that a very natural way to approach the writing workshop is to start by using journal writing. When students write for several days on a topic and receive feedback from the teacher on high standards and the need for correctness in writing conventions, students sense that writing is an important endeavor. The key for the teacher, in using the journal writing procedure to implement the workshop approach, is to monitor students' work and progress and to raise their expectations for good, legible writing.

Upsetting the Balance

There's a current movement underfoot that appears to be upsetting the harmony temporarily achieved with the whole-part-whole instructional framework and the balanced-literacy concept. This movement is related to a type of writing used for children's early reading books called **decodable text**. This concept reverts back to the issue of who is controlling the words children initially read. A decodable text is composed of two primary features, notes Heidi Anne Mesmer (2001). First, the majority of words presented to children conform to the alphabetic principle, and second, the words children actually read match the sound-symbol relationships they have been taught.

Teachers in the primary grades and teachers who have been assisting children with reading difficulties have been employing this concept for years. That is, they would write their own little stories to reinforce the learning of words containing a previously taught phonic element or phonogram cluster. In the next chapter, I will present a phonic lesson format whereby the phonic element to be learned is initially heard in a story or literary selection, as in the reading of a patterned book, and then practiced in contextual application with a second teacher-written selection.

However, the idea of decodable text gives license to publishing companies to produce little, marketable booklets to match the potential 166 phoneme-grapheme lessons. Witness some beginning and concluding lines of the four-page booklet of *A Fake Snake Tale*, number 5 in the Step-by-Step Practice Story sequence of Open Court Publishing Company (Meramec, 1995):

> Jake made a fake snake from paper. "A snake is just a tail and a face," said Jake. . . ."That fake snake can stay in the lake," said Jake. "I can make a different snake another day."

As a tale reinforcing the long *a* sound, it's great; as a work in the literary tradition of the narrative with plot, conflict, and problem resolution, it leaves much to be desired. After weeks of reflecting on a number of studies that allegedly supported the recommendation of the use of decodable texts with beginning readers, Richard Allington (1997) found that no such support actually existed.

Summary

The major focus of this chapter has been on the systems that control the initial words children encounter in print. The issue of control is highly related to one's belief of how to work with the alphabetic system of the English language. We saw that the whole-part-whole instructional framework is one way to achieve a balance in the way children learn words. The "whole" focuses on whole units of learning arising from stories, trade books, or children's writing, and the "parts" focus on skills development that occurs with sound-symbol relationships, sentence construction, and analysis of word parts.

Concept Words and Terms

alphabetic principle
balanced literacy instruction
basal reader
blend
controlled vocabulary
constructivism
creative spelling
decodable text
grapheme
grapheme-phoneme
    correspondence
literature anthology
miscue
miscued text

onset
phonemic awareness
phonics
phonological awareness
readability
readability formula
Reading Recovery
reading workshop
rime
running record
segment
whole language
whole-part-whole instruction
writing workshop

Word Challenge for Teachers:
Crossword Puzzle

This word challenge activity is a favorite (for children at least): a crossword puzzle. This crossword puzzle taps into the thinking of synonyms. With the longer clues, the reader has more context and thus more words to process and thereby may derive more information to achieve the correct answer. Answers may be found in Appendix A. Once again, to create such a puzzle go to www.puzzlemaker.com. Go through the provided list and select "Criss-Cross Puzzle."

Across

4. The smallest distinct unit of sound in speech
10. Refers to the choice and use of a limited number of words in a printed text to be used by children
11. Vowel elements and letters that follow after onsets

Down

1. A program in which students learn aspects of the writer's craft
2. The recording of how a child reads an actual text

3. The idea that long sentences and little-known words make for difficult reading, and short sentences with simple, high-frequency words make for easy reading

5. Another word for "word inaccuracies"

6. Majority of words conform to the alphabetic principle, and words match the sound-symbol relationships one has been taught

7. Universal word that means the grapheme unit

8. Type of instruction that incorporates both phonics and whole language

9. The visual symbols of which a written word is composed

3

Pathways to Word Identification

Focus Questions

1. What characteristics make phonics instruction so appealing?

2. What are the different ways that phonics instruction can be approached, and what are the advantages and disadvantages of each approach?

3. How might you use other ways to teach sound-symbol relationships, and what might be the appeal of these approaches when compared to phonics-systems approaches?

4. Why is the vowel a major consideration in the various English language sounding out systems?

5. How does writing it out, as in spelling, employ similar and different mental processes than sounding it out, as in decoding?

Word identification, also known as word analysis or word attack skills, refers to one of the cue strategies used by readers to figure out unknown words. Although word identification can be cued by grammar and meaning associations, educators generally acknowledge that the graphophonic system holds a major key in helping emergent readers with symbol-sound associations necessary to decode or attack words. Of course, in the context of word identification through letter-sound relationships, phonics is the big player.

The Appeal of Phonics Instruction

With all that was said about the depth of the alphabetic system and the spelling-sound rules presented in the last chapter, why are the phonics advocates so enthusiastic about teaching phonics as a primary system of initial reading? There are a number of explanations to account for the appeal of phonics. First, phonics as a system of instruction is created by adults, who publish books and phonics systems to help teachers make sense of the spelling-sound rules when teaching children. These adults understand the alphabetic system, so they are looking analytically at the symbol-sound regularities that make up words. In other words, familiarity with reading has already been attained, making phonics look "deceptively easy and useful," suggests Frank Smith (1999). The wise phonics author would not suggest to the instructor to include words such as *have, gone, the,* and *been,* in their lessons on long vowels. These words violate the alphabetic principle even though they are high-frequency words.

Thus, phonics instruction may work well because spelling-sound relationships are taught in a regular, patterned way to children, who have not yet mastered the reading of words and don't know what to look for in words in order to say them. When brought to children in a systematic way, phonics is useful. Probably any literate adult can create a systematic phonics program once the person is mindful of the 166 spelling-sound correspondences and is careful to include exceptions and irregularities. This way, children won't be confused. Children can read with success those materials that follow the instruction of the regular rules but would have great difficulty with the written language of award-winning children's authors, who use words to communicate stories of meaning, interest, and intrigue.

The second reason phonics may work is that it *appears* to be successful. This statement needs a bit of explanation. Many authors will tell us that the goal of phonics instruction is to help students learn spelling-sound correspondences, which will consequently allow them to sound out new and unfamiliar words. We might consider this goal to be one of **transfer**, requiring the thinking processes of **substitution** and **blending**. For instance, we would hope that teaching the /ou/ phoneme as in the word *out* would transfer to the sounding out of *flounder* and *boundary*. However, in lessons I have witnessed of teachers using phonics instruction, it appears that most children can already read all of the words offered in that spelling-sound pattern. Phonics appears to be successful because children can already read the words; they're not working out new or unfamiliar words through application of the targeted spelling-sound pattern or rule for that lesson. Teachers need to get to the transfer stage—to actually determine if children can get to a new word's identity by sounding it out.

Finally, phonics can be very successful by providing children with a large storehouse of words, if the presentation of each phonic element—meaning the grapheme-phoneme correspondence—does not become an end in itself. The goal of each phonics lesson should not be just to practice the spelling-sound correspondence of that lesson such as would occur for a lesson on /ee/ as in *meet*, /ai/ as in *rain*, or /dr/ as in *drop*. There could be at least 166 such lessons. The goal should also be to practice rapid reading of the words introduced in that lesson and rapid recall of the phoneme equivalent as the graphemes, or letter features, are perceived by the eyes.

We noted earlier that a phoneme is an abstraction. A difficulty for many children occurs when phonic elements are taught too hurriedly without practice time to learn the words of one phonic pattern before another is introduced. With too many phonic elements introduced too rapidly, children can't recall the phoneme abstractions as they stare at particular letters. This behavior in particularly bothersome with medial vowels. Think a moment. The child is reading the sentence, "After the ball was hit, it bounded across the playing field." The child reads quite fluently until the word *bounded*. The child hesitates and establishes the /b/ phoneme in her mouth because that grapheme-phoneme correspondence was learned and is solidly entrenched in her memory. She sees the *ou* and remembers that there was a lesson on those letters. The mental fishing begins. Was it the sound of /oo/ as in *moon*, /oi/ as in *oil*, or /ow/ as in *bowl*? Who is going to cue the child with the right phoneme equivalent if the teacher, mom, dad, or another child is not around? The phoneme cue has to come out of the child's own head.

Thus, if the teacher plans to cultivate the phonic elements in some systematic way, the teacher must be reminded to "sow the field" with different levels of words pertaining to each phonic element. First, plant visual recognition of the many words children already know in the oral language. These would become new reading words. Then present less familiar words so that they can practice and transfer the element to the sounding out of new words. Before moving on, make sure that they have that phonic element on the tip of their tongues. In this way, phonics helps children to develop a large storehouse of new reading words that are recognized accurately, immediately, and with little or no effort (Ehri, 1997). That is, a printed page can be read quickly and easily due to the overlearned knowledge that skillful readers generate regarding letters and spelling patterns (Adams & Bruck, 1995).

Automatic word reading can be achieved when children have **word recognition**—enough visual and auditory encounters with words so that they're recognized instantaneously. This means that many children need to practice with teacher-introduced words containing a phonic element in varying contexts—lists, games, sentences, stories—so that they have the words containing that spelling-sound pattern on sight. The goal of phonics instruction is not the teaching of each and every spelling-sound correspondence as an end in itself. The goal should be to guide children to use phonics instruction as a means to an end: fluent and meaningful comprehension. The process of phonics would then be to familiarize children with letter-sound correspondences, use this familiarity to transfer to the rapid reading (and spelling) of words, and use rapid, fluent word reading and spelling to achieve such good efforts as the reading of books and the writing of stories.

Phonics and Word Attack Approaches: To What Depth?

Recent national reports have noted that there is no consensus on what is the best way to teach phonics and word attack skills (National Reading Panel, 2000; Snow, Burns, & Griffin, 1998). This brings us to still other areas of controversy in ways to approach the graphophonic system. First of all, there are issues relating to the depth and sequence of the word attack, phonics program as the language arts curriculum shifts perspective through the grades. Those favoring a code-emphasis instructional focus want to get phonics and decoding done quickly in the early grades so that children can get on to regular reading, whereas the meaning-emphasis group believes that if children attain meaning first, they will consequently learn how to associate sounds with letters (Pearson & Raphael, 1999). If phonics instruction is done in the early grades, the belief goes, children in grade 4 and above will have the letter-sound foundation to focus on the next stage: the multiletter structural features of words that include prefixes, suffixes, root words, contractions, and syllables (Fox, 2000).

Then there's the issue of the vigor and intensity of the word attack program in the curriculum. Is the instruction in word attack, particularly as related to phonics instruction for early readers, going to be explicit, implicit, or incidental? Another way to phrase this question is "Who's in charge of the way phonics is going to be taught?"

Those who favor **explicit phonics** instruction want a structured phonics and word attack curriculum approach taught by direct instruction in sequenced lessons. Therefore, the curriculum itself is "in charge," and the teacher merely implements it. One such program is the Orton-Gillingham multisensory approach to language and word learning, which uses visual, auditory, kinesthetic, and tactile modalities in the learning of words. Each phonetic unit and sequence, as it appears in the oral language (the phoneme) and the written language (the grapheme), is learned through hearing, speaking, seeing, and writing, in coordination and reinforcement with one another. The Academy of Orton-Gillingham Practitioners and Educators (1999) believes that learners have a need for a program that is multisensory, phonetically based, structured, sequential, cumulative, and rational.

An **implicit phonics** curriculum framework would allow for phonics and word attack strategies to be taught within the context of particular readings, such as selections found in basal anthologies or children's literature. A teacher, a group of teachers, a school, or a district may preselect particular readings to be used at particular grade levels from aesthetic and meaning-oriented viewpoints. However, the readings may also lend themselves to the teaching of a **phonic element,** defined as a grapheme-phoneme correspondence. In this regard, teachers often use pattern books and books of rhyme. In a **pattern book**, a phrase or even a whole line or sentence is repeated over and over, so that the reader predicts the words that are coming. Reading these pattern books to children helps them build sensitivity to the sounds of speech, or phonemic awareness. Some patterns may also have rhyme, as in this verse from *Brown Bear, Brown Bear, What Do You See?* by Bill Martin (1983):

> Brown Bear, brown bear, what do you see?
> I see a red bird looking at me.
> Red bird, red bird, what do you see?
> I see a yellow duck looking at me.

Some of the most famous books that use rhyming words and bring smiles to children's (and adults') faces are those written by Dr. Seuss. In the *I Can Read With My Eyes Shut!* book, he writes about reading (Geisel, 1978):

> You can read about trees . . . and bees . . . and knees.
> And knees on trees!
> And bees on trees!
> And bees on threes!
> And when I keep them open
> I can read with much more speed.
> You have to be a speedy reader
> 'cause there's so, so much to read!

From one or both of these books, teachers may have focused on the /ee/ phoneme (the long *e* vowel sound) that is prompted by the *e* or double *ee* spelling at the end of words such as *me, be, see, tree, bee, knee, three.* Teachers can add *he, we, she,* but obviously not *the.*

In the implicit approach to phonics there's a plan of sorts, and a teacher formulates the plan based on striking the right balance between getting the most for children out of a meaning-oriented, context-driven approach to materials and out of using a sound-symbol reference system to help them learn words. Because teachers—and most likely school administrators and school boards—have different views on the right balance, they place different emphasis on the role of phonics in their literacy programs (Freppon & Dahl, 1998).

Incidental phonics and word attack instruction places the teacher completely in charge. As opportunities arise out of children's classroom reading and writing experiences, teachers pursue the teaching of a phonic element. In essence, phonics instruction arises out of a **teachable moment**. That is, when a student can't unlock the identity of an unknown word, but the teacher sees that a graphophonic element provides a clue, the teacher would, at that moment or soon after, provide a lesson on that element. This type of instructional stance might be linked to that of **embedded phonics**, in which phonics instruction is an aspect of authentic reading and writing experiences (Stahl & Stahl, 1998). **Authentic** has become a term used by many educators to mean the reading of unexpurgated children's literature—not basalized or controlled versions—and the writing children themselves accomplish, not the writing needed to fulfill the requirements of ditto and work sheet pages.

Thus, the issue of the intensity of the phonics program is somewhat rooted in the issue of control. The higher the controlling authority—from state to district to school to teacher—the more likely that its philosophical view on how to teach phonics and word attack in the curriculum will prevail. It is into this educational climate that the whole-language movement surfaced. The whole-language proponents held very strong negative beliefs about the issues of control and piecemeal skills instruction that occurred with the use of books that regulated vocabulary and language structure. This instruction was usually direct and isolated, particularly in regard to spelling-sound correspondences, and placed undue emphasis on accuracy (Adams & Bruck, 1995). Moreover, whether to teach spelling-sound relationships became the best discriminator between polarized groups, giving rise to two sides in the "Great Debate"—phonics and direct instruction versus whole language.

Into this whole-language versus phonics curriculum debate came a research study that investigated how and to what depth phonics was taught in whole-language classrooms. In eight different urban and suburban classrooms, involving primarily 178 Caucasian and African-American children, the researchers found that nine whole-language teachers covered the concepts of phonological awareness and phonemic representation during a full third of their instructional time. Phonics instruction became part of their daily whole-language activities, with 45% of phonics-documented activities occurring during writing time.

Across the eight classroom environments, researchers Karin Dahl and Patricia Scharer (2000) found three common threads:

1.   Teachers were able to assess and respond to learners' individual needs during reading and writing conferences. Teachers showed that they had deep knowledge about each student and could provide appropriate individual instruction as needed.

2.   Phonic skills were taught within the context of meaningful reading and writing activities. Moreover, students applied phonics concepts and skills in reading and writing new words. They appeared to demonstrate a real interest in how words worked and profited from the inquiry procedure in word-pattern searches and the exploration of letter-sound relationships fostered by their teachers.

3.   Phonics instruction was not just part of the reading curriculum but was featured during writing time, when children wrote and discussed their own pieces, surfaced during teacher conferences and flourished again when children participated in shared writing events.

Two Major Variations in Traditional Phonics

Within the phonics approach to word recognition, there have been two traditional variations in how the actual instruction is to be implemented. Phonics methods overall are based on the premise that the written symbols, or graphemes, of our alphabetic language represent phonological information. Such phonics methods intend to provide beginning readers and writers a basis for recalling the ordered identities of useful letter strings and for obtaining the meanings of printed words by making the relationships between spellings and sounds explicit (Adams & Bruck, 1995).

It is with the explicitness of the approach in showing children the spelling-sound relationships that the phonics methods differ. One very direct approach has been called **synthetic phonics**, deductive instruction, or the explicit phonics method (Leu & Kinzer, 1999). In this approach, the teacher focuses on the sound-symbol features of letters first, often in isolation. Next the teacher proceeds to the construction of words, followed by the use of the targeted words in larger meaning units such as stories or poems. It is an approach that is generally quite structured, such as with the Orton-Gillingham method previously discussed, in that when a word is taught, children are directed to visually sequence letter by letter, to assign sounds to the letters as they are encountered, and then to blend the letter-sound combinations to make the targeted word.

Synthetic phonics is based on a "bottom-up" theory of learning, suggesting that readers need to mentally process information letter by letter, word by word, and sentence by sentence until comprehension occurs (Reutzel & Cooter, 1999). As the sequence of such phonics skills instruction is from individual graphemes and phonemes to actual reading texts, synthetic phonics is regarded as part-to-whole instruction (Fox, 2000). This approach would undoubtedly be favored by those who advocate an explicit, direct, structured approach to teaching phonics—one in which the phonics system itself is in control.

A second approach to teaching phonics that is less explicit in its methodology is known as **analytic phonics**, inductive instruction, or the implicit phonics method. This approach starts off with a context, which could be a poem, a rhyme, a story, or even a string of sentences. Within the context are words that contain the phonic element or the spelling-sound feature of that day's lesson. After the story or poem is read or heard by the children, the teacher asks them to identify or name some words that contained a particular sound. If the children read the particular contextual selection, the teacher asks them to focus on the letters that made the sound of the day. After the grapheme-phoneme focus and identity, children practice words with that letter-sound correspondence. Finally, children apply their learning by using the day's words in reading and writing activities. Basically, there are four major procedural steps in the method framework of analytic phonics, as outlined by Leu and Kinzer (1999):

1. Provide examples of the rule or principle.
2. Use the examples to help students discover or induce the rule, principle, or pattern that applies.
3. Provide guided practice in which students practice the insights they have discovered—for example, by using the new principle to decode new words.
4. Provide independent practice, such as by having children read a story or content selection with words having the phonic element of the day's lesson.

The analytic approach has been called whole-part-whole instruction because it begins with a whole, meaning context and words, usually presented through the oral language, continues to the study of isolated parts of letter-sound relationships within the words, and then back again to whole words and reading and writing contexts using those words (Fox, 2000). In this approach, the teacher provides a procedure, a plan, for helping children to discover or induce the phonic insight governing a symbol-sound relationship. Teachers preferring this procedure would undoubtedly be more favorably inclined to a whole-language approach to literacy and would have more integrated or holistic language beliefs regarding how children learn to read and write.

A Report on Systematic Phonics Instruction

The National Reading Panel (2000), in its landmark report *Teaching Children to Read*, presented five possibilities of phonics instructional approaches. Four of the five would be considered systematic in their approach: analogy phonics, analytic phonics, phonics through spelling, and synthetic phonics. The fifth, embedded phonics, was described earlier in this chapter as being incidental and as arising out of opportunities in which phonic elements can be taught in the context of textual readings.

The Panel conducted a literature search of studies that investigated the use of phonics instruction to improve reading ability. From an initial identification of 1,373 studies conducted since 1970, the Panel analyzed 38 studies that had a clear research methodology in which a phonics treatment group was compared with a control group. The overall findings are important in considering the merits of phonics-oriented instructional methods and approaches and are summarized as follows:

- Overall, the analyses revealed that systematic phonics instruction improves children's success in learning to read and that systematic phonics instruction results in more effective learning than instruction that has little or no phonics instruction. The Panel defines *systematic phonics* as an explicit approach that occurs when phonic elements are planned and taught in sequence.

- For children in kindergarten through sixth grade and for those experiencing reading difficulties, systematic phonics instruction resulted in significant benefits.

- Those kindergartners who received systematic beginning phonics instruction increased in the ability to read and spell words.

- First graders who were taught through a systematic phonics approach were stronger in their ability to decode words and spell, and their understanding of text was higher.

- Phonics instruction for older children resulted in a stronger ability to decode, spell words, and orally read text, but not to understand text.

- Low-achieving students with reading problems and students identified as learning disabled benefited substantially in their ability to read words with systematic synthetic phonics instruction.

- Children of low socioeconomic status improved in alphabetic knowledge and word-reading skills with systematic synthetic phonics instruction.

- Systematic phonics instruction helped good readers across all grade levels to spell more accurately. This effect was noticeably stronger for kindergartners. Interestingly, the impact of phonics instruction in helping poor readers spell better was small.

The Panel did caution that phonics instruction is "a means to an end." That end is the ability to apply letter-sound knowledge. The purpose of learning sounds for letters is for children to be able to apply the phoneme-grapheme correspondences "accurately and fluently in their daily reading and writing activities."

A phonic element lesson that has served me well for many years is shown in Table 3-1. The lesson is in 10 steps, having been altered from a 9-step lesson format initially presented in one of my own college reading classes. Unfortunately, no citation was provided then; I can only say that I gratefully build on the work of a colleague. I have used the lesson format through the years, initially as a classroom teacher and reading specialist working with referred children through the grades, and later as a college instructor to assist forthcoming teachers in their work with children.

Table 3-1. A 10-Step Phonic Element Lesson, Using */oo/* as in *Moon* to Illustrate

Step	Explanation	Directions	Learning Principle
1. Reading Aloud	Read aloud a selection that contains the targeted phonic element. If a published selection is not available, the teacher could write a short selection or poem. In this case, the teacher used *The Day the Goose Got Loose* by Reeve Lindbergh.	After reading the selection a few times, ask children to name words that had the same sound. The teacher can reread parts so that children can isolate and pronounce words that have the */oo/* sound, as in *goose*. Then the teacher can follow the steps of the lesson by using the directions below.	Beginning with a meaningful "whole" before the "parts" are analyzed provides children with a larger context.

cont.

Step	Explanation	Directions	Learning Principle
2. Auditory Sensing	Read aloud groups of words that contain the day's phonic element. It's best when three or four words are in each group. The words could come from the read-aloud selection.	Listen to the first group of words. Tell me what sound you hear in each word. Also tell me where you hear that sound (beginning, middle, end). Repeat the procedure for more groups of words. For example: Group 1 – *goose, noon, spoon, loose* Group 2 – *moon, pool, boot, tooth* Group 3 – *broom, roof, spool, proof*	Sensing the auditory properties or phoneme equivalents as they sound in words.
3. Visual Sensing	Have the groups of words that were pronounced in step 2 ready on chart paper or the chalkboard. The printed words will appear in grouped lists.	Look at the words printed in column 1. Who can tell what letters are the same in each word? Come up to the board and circle the letters that are the same in each group.	Sensing the spelling pattern or grapheme components that correspond to the phonemes.
4. Auditory Fixing	Read aloud word groups in which one word contains the phonic element of the day. Students have to raise their hands, hold up a response card, or show in some visible way that they are phono-logically aware of the sound.	Listen to the group of words. When you hear a word with the day's sound hold up your hand (card, banner). What is today's sound? (elicit) Group 1 – *name, nine, noon, next* Group 2 – *feel, foot, fall, fail* Group 3 – *heap, hope, help hoop*	Discriminating the phoneme from others found in similar positions in words
5. Visual Fixing	Have groups of words listed (could be similar to those of step 4) on the board or chart paper. One word will contain the day's spelling pattern while the other words would look similar in configuration but have other vowel clusters.	Look at the words printed in the columns. One word has our letters (spelling pattern) of the day. Come up to the board and circle (box-in) the word that has our letters. What sound does our letter group make? Also what are our letters? (elicit) Group 1 – *beam, bowl, boot, beak* Group 2 – *pail, pool, peel, Paul* Group 3 – *stale, stove, steel, stool*	Discriminating the letters (graphemes) from other letters found in similar locations in words. Also beginning to internalize the phoneme-grapheme correspondence.
6. Auditory Blending and Substitution	The teacher's goal is to pro-vide a way through guided practice to help children accomplish the essence of phonics – that of transferring the phonic element. Children substitute the targeted phoneme into another word and blend the sounds to make the appropriate word. Teachers need to be skillful in selecting similar words in spelling pattern structure, so that the day's phoneme can be appropriately transferred.	Listen to the word *seen*. Does this word have our sound of the day? Let's take the /ee/ out of *seen* and put in /oo/ is in *moon*. What word did we make? Yes, *soon*. Then do *feel, fool* *boat, boot,* *bream, broom* *neat, noon*	This step is the real "bread and butter" of phonics. The child accomplishes substitution, segmenting, and blending of the phonic element to make a word. This step is auditory discovery of the principle.

cont.

Step	Explanation	Directions	Learning Principle
7. Visual Blending and Substitution	The goal here is to provide a printed way for children to transfer the grapheme elements or spelling pattern of the phonic element to make a new word. Again, the teacher needs to be careful in selecting appropriate words so that the correct transfer can take place.	Look at these words on the list. Do they have our letters of today? (the *oo* letters) Take the underlined letters out of the words and put in our letters. What words did you make? For example: Let's change: Steep to st_ _ p Leap to l_ _ p Bait to b_ _ t Roam to r_ _ m	Children see the position of the *oo* element in words and practice transfer of the letters. When they write in the grapheme(s), they blend to read the new words containing the sound of the day.
8. Listening Context	Read aloud sentences or two-line rhymes in which children have to use a word(s) containing the sound of the day.	Listen to the sentences or poems I will say. A word will be missing. Can you give a word that makes sense in the sentence that also has our sound of the day? For example: Twist the rope to make a _____ (loop). Or Mom said, "Go to your _____ (room, roam, ream) and sweep the floor with a _____ (broom)."	Use of context to facilitate meaning while focusing on the target sound to apply an appropriate word to obtain meaning.
9. Reading Context	Provide written activities so that students use the new words appropriately in differing contexts. Such activities could be: • Sentence completion • Definition matching • Crossword puzzles • Mix-ups and fix-ups • True-false statement choice	Let's read the direction to the activities. Follow the directions and select the best word that make sense in the sentence, puzzle, or other activities.	Use of written context to facilitate meaning while focusing on words containing the day's letter pattern(s) . . . also providing reading opportunities with the new words to promote fluency.
10. Story (cloze) Application	Write a short story using words that have the day's phonic element. Then delete the words to make a cloze selection. Arrange the words in a word box above, below, or alongside the selection.	Read the story to the end to get a sense of the meaning. Then choose words from the word box that make the best sense in the story. For example: "One wet night Tom wanted to take his pet _____ for a walk. He put on his coat and _____. He started to walk the dog but tripped on a tree _____. He fell, hit his head and out came his _____." Word Box boots, root, poodle, Booth Lesson provided by: Amy Housel, St. John's University, Reading Graduate Student	Applying the new words in a reading context . . . shows the ability to read and use the new words appropriately . . . also began with a meaningful "whole" by listening to a story, now close with a meaningful "whole" through reading.

The lesson is primarily analytic in nature in that children have to think and discover rules by induction. The blending and substitution aspects in steps 5 and 6 require children to deal with the basic constructivist thinking of phonics. They have to transfer the learning of auditory (phonological) and visual (graphemic) elements to the construction of new words. (The auditory sensing step that begins the lesson would today be called phonological awareness.) Within the lesson is enough practice with the phonic element and with words containing that phonic element to find favor with those who prefer a direct phonics approach. However, flexible, resourceful teachers will use the best of both the direct and indirect approaches to get the job done right (May, 1998).

Remember to conduct the phonic-element lesson focusing on one spelling-sound correspondence at a time. In other words, the long *u* sound would have three separate lessons because it is found in three distinct spelling patterns that each yield a fair number of words. The double /*oo*/ in *moon* lesson found in the table would be a separate lesson from the /*u-e*/ pattern in *cube* and the /*ew*/ lesson in *blew*. However, once one spelling-sound correspondence is learned well, the teacher can compare words from two patterns and then from all three patterns. A potential 30-lesson sequence focusing on the vowels will be given later.

The Word Family and Analogy Approach

Teachers often display lists of words that rhyme and have the same spelling pattern on charts and within visual displays that pertain to a lesson or story. For instance, with Lindbergh's selection *The Day the Goose Got Loose* (1990), the teacher may display a shape of a goose. Within that shape may be the other words that rhyme with *goose* from the story, plus additional words that have the spelling of -*oose* (*loose, noose, moose*). Many words from Dr. Seuss and other rhyming word books could appear in teacher-prepared, spelling-pattern lists. Such a spelling-pattern technique offers an alternative approach to the phonics system that focuses on the correspondence of smaller units of phonemes and graphemes.

The **spelling pattern**, or rhyming technique, is also called the **word family**. This technique of teaching has been called the phonogram approach and, more recently, the analogy approach. The National Reading Panel identified these as analogy phonics and phonics through spelling. The derivation of "word family" is not clear, but conventional wisdom suggests that members of a family have the same last name but different first names; similarly, the words in a rhyme family have the same last letters, or **phonogram**, but different initial letters (Cunningham, 1994). A phonogram is defined as a series of orthographic letters that have the same phonetic or sound value in a number of words (May, 1998). It is the initial letter that makes the distinctive difference in the way the word will be named (*hop, mop, pop, top,* etc.).

Analogy refers to the fact that readers search for letter patterns rather than individual letters as they attempt to sound out words. In this search, they find it easier and more advantageous for word recognition to focus on the onsets (the consonants and consonant clusters in front of words) and then blend the initial sound with the rime (the vowel element and letters which follow) (Goswami, 1993; Goswami & Bryant, 1992). Thus, it is easier to divide *bell* and *tell* into *b-ell* and *t-ell* than into *b-e-ll* or *t-e-ll*. Moreover, because *bell* and *tell* are known words, the reader will use, by analogy, the regularity of the rime to work out the unknown word *swell*.

Two researchers examining the words most frequently used by 900 children in grades 1 through 3 found that just 37 phonograms account for a potential vocabulary of 500 words (Wylie & Durrell, 1970). Their published list of 37 phonograms, shown in Table 3-2, are of high utility in generating the reading of words.

Table 3-2. The 37 Phonograms

-ack -ail -ain -ake -ale -ame -an -ank -ap -ash -a t -ate -aw -ay

-eat -el -est

-ice -ick -ide -ight -ill -in -ine -ing -ink -ip -it

-ock -one -op -ore -ot

-uck -ug -ump -unk

Nearly three decades later, Edward Fry (1998) reported that 38 phonograms can produce 654 one-syllable words. Fry acknowledges the accomplishments of the earlier phonogram researchers and notes that his phonogram list forms the basis of many polysyllabic words as well. Familiar phonograms occur in many syllables that are found in thousands of multisyllabic words (Johnston, 1999).

For those teachers who are not enamored with the various phonics systems and approaches but do wish to ensure that children have a strong foundation in the alphabetic principle to serve their reading and spelling needs, the word-family, spelling-pattern approach presents a good alternative, possibly with some advantages. First, there are just under 40 high-utility spelling patterns that yield the potential to read and spell many words and syllables, compared to the 166 or more graphophonic correspondences that would be covered individually in a phonics approach. By initially focusing on the 37 phonograms in the Wylie and Durrell list, the teacher can add patterns, build words, and generate student motivation with the procedure. For instance, in the shape of the goose discussed earlier were written the words *goose, loose, noose,* and *moose.* When a Native American selection is read, the word *papoose* can be added. When the little blue engine finishes pulling the circus train over the once insurmountable hill, the word *caboose* can meaningfully end the list.

A second advantage has to do with the vowel. We noted that the phoneme is an abstraction and that vowels pose the greatest difficulty for beginning readers because there are 106 graphophonic correspondences generated by six vowel letters. You'll notice that each of the spelling patterns is headed by the vowel and followed by the consonant(s). The spelling pattern itself controls the ambiguity of the vowel sound because the vowel is blended with the consonant unit to make one distinct sound, such as /ack/, /ice/, or /ot/. Blending the onset (an initial letter) with the rime (the spelling pattern, phonogram, or word family) is easier for young children because there are only two items, rather than all the letter-sound correspondences necessary to sound out an individual word with phonics, such as with *best* (/b/ + /e/ + /s/ + /t/) (Fox, 2000). Thus, the spelling-pattern approach presents a larger alphabetic chunk of visual information to assist children's mental processing in sounding out words.

A third aspect of the spelling-pattern method would be the way it is done: quite straightforward and of high immediate usefulness to children. A major way to display the patterns and have children use the words within the pattern is to create "pattern boxes," which are shown in Table 3-3.

Table 3-3. Pattern Boxes

	-at			-ight			-oose
b	at		n	ight		g	oose
h	at		s	ight		l	oose
c	at		l	ight		n	oose
s	at		t	ight		pap	oose
						cab	oose

The teacher should note that the vertical line separating the on-set from the rime can stay, be reduced, or be eliminated as children get used to the procedure. Such pattern box displays were very popular with linguistic reading series produced in past decades. I can recall witnessing, after a few weeks of using pattern boxes such as -et, -en, -ot and -at, young first graders going spontaneously to the chalkboard and writing, "A wet pet sat in a pen" or "A wet fat cat met a hen on a cot." The children would try to outdo themselves by producing the most linguistically correct sentences using the words available in the pattern boxes. The words were also spelled correctly!

Once children see the alphabetic principle at work, they become knowledge seekers and inventors. I recall one youngster who returned from a vacation and announced, "I visited a launching site, and the spelling is different from the one we learned." What a wonderful opportunity to launch into the -ite spelling pattern. A new pattern box is created showing the -ite rime with the words *bite, kite, white,* and *site.* Children can now write sentences, poems, and short selections using both -ight and -ite spelling-pattern words. The pattern boxes are displayed throughout the classroom or on one wall and become an organized display called a **word wall**. Be sure to leave space on the bottom of each pattern-box chart so that when a child deduces a word containing a rime, the word can be correctly added to an open slot in the pattern box (as was done with *papoose* and *caboose*). Margaret Moustafa and Elba Maldonado-Colon (1999) suggest that words containing particular onsets and rimes in the English and Spanish languages drawn from different stories can be placed in a pocket chart or on a movable word wall.

The final potential strength of the word-family approach is found in the analogy concept. Once some key words are learned in their spelling patterns, children can transfer this knowledge to read new words by analogy. That is, once -eep is learned in words like *keep* and *peep,* the child can transfer the symbol-sound properties to blend and synthesize /st/ to make *steep* and even *steeple.* It is not necessary to teach every common spelling pattern or phonogram to show children how the alphabetic principle works. Once children have learned some patterns, they become good at generalizing the visual pattern of the rimes and using that knowledge to read and spell new words while building an intuitive understanding of rimes. Both the onsets and the rimes provide rather dependable visual maps to sound, thereby allowing readers to gain confidence in word attack skills (Fox, 2000).

Furthermore, knowledge of spelling patterns is crucial to readers even if they are unaware that such orthographic knowledge allows them to recognize words holistically, all at once (Adams & Bruck, 1995). When readers read and when writers write, they unconsciously use a visually driven plan to cluster letters into familiar spelling patterns to process known and unknown words efficiently.

Remember those little wooden blocks you played with when you were a child? I remember "borrowing" some from my first daughter's toy box to use with my struggling readers. In those days, I didn't know the vocabulary of onset and rime as a teacher, but I understood the utility of the phonogram, or word-family, concept. On the side of each one I pasted a small cutout of cardboard (usually an old manila folder would work fine). Thus I had a block with six blank sides. Depending on the reader, I would crayon phonograms (rimes) such as *-end, -ent, -ell, -est, -et,* and *-ead* on the cardboard faces of one block and consonant or blend (onsets) on the six faces of another block. The trick was to try to select onsets and rimes that would match up when the blocks were rolled like dice to make a real word. Thus the consonant *b* would produce either *bend, bent, ball, best, bet,* or *bead* when the two blocks were rolled, and a student had to combine the elements to form the word.

Now those little wooden blocks of days past are collector's items! Nevertheless, you can make your own onset and rime cube by using two empty pint-size milk cartons (Cernek, 2000). First you cut off the tops of the milk cartons, and then fit one carton into the other to create a small cube. Using butcher paper, cardboard, or white mailing labels on each side, you can write onsets on one cube and rimes on the other. Teachers tell me they also use those small, equal-sided tissue boxes. Cernek suggests an alternative activity to create two spinners alongside each other. One spinner, acting like a game wheel at a carnival, would point to an onset when it stopped, and the other would point to a rime. Once the students rotate the two spinners, they would blend the onset selection such as *fl-* with the rime selection such as *-ing* to make the word *fling*.

One school uses the analogy approach to decoding for students in grades 1–8. The school's program, called the Benchmark Word Identification Program, is divided into two levels: the beginning level is designed for emergent-level readers and those reading at a first-grade level, and the intermediate level is for those students reading from second-grade to sixth-grade levels. At both levels students are shown how to decode words by comparing an unknown word to known words called *keywords* (Gaskins, Gaskins, & Gaskins, 1991, 1992). The program was revised in recent years and features little books coordinated with the phonograms that are introduced in each lesson.

The keywords are words that contain the common spelling patterns, or phonograms. The program selects 120 phonograms for the beginning level and an additional 94 phonograms for the intermediate level. Both sets of phonograms are derived from published lists of keywords and phonogram patterns (Fry, Fountoukidis, & Polk, 1985; Sakiey & Fry, 1984).

Students are taught the following four major thinking strategies with the Benchmark Program:

- First they are shown how to use the spelling patterns within the keywords to decode an unknown word. For instance, if the unknown word was *replenish*, the student might be able to recall the *-e* spelling pattern from *he*, the *-en* spelling pattern from *hen*, and the *-ish* spelling pattern from *wish*. This type of thinking is known as the compare-contrast strategy. The strategy is initially teacher directed and taught in an explicit way, with a gradual lessening of responsibility by the teacher so that students can apply the comparison-contrast thinking on their own (a good example of the scaffolding procedure).
- Once words are decoded, students work to achieve automatic or instantaneous recognition of the words. Context is used to support understanding of meaning, so that if a new word is met during reading, the student determines if it makes sense in a sentence or in a larger context.
- Besides the phonogram units, students are shown how to break down words into the units of prefixes, suffixes, roots, and syllables.
- Finally, because of the unevenness of sound-symbol correspondence in the English language, students are encouraged to be flexible when attempting to apply word parts they know. For instance, if the unknown word is *objective*, students have to be able to take the *-ive* from *five* and *give* to figure out the correct word pronunciation.

Additional information about the program may be obtained by contacting the Benchmark School, 2107 North Providence Road, Media, PA 19063.

Other Approaches to the Alphabetic Principle

This section presents three other ways that the teacher can help children read and write words as the teacher remains cognizant of the alphabetic principle. In keeping with the discussion of the preceding section, with its emphasis on spelling-pattern clusters and combining of onsets and rimes to make words, the next procedure is a similar strategy technique.

A Perceptual-Conditioning Decoding System

This technique is known as the **Glass-Analysis System for Decoding Only**. Its intent is to help children focus on the letters and sounds within words, blend them, and use letter-sound clusters to unlock bigger words. It was developed by a friend and colleague, Dr. Gerald Glass, and his wife, Dr. Esther Glass. The Glass-Analysis approach to decoding words became very popular in the districts of Long Island. In fact, once teachers were trained and had practiced the procedure with their own students, they swore to its effectiveness.

The Glass system encourages children to look at and say letters and sounds in words to develop a kind of **perceptual conditioning**, particularly with vowel clusters and the structural parts of words. It is quite closely aligned with onset and rime conditioning, except that the Glass system always has five major steps in the decoding analysis. It is structured in that the teacher leads the five steps of the decoding drill. The teacher is also requested to call upon different children for answers to the perceptual conditioning questions. In this way all the children in the group remain mentally active with the sounding, blending, and subtraction of elements. Let's follow the steps with the word *sing*:

1. The teacher says the whole targeted word—*sing*—and the children repeat it.
2. The teacher provides a sound and asks children what letters make the sound. For instance, "In the word *sing*, what letters say /*s*/? What letters say /*ing*/?"
3. The teacher now gives the letters and asks what sound the letters make. "In the word *sing*, what is the sound of *s*; what is the sound of *i-n-g*?"
4. Now the teacher takes off letters and asks for the sound that remains. "In the word *sing*, if I take away the *s*, what sound is left? If I take away *i-n-g*, what sound is left?"
5. The teacher closes this one-word perceptual conditioning drill by asking, "What is the word?"

With this technique, the word *singer* would involve more procedural steps. The teacher has to deal with the letters and sound of the structural element *-er* and take away sounds and letters from both *sing* and *singer*. With a word like *marketing*, the first targeted word may be *mark*, followed by a second drill with *market*, and concluding with a third round with *marketing*.

The Glasses emphasize that their system is a behavioral approach in learning a process. The student's behavior is shaped to respond to letter clustering in whole words through the repetitive use of the five-step procedure. The teacher-directed questioning involved in the steps is designed to help students learn to decode words through analysis of "service words." The service word generally contains the onset and rime clusters, just as in the analogy approach. However, instead of the comparison-contrast conditioning, the Glass-Analysis method focuses the learner on a visual and auditory conditioning pattern to react to specific target letter clusters and other structural parts of whole words.

The words for each letter cluster were arranged in sets of cluster-word booklets to accommodate more than 3,000 service words for 119 letter clusters. The booklets were coded at four difficulty levels—easiest, average, difficult, and hardest—to provide for the sets of 119 letter-cluster lessons. Although the sets of letter-cluster booklets were made available for classroom use by teachers (Glass & Glass, 1976), the perceptual conditioning system can be implemented by any teacher following the five-step procedure. The teacher just needs to be mindful of the patterning procedure, the questioning, and the understanding not to break up a cluster. For instance, the *-ing* is a letter cluster pattern and should not be broken down in smaller sound-symbol units. With the *-at* cluster, in many three-letter words (*sat, hat, bat, cat, fat,* etc.), the teacher could extend the Glass-Analysis procedure to such words as *patting, flatten, battery, clatter, attack, scratching, platform, attic,* and *satellite.*

A Vowel-Pattern Emphasis

A second technique focuses on **vowel patterns**. Vowel patterns have generated sets of rules that often appear in children's textbooks and phonic books. Such rules are known as the "silent *e*" rule, the "two vowels go walking" rule, the "short vowel" rule, and the "*r* controlled" rule. My direct experience with children and teachers leads me to believe that the concept of rules should be minimized. The focus instead should be on letter groups, particularly involving vowels as patterns. Also, experience has taught me that once children and youth have not succeeded with reading—an event occurring often as early as first or second grade—the difficulty is often due to word reading, with the specific problem residing in the medial parts of words. Many teachers will say that children with reading difficulty can get the beginning part of the word, but after that it's all "downhill." The technique of focusing on vowel patterns has come to me through actual work with students who have experienced reading difficulty through the grade levels. These students often carry labels such as "at risk," "remedial," and, more unfortunately, "learning disabled," depending on the group or place that assigns the labeling.

In Table 3-4 the teacher can see the suggested lesson sequence with the actual letter and vowel patterns that would be taught from lessons 1 through 30. The teacher might note some major departures from lesson sequences that appear in most phonics systems. Generally, phonics instruction begins vowel emphasis with the short vowel sounds, like /a/ in *cat*, /o/ in *hot*, or /u/ in *nut*. However, the focus with this vowel pattern technique is on those students who have experienced major difficulty with reading regardless of grade level. These older children and youth know the names of the long vowels; they are less abstract because they sound like their alphabet names. Thus, in order to rapidly return these children to word reading ability, the focus should be from less abstract to more abstract.

Table 3-4.
A Letter-Pattern Approach Based on Vowel Rules and the Alphabetic Principle

Lesson Sequence	Letter Patterns					Major Rule
1–5	a-e 1	i-e 2	o-e 3	u-e 4	-ee- 5	Long Vowel Silent e CVCE (1–4)
6–10	ai 6	igh 7	oa 8	ew 9	ea (eat) 10	Long Vowel CVVC
11–13	ay 11		ow (snow) 12	oo (moon) 13		Long Vowel CVVC
14–18	a 14	i 15	o 16	u 17	e 18	Short Vowel CVC
19					ea (head) 19	
20–22		oo (cook) 20	oy (boy) 21	ow (owl) 22		Vowel Clusters
23–24	aw (saw) 23		oi (oil) 24			
25	au (haunt) 25					
26–30	ar 26	ir 27	or 28	ur 29	er 30	r controlled vowels

C = consonant
V = vowel
E = the letter *E* when it is silent

Here's how the technique works. Lessons 1 through 4 present the major long-vowel pattern for visually identifying words. This pattern is also known as the consonant, vowel, consonant, silent *e* rule. The silent *e* acts as a major visual signal in the pattern. When the reader sees a letter cluster consisting of a vowel, a consonant or consonant cluster, and the trailing *e*, the reader activates the long-vowel sound to say the word. In other words, the cluster of letters—vowel, consonant, silent *e*—signal to the reader that the long-vowel name is to be called in the word.

The reader will note that lesson 5 is not labeled *e-e* because that is not an extremely productive pattern in English (*Pete, complete*). However, children will see many words with *-ee-* in the middle (or even at the end) of words. To complete the long vowel patterning of lessons, it's wise to introduce the long *e* sound here. The teacher should present each vowel pattern in an individual lesson quite like the procedure with word families, or phonograms, previously discussed. The teacher could create letter pattern boxes that look like Table 3-5, with the understanding that the "C" can be a single consonant or a consonant cluster:

Table 3-5. Long-Vowel Pattern Boxes

C	aCe		C	oCe		C	ee	C
l	ake		r	ope		s	ee	n
s	ame		h	ome		wh	ee	l
sh	ape		st	one		sw	ee	p
pl	ane		wr	ote		t	ee	th

In some cases, when children have difficulty blending the initial consonant or consonant cluster with the long-vowel sound, the procedure of capitalizing the vowel helps, such as *lAke, hOpe, sEEn*.

There are many words that can be generated in each pattern. Once a pattern is introduced and the words are practiced and learned, the teacher goes on to the next pattern. After the second pattern is learned well, the teacher might compare similar-looking words from both patterns that differ only by one graphophonic element, such as *lane* and *line*. The goal is rapid visual identification, so that by showing two or three words that look the same, the reader has to see all the features of the word in order to name it rapidly (next add *lone*). Besides building up a visual storehouse of words from each letter pattern, the lesson sequence shows that other letter patterns produce the same phonemic sound. Lesson number 6, as shown in Table 3-4, is another way that the long *a* is achieved, and lesson 11 is yet another way. Constantly building on a letter pattern that the child already knows makes the second and third patterns easier for the child. The abstract phoneme sound remains constant; only the spelling pattern changes.

Table 3-4 also shows that lesson sequences make alphabetic sense horizontally and vertically. By the end of lesson 13, students have been faced with the major spellings of the five long-vowel sounds of English. Then there's a shift to the short-vowel sounds and spellings. Note that in lesson 19, *ea* as in *head* is found in enough words to warrant a separate major letter-pattern lesson. Don't introduce words that were in lesson 10 with /*ea*/ as in *eat*. Both groups can be compared after each is learned well.

Lessons 20 to 25 have to do with a vowel cluster often called a **dipthong**. Dipthongs produce their own sound by a blend or "glide" of each of the single vowels. Readers having difficulty with word recognition will probably experience the most difficulty with words containing the dipthongs. One author, tongue-in-cheek, suggests that you "teach them separately and alone, in a dark closet, without bread or water" (May, 1998). Lessons 26 through 30 have to do with vowels whose sound is controlled by the *r* consonant; these are often called "*r* controlled vowels." Lessons 26 and 28 are quite straightforward; the sounds of /*ar*/ as in *car* and /*or*/ as in *horn* are quite distinct for children. The /*ir*/, /*ur*/, and /*er*/ and sometimes the /*or*/ (as in *worm*) produce the same sound, as in *bird, church, herd,* and *worst*. So while students have one major sound to remember for word reading, they may experience problems with spelling because of the four choices.

The vowel-pattern technique is based on the premise that English as an alphabetic language has sounds that are spelled by more than one letter, by different letter patterns, and by a combination of vowels that create their own unique sounds. Letter patterns are presented particularly as they affect the sounds of vowels, which, as noted throughout this section, pose the greatest difficulty for readers and writers of English. The search for patterns that guide the grouping of letters not only provides a sense of consistency but also makes the alphabetic principle more understandable (Bear, Invernizzi, Foorman, Lundberg, & Johnston, 2000).

Children often create their own words to fit the spelling pattern as they use their phonological awareness skills. For instance while looking at the -*a-e* pattern, they might offer the word *train*. This provides an opportunity to say, "Good thinking! But train is in another pattern that looks a bit different. We'll do that pattern later." Although the technique is basically teacher controlled, in that the teacher is guiding students through the letter patterns, students do begin to mentally manipulate sounds and symbols to make words that they know in the oral language but haven't been able to read. Teachers have to weigh choices depending on their students. For instance, should the teacher do *pain* when the *ai* letter-vowel pattern is offered, or should she introduce *pane* when the *a-e* is covered? Almost all children would know the meaning of *pain* and some might know *pane*. If the teacher believes it's fortuitous to add the new meaning word *pane* at the time the letter pattern is taught, then the timing might be right. The advantage is that the teacher has skillfully used sound-symbol associations to achieve a new meaning word for the children. The teacher has used a letter pattern system as a way of guiding students through the alphabetic principle to obtain word meaning, thereby adding on several layers of knowledge to the students' knowledge base.

Constructing the Alphabetic Principle With Invented or Creative Spelling

A procedure that is extremely child centered is called **invented spelling** or creative spelling. Here the individual child is in control and mentally constructs grapheme-phoneme correspondences to make words. Through the act of writing (not as adults know it, with correct spelling and sentence structure), the child discovers how the alphabetic principle works, and the child's own written products set the stage for reading. Invented spelling is a cornerstone of the emergent literacy and whole-language movement, as the child is developing the use of print to communicate meaningful messages. Invented spelling maintains that learning to spell and write, like learning to speak, is developmental. Children have to engage in it, practice it, and receive appropriate feedback about the meaning of the message and the risks taken with the spelling. A major concept of invented spelling is that children are not expected to achieve correct spelling and writing right away. Spelling and writing take time. Children need the time to experiment with printed language and learn from their mistakes. In fact, the very word *mistake* is often toned down with use of the word *miscue* instead.

Emergent writing and spelling progress through a series of stages. In its earliest form, the writing is "pretend" in that children initially make random marks or scribbles on a page and then move on to create a representative drawing to communicate a message (Hiebert, 1994). Later children produce a drawing with marks or scribble writing alongside but distinct from the drawing. Then they create letterlike words in a linear way across a page, and finally, at the invented spelling stage, they produce alphabetic letters that represent sounds in words. In order to invent a spelling such as *DD* for *daddy* or *tr* for *train*, children have developed insights and are attending to sounds in words and the distinct phoneme sounds that make the letters within the words.

Children need four skills in order to invent a spelling (Bear et al., 2000): (a) They need to know just enough letters of the alphabet to get started; (b) they have to be able to produce the letters they know by writing them; (c) they need to understand that the known letters represent sounds (phonemes); and (d) they have to attend to the sounds within syllables and correspond the sound segments to letters to get started. Thus, with emergent writers, we see the condition in which whole words and syllables are represented by one or more letters. Moreover, just prior to producing conventional spelling, a transitional stage occurs in which a vowel character appears in every syllable (Hiebert, 1994).

Teachers will sense that they need to be both tolerant and respectful of children's attempts with writing and spelling in the emergent literacy framework. In the developmental process, nonstandard handwriting, spacing, letter formation, and spelling will occur (Leu & Kinzer, 1999). It is through teacher encouragement, modeling, and instruction with continued works in progress of individual children that variations in nonstandard form will move toward more standard form. In essence, what adults call mistakes will be made as children move toward more conventional style. The attitudes of teachers to children's use of invented spelling must be one of discovery, exploration, and risk taking. Children who are engaged in such exploration in emergent literacy classrooms are discovering sound-spelling relationships to spell words in ways that children who are taught through didactic spelling instruction do not receive (Hiebert, 1994). Furthermore, research emphasizes that the association of spelling with sound is a fundamental step in early literacy development and that when spelling-sound and speech-sound correspondences are developed concomitantly, phonemic awareness will develop to enhance early writing and reading (Adams, Foorman, Lundberg, & Beeler, 1998).

In the photo, one can note the intentness of the young kindergartner as he's putting the finishing touches on his story. Some words are spelled correctly, such as *the, boy,* and *carrot.* Since there was a springtime planting theme in progress, the word *carrot* was displayed in the classroom, and possibly he cued in on that word card.

This learner has invented the spelling for *planted* with *Pa* and for *ate* with *et.* He does have a sense of writing for meaning and of story construction.

When Spelling Occurs

Figure 3-1 illustrates the mental process and modalities that are undoubtedly involved in the process of spelling words that are not automatically recalled during the act of writing. The figure is focusing on a learner wishing to spell the word *truck*. Notice that the visualization of the word involves both visual and kinesthetic pathways if handwriting is to be involved. The learner may say the word back to herself to capture the whole sound and phoneme representations. Then she attempts to recall the letters that are in the mind's eye or thinks of the letters that match the phonemic sounds. Then she writes the word. Sometimes, after the very act of writing with the visual feedback of seeing the word in its whole form, the child may perceive that the spelling is incorrect, smudge out the word, and try again.

If the word is spelled correctly, it usually goes by unnoticed. The child may get a pat on the back from an adult or teacher if it is a newly learned word, and, of course, the child will get those needed points on the weekly spelling test. If the word is misspelled, a number of possibilities may emerge. It is the eye of the beholder that determines various points of view on what to do with the spelling "mishap." If the young child is in an emergent literacy classroom setting, and learning to write is viewed as a creative, inventive process, then the invented spelling is accepted and the child is positively reinforced, particularly for those letters that were perceived correctly (as with the kindergartner in the picture). The teacher may wish to display the correct spelling as well so that the child can work with it and add the unknown to the known.

If the child is in the later elementary grades and has been experiencing difficulty with spelling, and writes the word *truck* as *trok* or *chuk*, he might be considered for referral to a reading or language arts specialist for additional help with grapheme-phoneme correspondences. Systematic phonics instruction, a word-family approach, or an analogy approach may help him to perceive letter-sound relationships to a stronger degree.

If the child is in the later elementary grades (or, unfortunately today, even in kindergarten or first grade) and there exist many misspellings with another "mishap," such as reversed or inverted letters, then the child might be eligible for a label. With the right parents and/or school system pursuing the "disability" of the child, she might event warrant a medical diagnosis. The labeling and granting of medical terms and remedial prescriptions usually means that she could receive special services to help her overcome the school-related difficulties—in this case, the irregular spellings of words with letters and/or numbers not facing the prescribed direction.

Figure 3-1. The Process of Writing It Out

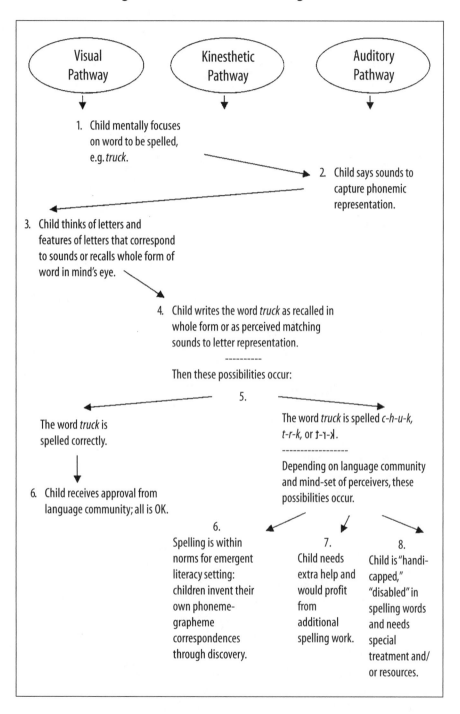

Over the years, in my capacity as director of a reading clinic for a large metropolitan university, I have become involved with the families of many children who have had deep-rooted spelling difficulties. There are two major observations I have made in the treatment of these children. First, the parents often report that even though their children are receiving special services at their school or at an off-campus site, they aren't improving in spelling or writing. A parent will say that many activities are going on, but the program isn't working on the disability area in which the child was supposed to receive help. The second observation may be related to the first, and it has to do with the treatment remedies pursued at the academic facility. The general treatment for those students having difficulty with the **encoding** process—the writing of words; opposite of the decoding process—is a heavy dose of structured, systematic phonics. Very often, the phonics instruction appears to have been well done, as indicated in the child's individual educational plan.

However, what is being missed is the understanding that the encoding of words involves a visual and a visualization process. If the words are to be handwritten on paper, then a **kinesthetic**, or bodily movement, process is involved as well. The visual process comes into play when one sees and analyzes the letter features of a whole word. Visualization is seeing the word in the mind's eye, one's visual memory, as a whole form with letters in particular sequences, arrangements, and orientations. Visualization is based a great deal on the original visual process and how one perceived a whole word form and captured it to be stored in memory. Many good readers excel at this visual recall process; they're good spellers. By extension, they have a good chance of being capable writers as well. Many poor readers, especially those who have been poor readers for a number of years, are poor spellers. Also, by extension, they are very often perceived to be poor writers.

Yet the opposite scenario very often occurs as well, as aptly pointed out by Patrick Groff (2001). Whereas poor readers are usually poor spellers, some very poor spellers can be good readers. Likewise, some very good readers may be poor spellers. This anomaly occurs because the reading of a word may be based on the intake of a few features of a word while correct spelling requires accurate recall and production of all of the word's letters.

I have described the visual processing behavior of 14 young males whom I tracked over a number of years in a case study approach. My research was reported in two sources: a short version (Sinatra, 1989) and a lengthier version (Sinatra, 1988). I administered five tests involving the phonetic and nonphonetic spelling of words and one test involving the visual memory of word forms. Although the young males' average age was 17 years and 8 months and their average grade level was 10th grade, their averages on the spelling and visual memory tests ranged from second to fourth grade. Of the 14 boys, 12 had been retained at a grade level, and 6 had been in a special education placement.

The reader can sense that these young males, who had achieved in the average range of intellectual functioning, had pronounced deficits in the ability to recall the correct spelling patterns of words. Although their capability with verbal and written language proficiency decreased over time when compared to their peers, their strengths in visual, spatial, nonverbal processing remained constant over time and was a strength in their thinking styles.

For instance, one father commented that his 16-year-old son was "excellent with his hands, a bike doctor, great in science." A custodian who could hardly spell on the second-grade level reported that he had always built things and taken them apart. His hobby was customizing cars and motorcycles, and he exhibited a scrapbook that showed pictures of his work along with the trophies and certificates he had won. A third was a specialist in wiring the electrical circuits of cars; he worked by studying the diagrams in the auto books. What are the factors in brain processing that allowed these talented young men to be so gifted in some areas requiring visual processing yet be so deficient in another, the learning of printed words?

The report of the National Reading Panel (2000), in its findings on the effects of systematic phonics instruction with various populations, makes a clear statement about the relationship of poor decoding ability with poor spelling. The Panel noted that the results of phonics instruction to improve the spelling ability of poor readers was small, perhaps in accordance with the consistent finding that disabled readers have difficulty learning to spell well. More recently, Gail Tompkins (2002), who writes about writing, observed in a seventh-grade class for struggling readers that their most severe problem with writing mechanics was spelling words. Most students were unable to spell common, high-frequency words, and most of their errors were related to the incorrect use of long and short vowels.

What's the point, then, in the long discussion of different possibilities of writing-it-out outcomes for children who spell words poorly or spell a target word such as *truck* a number of different ways? The treatment outcomes are, more often than not, conditioned by the eyes of the beholders. Teachers need to be aware that encoding, like decoding, is a developmental process and that deep-rooted problems with the spelling of words are often aligned with deep-rooted problems in decoding, or the breaking down of features of words in order to read them. Teachers need to be aware as well that strong instruction in word attack through phonics, word family, or analogy approaches may not be enough to help children with writing-it-out problems. Visualization of word forms, the correct embedding of words in long-term visual memory, and hand and arm movements are essential aspects of the writing and spelling processes.

The daily copying and rehearsing of words for the weekly spelling test may not be enough for children who have difficulty with the spelling of even basic sight or function words. I can recall seventh-grade Milton, who had an astonishing IQ of 140 or more on a well-known intelligence test. He spelled the word *with* three different ways on a little paper he wrote for me as I sat beside him. What helps are good old-fashioned remedies, such as (a) writing the word (cursive is best) in the air with closed eyes a number of times; (b) writing the word with large arm movements on the chalkboard, studying it, erasing it, closing the eyes, and writing it again from memory; (c) using the same procedure with regular writing paper instead of the chalkboard to get the word feel into small motor movements; or (d) tracing the word form in sand contained in a small flat box. Rather than sand, which tends to collapse into the trace, you might use course crystal salt, which is a great tracing medium.

What I advise parents to do, often as soon as they are financially able, is to ensure that their children do their written work on a computer. This advice is not just because of the spell-check feature of word processing programs. What also occurs, as soon as the child types the written work, is the visual feedback of what has been typed. The appearance of what's on the screen may not be in accordance with what the child remembers the word to look like on a printed page. Thus, the feedback process of self-correcting may begin as the child self-monitors the work. Then there is the spell-check input, followed by the printout of the child's written work. A parent, a peer, or an older sibling now has a chance to read the work in a somewhat standard manuscript form and may offer additional assistance to the writer.

Summary

This chapter has discussed major routes to word identification, or word recognition. We know from chapter 1 that words can be recognized as a whole, meaning immediately and on first sight.

Words can also be sounded out, meaning the use of some system (or systems) based on the alphabetic principle to work out the name or identity of unknown words. This discussion of the alphabetic principle and the ways to implement it in English may be considered the "technical" aspects of teaching reading, or decoding in particular. Teaching decoding requires knowledge of phonology and orthography, of how children learn language, and of ways to approach the writing system while the skills of reading are maintained in focus (Moats, 1998).

We noted that there were a number of methods and techniques available to help learners make use of the alphabetic principle to decode words, the major ones being invented spelling, analytic or synthetic phonics, the spelling-pattern and analogy approach, or the use of letter patterns. Each sound-symbol technique or combination of techniques is available for the teacher to use with students of different ages and abilities and for different purposes. For instance, a teacher who believes in fostering constructivist thinking in children could begin with invented spelling and move to an implicit phonics or an analogy approach. The two latter approaches support the teacher's thinking framework about how children learn through discovery.

This relationship is illustrated in Figure 3-2. There are a number of ways to help children identify words based on systems that attempt to match grapheme-phoneme relationships concordant with the alphabetic principle. Whatever the sound-symbol system or approach, its ultimate purpose is to provide a processing pathway whereby learners can unlock new words' identities and facilitate the rapid reading of words by sight. The figure suggests that word attack routes have to eventually lead to help learners read whole words on first sight. The time necessary to match the grapheme-phoneme units has to diminish with each encounter of the word so that it is understood and recognized (it doesn't have to be pronounced) accurately in its whole form.

Whatever approach or technique is used to help children decode (read) words and encode (spell) words, the teacher needs to remember that these are means to ends. One major end for the child is to transfer the words taught through any of the spelling-sound approaches to sight vocabulary. A second end is to learn the meanings of the words as they appear in different contexts so that as the child rapidly recognizes the words, understanding occurs as well. We need to keep in mind that the ultimate goal of reading is to read with understanding and enjoyment.

Figure 3-2. Pathways to Word Identification

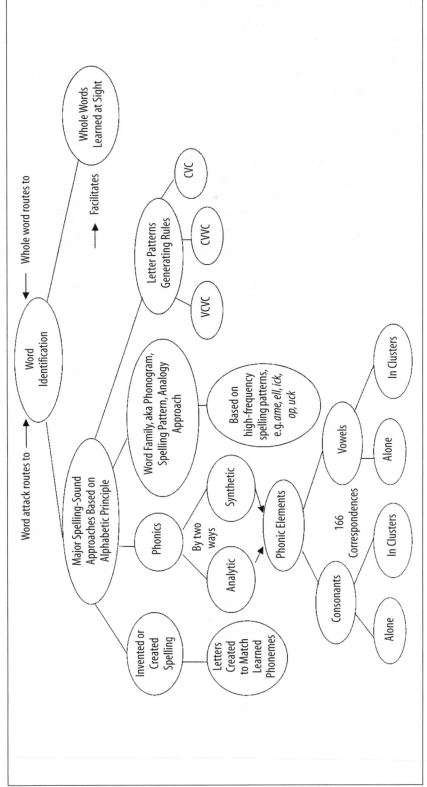

Concept Words and Terms

analogy
analytic phonics
authentic
blending
dipthong
embedded phonics
encoding
explicit phonics
Glass-Analysis System
    for Decoding Only
implicit phonics
incidental phonics
invented spelling
kinesthetic

perceptual conditioning
pattern book
phonic element
phonogram
spelling pattern
substitution
synthetic phonics
teachable moment
transfer
vowel pattern
word family
word identification
word recognition
word wall

Word Challenge for Teachers:
Tic-Tac-Toe Synonym

You know the rules for this activity from your childhood. Try to connect the three in a row—either horizontally, vertically or diagonally through the middle—that most nearly mean the same or refer to the same thing. This is a really fun way to use your new words and concept terms with children. Once you line up your three synonymous relations in the spaces on your game board, you place other "distractor" vocabulary words and terms in the other six spaces. Just be careful. Remember some words have multiple meanings, and children are sharp! You probably could plan a Tic-Tac-Toe Antonym as well. Answers are given in Appendix A.

	Game 1	
Phonogram	Perceptual Conditioning	Vowel Patterns
Encoding	Word Family	Kinesthetic
Diphthong	Pattern Book	Spelling Pattern

	Game 2	
Systematic Word Attack	Inductive Word Attack	Transfer Word Attack
Implicit Word Attack	Mastery Word Attack	Pattern Book Word Attack
Incidental Word Attack	Analogy Word Attack	Word Wall Attack

	Game 3	
Rimes	Kinesthetic	Writing a Word in the Air
Synthetic Phonics Instruction	Encoding	Transfer
Spelling	Perceptual Conditioning	Onsets

How the Written Language System Works

4

Focus Questions

1. How does prior knowledge influence reading success even at the word reading level?
2. How do distinctions in the oral and written language influence children's and adults' successes with either mode?
3. What makes fluent readers fluent?
4. Why must the graphophonic cuing system be abandoned in order to become a fluent reader?
5. Can you consider how the eyes work in conjunction with the brain during the reading process for fluent and non-fluent readers?

Although viewing, listening, and speaking are universal ingredients of human life and cultures, written literacy practices require extensions of the oral language codes. Visible marks have to be produced on a surface to represent sounds (phonemes), words (morphemes), and even movement, as in a musical or dance score. A text is produced by a writer. To be read, the reader has to know how to negotiate the symbols or the code of the printed language. To understand, the reader has to decipher the language of the code to approximate the same representational thinking that the writer is using. For the writer, the words, sentences, and paragraphs laid out on the printed page represent a technology. This technology has been with the world for some time and has undergone change as newer ways have been discovered to stylize writing. The world has moved from clay tablets and scrolls to the printing press and mass-produced paper to electronic networking. Whatever the means of the technology, the reader and the message composer need to be literate in interpretation and use of a printed language code.

Proficiency in reading and writing is considered to be essential by members of the educational community. In fact, it is thought to be the first, or basic, skill of school success because they are intended to be mastered by young children as they begin their formal schooling. This initial literacy experience lays the foundation for all subsequent book learning. What happens, however, when young children experience difficulty at the written literacy level? Does the learning difficulty reside at this level, or with a lack of experience and/or exposure at the earlier levels of formulating mental representations and oral language proficiency?

It's What's in the Head

Many people believe that reading and writing are natural processes and that children learn reading and writing simply by doing reading and writing. Children's experiences with talk and with stories provide the natural base from which to shift into a print environment. One well-known literacy author maintains that because proficiency with the oral language gives the forthcoming reader a meaning-based structure for the analysis and recognition of unfamiliar words, direct instruction in word attack skills, phonics, phonemic awareness, and even reading comprehension is probably unnecessary (Goodman, 1996). Likewise, Lucy Calkins (1997), presenting suggestions to parents about children's early reading and writing experiences, notes that the foundation for reading is not to be found in the sound-symbol code but in children's play, in their talk, and in the sharing time when they listen to adults read. It is quite natural, and even essential, that young children attempt to write stories and spell words to the best of their ability even before they begin formal reading instruction. For Calkins, such early writing assists children in making discoveries about how words are written.

I witnessed this discovery process myself while working on this book. Three-year old Marco initially told me that he wanted to do his "skibbling" to "keep me company" as I did my writing. I allowed him to pick his pencil or pen of choice and gave him a few blank pages, and off he went to another end of our table to do his scribbling. The effect on a page was just that—a mass of lines directed every which way. Some days, after he finished a concentrated work, he'd say, "Grandpa, what's that?" I'd have to make up something to match what we'd been reading lately. I'd say, "That looks like the fin of the dolphin," or "That's the baby's head in the *Baby's Sleeping* book." After agreement or disagreement about my interpretation, we'd go off to another activity.

About 3 months later, Marco said, "I want to do writing with you." Now, it was the same scenario as before, with the 3-year-old standing before the writing table, looking at the pencils, pens, and the clean paper. But the word *scribbling* had changed to *writing*. How and why had this occurred? Had he heard me use the word in my writing context, or his mother, also a teacher, in hers, or his brother and sister as they did their homework? Does he understand the concept of writing to be associated with word usage, or does simply the act of using a writing implement mean the act of writing out, whether the end product is words, pictures, or scribbling? One would think that the discovery process of written literacy was developing as a natural process, because I also heard, "Grandpa, what does this say?" *This* refers to words he was pointing to in one of his books, on a toy package, or on his T-shirt.

When new learning experiences are brought to learners, they add on or accommodate the new to stored understandings already in the head. New learnings also include the understanding of new words used by speakers during events. In essence, children construct meaning associations for words as they are used in evolving, natural experiences. Likewise, many educational theorists believe that the understanding and writing of texts are acts of construction by readers and writers, respectively. Texts are regarded as reservoirs of possible meaning relationships to which the reader brings knowledge and background information that interacts with the text's meaning. This view of the reading of texts operates in sharp contrast to an earlier view of the nature of reading, which held that one obtained meaning passively from a text. However, in the metaphor implicit in constructivism, readers and writers themselves are the constructors, mental meanings are the constructions they make, and prior knowledge is the material in the head that assists in the construction process (Spivey, 1994).

Another name for this shift in assumptions about learning and teaching is the **transaction model**. This contrasts with the **transmission model**, which had been the prevailing view of classroom instructional practices for most of the 20th century (Monson & Pahl, 1991). Many features of the transaction model have been alluded to in this book: the construction of meaning, interacting and accommodating the unknown, whole-to-part learning, active engagement in learning, and student-centered learning. The transmission model is characterized by acquisition of knowledge with concentration on facts, defining the known, part-to-whole learning, skills-based learning, passive learning, and mastery of teacher-delivered segments of information.

A central feature of the transaction model is the belief that **prior knowledge**—what one already knows—influences new learning experiences. Because prior knowledge differs for each child in the classroom, the teacher needs to help each child construct meaning in a way that the information or factual knowledge presented becomes integrated with what the child knows. This teacher construction and designing of learning experiences is most critical to implement during the acquisition of new vocabulary, as many children come from different backgrounds.

Frank Smith, in his first edition of *Understanding Reading*, published in 1971 (now in its fifth edition, 1994), argued that readers, not prepared-reading materials, have control while reading. Because of processing factors and knowledge within the head, readers determine how a text will be handled and how information will be integrated with prior knowledge. Smith's position was far different from many others, who believed in placing the text in charge rather than the reader's processing skills. With the view that the text is in control of the reader's ability, Smith believed that the focus of reading instruction erroneously shifts to the study of letters and sounds, which in turn hinders fluent reading.

Smith points out that there are two major sources of information during reading. One source of information that the brain receives through the eyes as the eyes see print is called *visual information*. The second source reaches the brain behind the eyes based on what the reader already knows. Smith calls this "nonvisual information" or "prior knowledge." Reading always involves an interaction between the two sources of information, or between what is in the reader's head and the printed text. Smith adds that there's a critical reciprocity in reading. The more nonvisual information a reader has on a particular topic he is reading about, the less visual information he will need. The less background experience or prior knowledge of the topic that the reader has behind the eyes, the more that visual information or careful print reading will be required. Reading and writing may be difficult for young children because of this lack of prior knowledge and because of scant relevant nonvisual information. They can struggle with a line of print trying to figure out unknown words because they don't have enough clues about information in the reading. Providing background relevant information helps the eyes predict what to see.

James Moffett and Betty Jane Wagner (1992) also believed that it was erroneous for educators to think of reading and writing as the basic skills. They maintained that the real basic skills are thinking and speaking, with nonverbal thought at the core. The "basics" to them did not mean word recognition, spelling, and punctuation. They reminded educators that reading and writing occur last in the acquisition of coding skills, generally after proficiency with verbal learning and its interaction with nonverbal experience, or "raw reality." Schools have ignored the strong interaction between the nonverbal and verbal worlds and have tended instead to concentrate efforts on verbal learning without connecting such learning to raw reality referents.

Thinking, the oral language, and the printed language are nested within each other, and each is the foundation for the next. Moffett and Wagner noted that teachers can ask students to compose and comprehend orally, thereby assisting the word recognition and handwriting skills necessary to perform at the print level. If children have difficulty conceptualizing a topic or verbalizing thought before they read and write about a given topic, teachers should ask students to talk about it first. With the talk and the questions posed by the teacher to elicit more talk, the teacher can help students formulate their thoughts before they read or write about a topic. The teacher, then, is guiding students to use their own words in transposing their talk into written words.

Oral and Written Language Distinctions

There is a distinction, of course, between spoken and written language. The spoken language is meant to be heard, and generally the speaker is looking at the listener(s) or is addressing a particular audience via the broadcast media. The grammar and vocabulary of the speaker will vary according to the purpose of the talk itself and to the relationship of the people interacting with or listening to the talk (Smith, 1997).

The written language, on the other hand, is meant to be read. The written language is more complex in its vocabulary, its grammatical structure, and in its genre or text schemes. The writer brings an array of words to the printed page and follows written conventions of spelling and syntax to arrange words into sentences, paragraphs, and larger meaning units.

Moffett and Wagner (1992) use the term **discourse** to refer to these larger meaning units. A discourse is a whole unit of language used for a specific purpose. A discourse could be a conversation, a lecture, a letter, a response journal entry, a short story, an ad, or even a label on a particular product. It is the largest unit of language in which a complete message exists between the language sender, who can be a speaker or writer, and the language receiver—

the listener or reader. According to this holistic view, composing and comprehending words, sentences, and paragraphs should be done within the context of a complete discourse. When substructures alone are used as the learning units, readers and writers lose a sense of relevance and connectedness with the overall purpose of the message.

If discourse is the superstructure of the communication context existing between a reader and a message, the paragraph, the sentence, and the word itself, with its letters, syllables, and affixes, form the **substructure**. According to Moffett and Wagner, the paragraph is governed by the kind of discourse of which it is a part and is influenced by the ones that preceded it and set its purpose.

Sentences will also vary in style and complexity according to the kind of paragraphs in which they are used. Sentence structure, as we know, involves the set of relations between the words and the word arrangements found in any given sentence. These relationships are governed by the rules of grammar, such as word function, word order, and word endings. Moreover, the structure of any given sentence governs the meaning of each word in that sentence. The word itself is a structure because it contains parts related to each other, such as letters, phonemes, syllables, and the morphemic parts of roots, prefixes, and suffixes.

Thus, individual word meanings depend on the location of the word in the sentence; individual sentence meanings depend on the paragraph of which they are a part, and individual paragraph meanings are dependent upon the intent of the discourse. The reader must be aware, moreover, that global comprehension and creation of verbal (and nonverbal) works occur at the whole discourse level. In short, Moffett, Wagner, and Smith remind educators of the critical importance of background information and nonverbal experiences as being at the "core of knowledge."

How The Written Language System Influences Fluency

Although the emphasis in preceding chapters has been on providing clarity about word concepts, we know that words, with their phonological, orthographic, and morphological features, are used in larger contexts of sentences, paragraphs, and literary and informational selections. These larger contexts also flavor and shape word meanings, but how do readers process the printed page? Is the visual traffic flowing through the eyes to the brain different for a beginning reader than for a more advanced, or **fluent**, reader?

The fluent reader is not even aware of how his mind works to interact with the mind of the author, who has set down readable print on a page. When you process a text in a smooth and efficient way with understanding and have no need to use word attack skills, you are a fluent reader. You are influenced by the very nature of the author's style in communicating her message and by the experiences and concepts she brings to interface with your mental pictures and your conceptual understandings. You work through the author's sentences and hope that not too many ideas are **embedded**, or contained, in them. If too many pieces of information, especially those of a factual, technical nature, are embedded in one sentence or in a short series of sentences, you may not be able to make the meaning connections, and loss of comprehension occurs. Your efficiency may be temporarily halted as you activate other known skills. If the author presents unfamiliar words, you hope that she has provided some clues within the sentences to help you figure out the meanings of difficult words. If you can't guess at a word's meaning from context, you can approximate the way the word might sound in the oral language by trying to sound it out, or you can try to figure out the word's meaning by analyzing some of the morphological parts that are meaningful to you. You, as a fluent reader, can utilize these behaviors because you have internalized them over time through wide and diverse reading. But do beginning or emergent readers, who are in various stages of nonfluency with print, have the same processing capacity?

Cues Available to Readers in Written Texts

Authors and literacy experts talk about the clues available through the printed language that serve as **cues** for readers to help them process and understand text. These clues also highlight the symbiotic relationship that exists between the writer, who implicitly uses the clues of written language because they're the systematic features that allow writing to happen, and the reader, who implicitly uses the same clues because they're the cues for gaining meaning from reading. We can account for five **cue systems** that are available for readers. Most sources identify the **graphophonic cue system**, the **syntactic cue system**, and the **semantic cue system** as being the most important (DeFord, 1994; Goodman, 1999). Others add the **visual cue system** and the **pragmatic cue system**, which also influence the processing of text (May, 1998; Tompkins, 1998). These are all explained below. We also know that words themselves have four inherent features (see Fig. 1-2) and that these features become part of the cuing systems.

It is important for the teacher to understand the nature of the reading cuing system because the system works differently for readers at different levels of reading proficiency. It is also important for the teacher to note that the spelling-sound or graphophonic system provides just one set of cues, which eventually has to be discarded to reach a high level of reading fluency. The following discussion describes the features of each cue system and the information that is potentially transmitted to each and every reader during the act of reading. Table 4-1 provides an overview of the major features of each cue system.

Table 4-1. The Cue Systems of Written Language and Their Features

Visual	Graphophonic	Syntactic	Semantic	Pragmatic
• Word Configuration	• Symbol-Sound Associations	• Grammar • Word Order	• Meaning (Influenced by) ↓	• Social and Cultural Influences
• Paragraph Indentation	• Spelling Patterns	• Sentence Structure	• Experience • Concepts	• Affective Memories
• Punctuation	• Onset Rime Cluster Units	• Rules of English	• Prior Knowledge	• Situations and Settings
• Typographical and Text Features		• Syntax	• Rules of English Syntax • Vocabulary Understanding	

Visual Cue System

Each word has a visual **configuration**, or look, made up of its length, its shape, its ascending and descending letters, and the arrangement of its internal letters. The word occupies a visible space and is distinct from another word because of a space boundary. This configuration is what makes readers miscue or misread such words as *letter* for *little*, *month* for *mouth*, or *committee* for *community*. Don't be fooled or be misled into thinking that these type of miscues are indicative of a phonics or sound-symbol problem. Remember that there's a visual and a visualization process operating in learning words. What often happens is that at the moment of reading, the reader is "off task" with his or her mind—that is, not fully engaged in the reading understanding process. You'll find this out if you place the two words, the text word and the miscued word, side by side and ask the student to read the two words. If the student reads the two words without fault and knows the meaning, can this be a sound-symbol problem? If the word is *abuse* and the student reads *a bus*, is this also a sound-symbol problem? Probably not. Ask students if they've heard of the word *abuse* or if they know what it means. Most likely you'll discover that the student didn't know the meaning of the miscued word. Thus vocabulary development, not word reading, is in order.

This is a very sophisticated, diagnostic decision on how to proceed with remedies or treatments to help children overcome their misreading of words. It's troublesome for practicing teachers, even those who are about to earn their licenses from their respective states as literacy or reading teachers. More often than not I'll witness advanced-level teachers taking intermediate and junior high students back to the stages of rudimentary phonics instruction when the students are misreading polysyllabic, less frequent words with morphemic parts. Phonics may help to work out a few words, but the student may still not know their meanings.

On the other hand, if you're dealing with a second grader or higher, and the types of miscues are *of* for *for*, *but* for *by*, *this* for *that*, *was* for *saw*, or *for* for *from*, you need to take stock of the child's situation. This child has been exposed to these basic function words during many classroom encounters and possibly during home reading experiences. For whatever reason, these words are not secure in the child's mind. There are features in the words' configurations that prompt the child to misread. Once again, a phonics or sound-symbol program may not provide the key to help the child with these problem words. Once the miscalling of basic function words becomes deeply rooted in the child's mind, a good teacher has to go in and uproot the child's visual configuration problem. Some ways to do this will be suggested in the next chapter.

A second type of visual cue is associated with shifts in meaning. In written English, we have evolved a visual cue to help writers with a way to focus their evolving thoughts and for readers to process the changing, cumulative thoughts of the writer. We know this as **paragraph indentation.** Each new paragraph is indented, signaling to the reader that the author is offering a new idea or an addition to a previous idea. Also, the new paragraph signal "tips off" the skillful, purposeful reader to search for the main idea, which may be explicitly stated in a topic sentence.

Punctuation and **capitalization** also provide necessary visual meaning cues to both readers and writers. Without these two visual cues in the English-language written system, we would lose a sense of sentence. Punctuation, along with capitalization at the beginning of the sentence, provides the idea of sentence sense—that the sentence provides a unit of meaning. The different end marks of punctuation—period, question mark, exclamation point—also signal qualities of meaning. Most modern-day scales or rubrics for scoring writing proficiency include punctuation and capitalization in the mechanics section.

Typographical features such as page design, font size, boldface, italics, and underlining are used by authors to visually alert readers to ideas of importance. The larger the boldface heading, the more central the idea. This is a visual cuing feature that you should impart to your students, particularly as they deal with their content area reading selections and textbooks. By learning how to weigh the ideas presented in the boldface heads, students begin the mental process of cognitively mapping the text information.

Graphophonic Cue System

Grapho (from *grapheme*) refers to the alphabet letters or strings of letters that the reader initially perceives in reading text. *Phonic* refers to the sound or phonemes that readers have to call to mind to match the perceived letters. The graphophonic cue system may be called upon when a word is not recognized on first sight and the reader needs to decode (sound out) the word to obtain meaning. This system is connected to the person's understanding of the alphabetic principle and the different ways that words can be sounded out. These major sound-symbol methods were presented in chapter 3.

As noted in the previous discussion of the visual cuing system, the letters hold configurational information as well in that they can transmit rapid visual information while holding the key to the phoneme or spelling-pattern equivalents.

Syntactic Cue System

A great deal of syntactic information has been derived from the **grammatical rules** and structures that readers have come to learn through the oral language before reading occurs. Speakers have learned to create sentences and to transform syntactic structures such as phrases and clauses in compliance with the rules of English. Readers and writers will bring these same skills to the printed page. They process word order, function words, morphological structures that include inflectional endings, and pauses indicated by punctuation to both understand and write.

Some syntactic structures appear with regularity in formal written English but are not often used in the oral language. For instance, a syntactic structure that appears in writing but is not necessarily used in the oral language is the appositive phrase. The appositive is a single noun or noun phrase that immediately follows another noun to explain or identify it. Young children speak using single words and names as appositives quite regularly. They might say, "My friend

Susie came to my party," or "My friends, the Sanchez bunch, came to our house last night."

Direct teaching of the meaning of the appositive phrase and how it is punctuated in writing may be quite necessary in the lower and middle grades, when authors begin to use this structure in children's reading material. Students need to understand that one and not two ideas are explained in the sentence. For instance, in the sentence "The aging president, the great general of the war of independence, decided not to run for another term of office," many students may erroneously think that two people are indicated. They think this because they have not faced the appositive structure much in reading, nor have they used it in their own writing.

The teacher may therefore have to reword a sentence by making phrase and clause transformations to help students understand it. The **transformation** would retain the same deep-structure meaning but would appear as different **surface-level** writings so that students could connect the underlying meanings to structures they use in the oral language. The teacher would recast the original sentence as "The aging president, who was the great general of the war of independence, decided not to run for another term of office" or "The aging president decided not to run for another term of office. He was the great general of the war of independence." The reader can note that recasting these sentence with the clause transformation directly assists in the reading understanding process while providing good mental gymnastics work for students in composing and combining sentence structures.

Semantic Cue System

Semantic information is the meaning brought to the reading and writing experience. How does the writer know if the readers will understand all the ideas and content the writer has included? Writers undoubtedly make predictions about their style of writing based on projections of the reading audience they wish to reach. Writers of literacy works wish to engage their readers in the unfolding of a story and in the use of words to make their characters and plot come alive on the printed page.

Writers of information texts, on the other hand, have to use the necessary vocabulary to explain the substance and parameters of the information. For instance, if the information concerns the topic of photosynthesis, the writer needs to use such supporting vocabulary as *chlorophyll, carbon dioxide,* and *carbohydrates* to explain the concept of the photosynthesis process. Although each of these words can be separately defined, the author has a tough time substituting easier synonyms to make the reading user-friendly for a projected

audience. This notion leads us to understand how critically important **vocabulary knowledge** becomes in the reading comprehension process, and how aligned vocabulary becomes with the
understanding of concepts.

We have also noted that a great contributor to meaning obtained
during reading is the information in the head of the reader. Thus,
prior knowledge composed of one's experiences, concept understandings, and vocabulary volume all interact with a text as it is
being visually processed. The meaning obtained from sentences is
also highly related to the grammar of those sentences. That is, the
complexity of a sentence, the order of words within it, and the redundancy of signals, such as pronoun referents, all contribute meaning, or semantic cues.

Pragmatic Cue System

The pragmatic cue system is closely related to semantic understandings, but it encompasses a bit more. This system is shaped by
culture, social considerations, the setting in which literacy experiences occur, and one's affective state during literacy events. For instance, if a particular topic is not in favor in one's social group, the
reader may have negative or hostile feelings toward the topic even
though he or she can read it with understanding.

Language use is also influenced by one's culture and the social
considerations of when, where, and how to use particular language
styles, such as formal, informal, or slang. Situations influence the
language that is appropriate and the language style that one comes
to expect at particular times and circumstances. For instance, the
language expectations of school, business, and most professional
life is formal standard English, whereas informal language would
be the expectation of a close-knit group of friends. Particular types
of settings and groups in school may influence how reading and
writing are accomplished by students. For instance, for some students the pragmatic influence of a school computer lab may en-
gender far more productive writing than an in-class desk setting,
which they believe to be an old-fashioned way to conduct the writing experience.

Shifting Among the Cue Systems to Gain Efficiency

Although readers are influenced by all of these interactive cuing systems, Figure 4-1 shows that a major distinction can be made
between readers who are fluent and those who still are learning to
read or are nonfluent. While the chart is a bit of an oversimplifica-
tion, in that readers' reading behaviors change with the complex-

ity of texts, the processing routes through print are mainly influenced by the ability to use the printed language cues to gain efficient understanding.

Figure 4-1. How the Cue Systems of Written Language Influence Readers

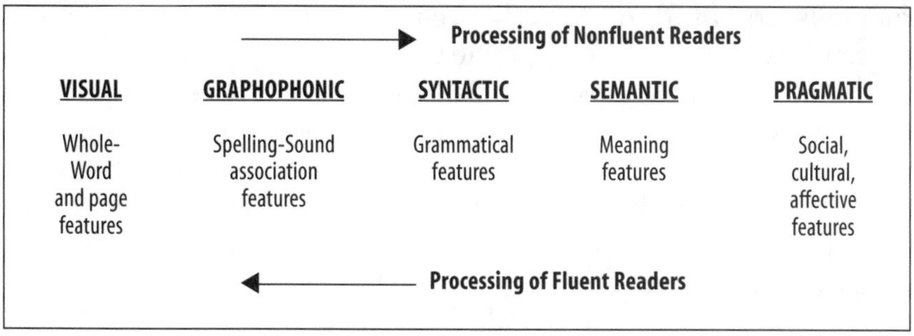

VISUAL	GRAPHOPHONIC	SYNTACTIC	SEMANTIC	PRAGMATIC

— Processing of Nonfluent Readers ▶

VISUAL	GRAPHOPHONIC	SYNTACTIC	SEMANTIC	PRAGMATIC
Whole-Word and page features	Spelling-Sound association features	Grammatical features	Meaning features	Social, cultural, affective features

◀ — Processing of Fluent Readers

Thus, beginning or emergent readers (kindergartners to second graders) and nonfluent readers (any older child, youth, or adult who is struggling with reading and is temporarily dysfluent) need to devote analysis time at the visual and graphophonic level to arrive at a word's identity. Yet the grammatical, semantic, and pragmatic understandings may be known in the head.

The fluent reader, intent on getting on with it, has knowledge, affective memories, and social and cultural know-how in the head and brings these experiences to the printed page. The fluent reader picks up visual cues with the eyes, and if these cues confirm words that bring a comfortable sense of meaning to satisfy the reader, the reader reads on. If the fluent reader has to stop to decipher a new or difficult word, as might occur with a Russian novel, the fluency process is stalled and the sense of meaning may be disturbed or even temporarily lost. This is because decoding the graphophonic features of words involves a different mental process than reading with meaning. As long as there's no text ambiguity to confuse the reader, the reader can rush purposefully through the text as "the eyes do the walking" and the mind "does the talking." The more that printed words become learned automatically with at-sight visual recognition, the more that the nonfluent reader gains proficiency and enters the more skilled level of fluent reading.

However, anyone who is a fluent reader most of the time can become nonfluent (or dysfluent, in this case). Although you handle your favorite authors and periodicals with ease, what happens when you are beckoned to read a lawyer's document, a mortgage contract, or an income tax manual? The same behavior that the emergent, nonfluent reader experiences with new words and new concept experiences now faces you. You become bogged down with the reading by placing your fingers on particular words as you study them and trace your finger under particular sentences as you try to fig-ure them out. Although the immediate issue facing you is unfamil-iar words in difficult-to-decipher sentences, the real issue here is that you don't have the background and semantic knowledge of the topics. Nor do you regularly read laws, legal cases, and tax code manuals, so you don't have the reading experiences of style and vocabulary use to call upon, either.

So it is with a young child as an emergent reader, or an older child, youth, or adult performing as a dysfunctional reader because of experiential, text, and word knowledge incompatibilities. When-ever the words get too difficult or the sentences and textual mean-ings are too far removed from their linguistic and experiential knowledge, these readers will become bogged down. A major con-sideration for the teacher would be to ensure that new words and sentence structures are practiced in contexts that emergent and strug-gling readers can understand.

Nor is fluency enough to achieve full benefit from an author's craft. I can recall an incident when I was a teacher of high-achieving eighth-grade students. We were reading "The Legend of Sleepy Hollow" by Washington Irving (1995). I smirked and laughed at the wonder-ful way Irving played with words and how he portrayed through humor the contrasting personalities of his three major characters. Yet the eighth graders didn't feel the same merriment, and, unfor-tunately, couldn't be made to feel it through the efforts of teaching. Why was this so?" These students could read, and they read well. However, they hadn't experienced the cultural and social niceties of Ichabod and Katrina's time. Nor could they relate to the imagery produced by Irving's powerful word choices relating to old-fash-ioned courtship and the rejection produced to make Ichabod "heavy-hearted, crestfallen," and feeling so "dismal." The colorful sentence follows:

> It was the very witching time of night that Ichabod, heavy-hearted and crest-fallen, pursued his travel homewards, along the sides of the lofty hills which rise above Tarry Town, and which he had traversed so cheerily in the afternoon. The hour was as dismal as himself.

Depending on the proficiency of the reader, the demands of the text in word difficulty and syntactic and semantic complexity, and the compatibility of pragmatic influences, the reader samples and uses the printed language cues in the most efficient way. The able reader processes and monitors each **word chunk**, or segment, based on the incoming visual information while attending to meaning. Less able readers and young children learning to read have not achieved a comfort level of fluency with the intake of words in con-tinuous text. Therefore, the novice reader is compelled to attend to print in a serial order while simultaneously considering what information to attend to in the hierarchy of whole meaning, discourse type, sentence, phrase, word, letter clusters, and individual letters (DeFord, 1994).

The Importance of Automatic Word Reading

Over the years a false dichotomy has arisen in teaching words: teaching words as "wholes" versus teaching words through decoding techniques based on the alphabetic principle. The latter is known simply as phonics. Basal reading systems, in an effort to control the words introduced to children and to capitalize on the utility of high-frequency words, offered a limited set of words in each of their series books published for children. Because many of the high-frequency, function words did not have symbol-sound regularities, they were taught as "whole words." In time, the basal-reading program approach was considered a **whole-word approach** that focused on controlled repetition of a small set of words in the early grades. It was also quite easy to merge whole language with whole-word learning for the critics of either one. This merger served to sharpen the divide between those who believed in whole-to-part instruction and those who favored part-to-whole instruction.

However, we have noted in the previous chapters that it's not a matter of how words are learned, but that they become committed to one's sight vocabulary. Even words that are learned through part-to-whole decoding techniques, requiring increments of time necessary to analyze the word and letter-sound features, must be read eventually as wholes, immediately and without hesitation. The learning equation that forms when the reader recognizes words as wholes looks something like this:

Rapid whole-word recognition

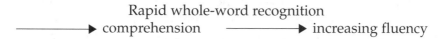 comprehension increasing fluency

The comprehension and fluency outcomes of rapid and smooth word recognition could be interchanged, but the two generally go together in skilled reading. Understandably, automatic word recognition does not always equal adequate comprehension. The factors of cues and clues discussed earlier and found in Table 4-1 remind us that there are written language conventions, author style, and in-the-head conditions that affect fluent reading with comprehension. Active readers shift their mental processing skills in four ways to achieve meaning: (a) they shift between what the text says and what they know about the topic; (b) they elaborate and make connections to what they have read; (c) they monitor their comprehension to see if what they read makes sense; and (d) they use the influence of the social context to select what is important and meaningful (Walker, 2000). Meaning, moreover, is highly related to smooth word recognition, making the ability to recognize words rapidly a distinguishing characteristic of the skilled, active reader (Juel, 1994).

To obtain meaning during the act of reading, readers need to be able to chunk or group words into meaningful units. This chunking of words requires that important processes occur between the eyes and the brain. First, the eyes remain in location, or **fixate**, on word parts, a word, or chunk of words as determined by the proficiency of the reader. Keith Rayner and Alexander Pollatsek (1994) note that a **fixation** in reading occurs when the two eyes come to rest for milliseconds to allow visual information to enter. The information obtained during each fixation pause is like viewing a slide show. An initial fixation, or "slide," occurs for about a quarter of a second, followed by a brief shift to the next segment of print on a page from which information is extracted in the next fixation slide of a quarter of a second. Contextual reading thus proceeds until the text is finished.

The mind of the reader is, in effect, in control of the eyes during efficient reading. The reader will direct the eyes to the next chunk, depending on what has been understood. Each subsequent fixation transmits additional meaning about the topic. If the mind of a poor reader, like the mind of a young, emergent reader, has been engaged in understanding what is to be expected from the reading context, then he or she will be able to predict meaning by visualizing the words that enter the visual field.

Word length patterns and letter shapes (visual cues) can be recognized by fluent readers many letter-character positions beyond the fixation span. This leads us to a second type of visual processing that occurs between the eye and brain: **peripheral vision**, which is vision that occurs beyond the fixation word chunk. This expansion of visual intake may influence a reader's predictions and anticipations of meaning. With information already in the head during a fixation pause, the fluent reader uses peripheral vision to project the mind further into the text to sample, anticipate, and corroborate meaning hypotheses. In a sense, fixations in connected text become extremely efficient when visual cues are picked up by the periphery to confirm expectations in the head. Fluent, efficient readers make constant predictions about the next word or next thought about to unfold in the text as their eyes leap ahead to confirm the information they have come to expect (May, 1998). All of this efficient eye-movement processing to gain meaning from words that are in and that enter the visual field accounts for fluency in reading.

The implications for readers who are poor in automatic word recognition become clear. If the reader becomes bogged down with actually figuring out words during contextual reading, the mind and the visual processing system have been diverted from efficient connections to meaning. Because the reader needs to look at the letters and the letter clusters of words (the orthographical properties) to trigger the sounds these letters make (the phonological properties), the mind has shifted from fluent connections to meaning to a process where words have to be sounded out to gain access to meaning. Decoding in context and word-by-word reading further serves to limit the development of rich visual images that often accompany the reading of literature and descriptive passages. When faced with a text that is overly challenging, problem readers have difficulty relating the text to their experiential backgrounds and elaborating the content (Walker, 2000).

It would be both important and efficient for beginning and problem readers to build a strong sight-vocabulary foundation, but learners are different. Although the visual processing system is available to achieve smooth, fluent word intake, children's memory is a factor. Let's consider this next scenario to see how challenging it is for the teacher to be certain of the words any given child knows by sight.

We overheard one of our Reading Clinic teachers saying to a child, "You know this word. It's a sight word." The young girl was seated, holding a book, and staring at a word while the teacher was bending over the child pointing to the word. There's something right and wrong with this scenario. The teacher earnestly believes that the child knows this word, probably because they had worked on learning it in a previous session. The child may have showed some mastery of the word in previous reading encounters, so the teacher thinks the child knows this word. The teacher also recognizes this word as being a basic reading word as recorded on a high-frequency, sight word list. Finally, the teacher is human, with fallible traits. She is probably a bit crestfallen because she thinks she has miscalculated the child's ability to remember, and annoyed because she has to review again and can't go forward as she would like to do.

However the child is the key here. We have to acknowledge what's really happening in the situation. The earnest teacher thinks that this is a basic word, it "should" have been learned. However, it has not been learned with full mastery; it cannot be retrieved automatically from the child's long-term memory. While the child is staring at the word, two major possibilities may be occurring in her thought process. She may be looking at letters within the word in an attempt to link individual letters or letter clusters to speech sounds in order to decode the word and be able to say the word's name. Or she may be reading ahead in context, trying to figure out what the unknown word may be by understanding the sentences and the surrounding context.

So the "wrong" here is that for whatever reason, the child does not know this particular word on sight. Even though the teacher thinks that the child should know this word, the child hasn't mastered it. The word has not been committed to long-term memory and is not a sight word yet for that child. Thus, it's not a matter of seeing it; it's a matter of calling or saying it correctly when one sees it. If the saying of the word is done rapidly, instantaneously, without analysis, then we would say the word is a basic sight word for that person.

This leads us to believe that every person's mastery of sight words, or words immediately recognizable in print, is different. That is correct. This one factor—a person's sight word vocabulary—is so important in reading success that it basically separates the "haves" from the "have-nots." Think about it. Suppose that every reader of English could master at first sight the first 5,000 words in the Carroll et al. (1971) frequency count. Then they would be able to read any given text with about 89% accuracy. If the reader could master the 40,000 plus words of that frequency count, they would be able to read any given text with 99% accuracy.

Thus, a major goal of reading instruction should be to assist all learners to add words to their individual basic sight word vocabularies as rapidly and as meaningfully as possible.

Summary

The above statement about the major goal of reading instruction is easy to write, but it's very difficult to do at the same time and at the same pace for all learners in the classroom. It's not a matter of children seeing the words, it's a matter of children retrieving the words from memory to be able to read them automatically. Teachers say statements like "They knew the words on Monday morning, and when they came back to their reading groups on Wednesday, many of them forgot the words." What's happening is that the children who forgot the words needed more exposure and recall opportunities with the words from Monday afternoon through Tuesday. The children who learned the words on Monday were able to commit those words to long-term memory, and in most cases the word configurations and corresponding word names were secure in the children's safe-deposit boxes of memory. The children who did not learn the printed words were not able to associate the look of the words—the visual configuration cues—with the word names to achieve a bond in long-term memory. The answer is that the children need more practice with the words so that they can retrieve them automatically and correctly from long-term memory as soon as they are perceived in print.

Concept Words and Terms

capitalization	prior knowledge
configuration	punctuation
cue	semantic cue system
cue system	substructure
discourse	surface-level
embedded	syntactic cue system
fixate	transmission model
fixation	transaction model
fluent	transformation
grammatical rule	typographical feature
graphophonic cue system	visual cue system
paragraph indentation	vocabulary knowledge
peripheral vision	whole-word approach
pragmatic cue system	word chunk

Word Challenge for Teachers: The Classification Concept Map

This activity is in the form of a concept or cognitive map. The objective is to classify the major cue systems of written language presented in the chapter. To make the task user-friendly, I have placed the word topics across the circles for the five subcategory areas. Once you have written in a topic, you select those features, characteristics, or properties that are part of that topic. If you need to refresh your memory with the appropriate feature details, you can turn to Table 4-1 or look through the chapter again. Answers are in Appendix A.

You could construct the same type of classification map for such major topics as "The Earth's Biomes," "Kinds of Rock on Earth," "Clouds," "Kinds of Squares," and "How Volcanoes Are Classified." It's a good way for students to match up that essential concept vocabulary noted in the feature details with the right category or subtopics.

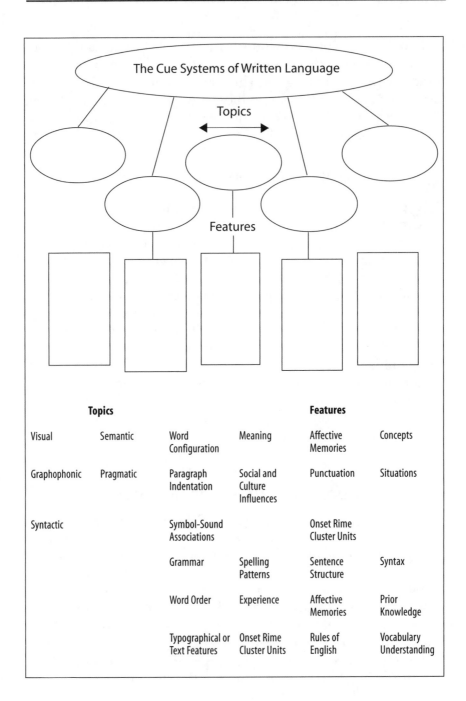

Topics

Visual	Semantic	Word Configuration	Meaning
Graphophonic	Pragmatic	Paragraph Indentation	Social and Culture Influences
Syntactic		Symbol-Sound Associations	
		Grammar	Spelling Patterns
		Word Order	Experience
		Typographical or Text Features	Onset Rime Cluster Units

Features

Affective Memories	Concepts
Punctuation	Situations
Onset Rime Cluster Units	
Sentence Structure	Syntax
Affective Memories	Prior Knowledge
Rules of English	Vocabulary Understanding

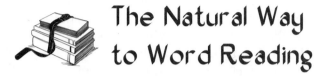

5

The Natural Way to Word Reading

Focus Questions

1. Why is reading aloud to children important for both the development of new vocabulary and the learning of syntactic and semantic conventions that children will later encounter as readers?

2. How does the construct of emergent literacy differ from historical ways that children were perceived to be ready for formal reading and writing instruction?

3. What components of the language-experience approach contribute to its status as being a natural way to build a reading vocabulary?

4. Why might the Visual, Auditory, Kinesthetic, and Tactile (VAKT) method of word learning be considered labor intensive?

5. What features of the retelling strategy make it a highly motivational and versatile way to build word reading and vocabulary development while capitalizing on children's use of imagery?

We noted in the previous two chapters that rapid and automatic word reading should be a top priority in children's early literacy development. With instantaneous recognition of words known in the oral language, a child can immediately attain success with initial reading experiences and not be tainted with the storm clouds of calamity that befall those who haven't "achieved" by the end of first grade.

We also noted that there are many prior knowledge experiences that influence how a learner approaches a learning task and succeeds with it. The in-the-head factors, such as oral language fluency, vocabulary understanding, concept knowledge, and early awareness of print have a great bearing on a young learner's success with beginning reading. This chapter will discuss natural ways that young children learn about print while additionally filling the head with prior knowledge factors. Techniques and strategies will be presented for teachers to follow, either for their own use or to suggest to parents as ways to assist their children with print-rich development.

Talk Language and Book Language

Through the oral language, the listener hears the talk of the speech community. For the young child, the talk community is usually composed of the child's immediate caretakers: mom, dad, grandparents, siblings, other relatives, and friends. As the child becomes older, the speech community becomes all of those who verbally interact with the child at home, in school, on the playground, and in other meeting and entertainment places. Interaction with peers and the influence of their language becomes an important factor in the talk used in social encounters. This local talk may be limited in its use of rich vocabulary to express meaning and also in its use of various grammatical structures. There will be a generous use of basic sentence patterns, normally those with a subject, a verb, and an object. We see these patterns reflected in children's earliest writing attempts.

Then there's the talk of the pop culture. This talk, transmitted through radio and the visual media, may be even more limited in vocabulary and style than that of the child's immediate language community. Moreover, there are those who feel that the language used on radio and in the visual media to lure children into the mass or popular culture is cause for alarm. They believe that this is a troubling time in the overall mental health of our nation's youth, who are quickly losing the reflective power of their minds. They are losing their minds to a seductive message of fast and easy enjoyment that is pressed upon them by the entertainment media. Through the talk of shock radio and the quick-moving images packaged in video games, TV commercials, MTV, CDs, and whatever else the media comes up with next, our children are conditioned to think and talk like the models they hear and see in entertainment.

This is one reason why teachers caution parents to limit children's television viewing. Too many hours of television viewing after school, in the evenings, and on the weekends may result in a "softening" of children's minds. It's easier to watch and listen to be entertained than it is to watch and listen to be informed. Furthermore, if the vocabulary and concepts used in the discussion of an informative topic are alien to the children, they have to invest mental energy and put in reflective thinking time to obtain the ideas.

Vincent Ruggiero (2000) believes that a major reason for academic deficiencies in today's youth is that mass culture has undermined their desire to learn. Learning words and numbers takes mental effort, but today's teacher has to cope with a climate of schoolwork and text reading versus entertainment. The separation between the "haves" and "have-nots" in literacy success is widening today due to the influence of the talk and visions of the popular culture, maintains Ruggiero, and it is affecting more and more young children regardless of culture and socioeconomic status.

The world of the talk community may limit children's expansion of mind to absorb more complex vocabulary and syntactic structures that will be unearthed in the world of print. Indeed, researchers have indicated that speech is vocabulary-poor compared to the language used in the written language. In 1988, Donald Hayes and Margaret Ahrems analyzed the type of words that were used in different oral and written contexts. They looked at words used in three broad categories: (a) in printed texts ranging from preschool books, children's books, comic books, and adult books to abstracts of scientific articles; (b) television shows ranging from *Sesame Street*, cartoon shows, popular prime-time children's shows, to popular adult shows; and (c) the oral talk of college graduates speaking to friends and spouses and in expert witness testimony.

To analyze the number of times words were used in the different print and oral language contexts, the researchers turned to the frequency count of Carroll et al. (1971). The purpose of the count was to rank the occurrence of words in print by their frequency. Of the 86,741 words the three authors analyzed, they found that *the* was number 1, *it* was number 10, *know* was the 100th, *pass* was the 1,000th, *vibrate* was the 5,000th, and *amplifier* was the 16,000th.

When Donald Hayes and Margaret Ahrems matched their print and oral language sources with the Carroll et al. frequency list, they found that children's authors use a good number of less frequent, higher count words. Their analysis revealed that children's books had 31 rare (or less frequent) words per 1,000 words, whereas popular adult shows had 23 rare words per 1,000, popular children's shows had 20 rare words per 1,000, and *Sesame Street* had 2 less frequent words per 1,000. Interestingly, the TV category of cartoon shows rated just about the same number of rare words as the category of children's books. This may be because cartoon shows don't seem to be programmed just for children. Such shows contain much sophisticated, adult-oriented humor.

When the language of children's books was compared to adult speech, the results were even more revealing. The vocabulary used in children's books was just a bit more rare than the formal oral language used in the courtroom with expert witness testimony, and almost twice as rich and less frequent in word selection than the talk of college graduates, who recorded 17 rare words per 1,000. Even children's preschool books recorded 16 rare words per 1,000. When you compare the children's books finding with the words of adult speech, the implications become clear for children's word-learning development. Talk is not as strong as reading for developing vocabulary.

Some ideas may come to mind in this section on the differences between talk and book language. First, you're probably thinking of what might be the best way to prepare young children (even beginning with infants) to enter the visionary world of books. Second, and connected to the first, is this question: Why is it that teachers, professional literacy and child development organizations, and even noted personalities on afternoon and prime-time television urge parents to read to their children? What is it in being read to that prepares young children to read on their own?

Finally, there may be some wisdom in the use of children's literature as a vehicle of reading instruction. This wisdom may also be evident in some of the recent standards documents for the English language arts published by various states and large school districts. The first section of the reading standard for elementary and middle school students published by New York City for implementation in its 32 districts requires that students read at least 25 books or book equivalents per year. These materials can include traditional and contemporary literature as well as magazines, newspapers, textbooks, and on-line materials (Board of Education of the City of New York, 1997). Rather noteworthy in the Hayes and Ahrems finding was that the newspaper category contained 68 rare words per 1,000, popular magazines contained 66 rare words per 1,000, and adult books had 53 rare words per 1,000.

Reading Aloud: A Natural Bridge to the World of Print and Written Discourse

Educators and researchers have long acknowledged that book reading at home, reading aloud, or "on the lap" reading is a major contributor to children's language acquisition and to their anticipated success with schoolbook encounters. **Reading aloud** provides opportunities for children and adults to partake of sustained discussion of past, present, and forthcoming events in a book. Although pictures and illustrations may cue much of the discussion, the discussion proceeds through listening and speaking interchanges prompted by the language of the book. The adult or older sibling who is reading aloud becomes the author's stand-in and presents the author's version and vocabulary of a developing narrative. The different stories and authors ensure that children hear new vocabulary and syntactic constructions that may not be forthcoming in conversation. As children become familiar with a particular story, they may question more to gain a fuller or richer meaning, thereby increasing the likelihood that they will use the new words written by the author. Furthermore, as we noted earlier, repeated exposure to stories helps children internalize the structure of the narrative—meaning that the narrative has "good" and "not-so-good" characters, who do something (the plot), in particular places (the settings), and there are outcomes, resolutions, and conclusions to the characters' actions.

Thus, on-the-lap reading and hearing the written language of books prepares children for the conventions of the written language. Book reading to children may be considered a bridge between the world of familiar talk and the world of written discourse. Through storybook listening, children's range of new vocabulary will increase. In fact, Warwick Elley (1989) found that young children can learn the meanings of new words from hearing just one story read aloud.

Children hear grammatical structures not encountered in the oral language as they become immersed in the different story genres such as folklore, fantasy, mythology, biography, and realistic fiction. Being read to enlarges the child's fund of nonvisual, in-the-head information regarding the structure, conventions, and style of the written language. When children hear whole units of discourse such as that contained in informational trade books, children's literature, historical adventures, and articles from magazines and newspapers, they hear the language of writing to enlarge the discourse schema that they will bring to their school texts.

Figure 5-1 illustrates how reading aloud positively influences young children's language and thinking processes. After hearing the oral language of the speaking community, the young child is read to and adds the words and language patterns of books to his thought process. Because of the reading aloud influence, the youngster is motivated to read on his own just to enjoy the world of imagination that books bring. Understanding the words and craft of writing that authors have brought to books, the young person also uses writing to convey messages and complete school assignments for others to read or to hear as they are being read. Writing is also used to prepare talks and scripts that will be delivered to a larger listening audience. Such a prepared talk would use the words and language patterns that have been learned over time through the awareness of books and other written materials.

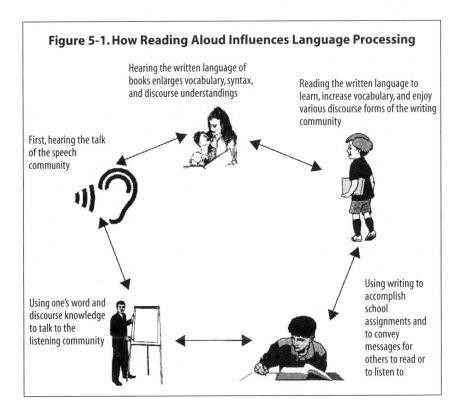

Figure 5-1. How Reading Aloud Influences Language Processing

Hearing the written language of books enlarges vocabulary, syntax, and discourse understandings

Reading the written language to learn, increase vocabulary, and enjoy various discourse forms of the writing community

First, hearing the talk of the speech community

Using one's word and discourse knowledge to talk to the listening community

Using writing to accomplish school assignments and to convey messages for others to read or to listen to

Getting Ready for Reading and Writing

As children approach the world of print, a shift in their language learning occurs. The process of becoming literate with print means a shift from natural, very meaningful uses of oral language to a somewhat unnatural situation of examining printed words in order to say or write each word's name to obtain meaning. Also, as noted in the last chapter, the process of becoming reading-literate means that the learner has to rapidly shift from being a word examiner to one in which whole sentence chunks are efficiently processed by the brain to obtain fluent reading with meaning.

The Reading Readiness Concept

Educators have postulated that there are particular routes or stages a child must undergo in order to be ready for formal reading and writing instruction in the school setting. For many years of the 20th century a concept of **reading readiness** prevailed. This belief focused on a mental age of 6 $1/2$ years as the ideal time for children to begin reading instruction (Franzen, 1994). Prerequisite perceptual and prereading skills had to be mastered before the reading of words occurred. This caused teachers to focus on training auditory and visual perceptual skills and on teaching children letters and sounds before attempting whole words. Thus, according to Franzen, instructional materials emphasized a "bottom-up" approach of learning to read, one that focused on the mastery of isolated parts of written language, like learning the alphabet or the letter sounds, before enough knowledge occurred to try to learn words.

Chall's Stage Model

A very comprehensive view of reading levels was the stage model proposed by Jeanne Chall in 1983 (reprinted in 1996). A **stage model** presumes that learners accomplish different tasks at different age levels or grade levels. One advantage of formulating a stage or levels model for reading is that it helps educators to focus on the skills and understandings that are necessary at each level. At each of the stages, the reader engages in different mental activities with print, and it becomes important for readers to "graduate" through each of the stages in order to become critical, efficient, lifelong readers. Therefore, a child operating at a higher level in reading will have different skills and understandings about the reading process than a child operating at a lower level or stage (Stahl, Heubach, & Cramond, 1997).

Chall's six stages of reading development are summarized below so that you can note the beliefs about the reading process that are still widespread today. You will also be able to make comparisons with a modern-day perspective of early literacy attainment, the perspective of emergent literacy that will be presented in the next section. Finally, the reading characteristics at the various stages are bulleted (a text feature!) so that you can focus on specific behaviors at each level:

Stage 1: Prereading—Birth to Age 6

The prereading stage covers a longer period of time and entails more developmental changes in the child than any of the other stages. The aspects of print acquisition Chall presented at this level can be summarized as follows:

- The child gains insight into the nature of words—that some rhyme, that some begin or end with the same sound; that words can be broken into parts, and that parts can be put together to make words.
- The child can visually discriminate and name letters of the alphabet, and some children can print their names and letters told to them.
- The child can say actual words in association with contextual experiences, such as seeing a fast-food restaurant, a TV commercial, a food container, or a special book.
- The child learns how a book works.

Stage 2: Initial Reading or Decoding Stage—Grades 1–2, Ages 6–7

During stage 2, children learn that letters and sets of letters are associated with corresponding parts in spoken words. Learners internalize cognitive knowledge about words and the reading process. They know the differences between words that the letters make (such as *cat* and *cop*), and they sense when a mistake has occurred. By the end of this stage, children have gained insight into the nature of the spelling system and sound-symbol relationships. The following behaviors occur at this level:

- Children are engaged in sounding out. They mumble and bumble along as they try to read with exactness.
- They are more glued to the print than to the meaning.
- They supply their own words when reading because they don't know enough about the author's words.
- They can learn to read many high-frequency words and read simple connected texts using these words.
- Their oral reading is far more proficient than their silent reading.

Stage 3: Confirmation, Fluency, Ungluing From Print—Grades 2–3, Ages 7–8

Stage 3 reading fuses and strengthens what was learned in stage 2. The learning in stage 3 is not so much the gaining of new information but the confirmation of what the reader already knows. For instance, when the child reads stories previously heard during on-the-lap reading, the child's fluency with print should escalate. Basically, the following generalizations are in effect:

- Most children apply their decoding knowledge, learn more complex phonic elements, and learn to use the redundancies of syntactic and semantic information.
- Because they begin to use the context with skill, they gain in reading fluency and speed.
- They have more success if the environment fosters an opportunity to read familiar books of familiar stories, of familiar topics, of familiar structures or genres (such as fairy or folk tales), and of familiar language patterns. The greater the practice time and immersion with books, the greater the chance that fluency with print will develop to set the stage for the acquisition of new learning through reading that will occur in stage 4.
- For those children who do not have the opportunity of practice and of immersion time with books to increase their volume of reading, they may experience a widening of the gap in the ability to read with fluency, success, and at higher levels of understanding.

Stage 4: Reading for Learning the New—A First Step

This is a highly important stage, because another "graduation" of sorts takes place. Before stage 4, the child has been learning to read; now the child is engaged in reading to learn. During the earlier stages, what the child learned about reading was relating print to speech. In stage 4, however, the child relates print to ideas. Earlier, the child gained new information about the world from listening and viewing, and now, with stage 4, reading offers another means of knowing. For some children, by the end of stage 4, reading efficiency may equal or surpass other means of gaining new information about the world. In our electronic media age, stage 4 children can also access information sources on the Internet through the World Wide Web. At this stage, the following also occurs:

- Children's reading is characterized by the growing importance of learning word meanings and of using prior knowledge.
- Children learn the process of using books and of locating information in texts, such as how to find information in a paragraph, a chapter, or in the book itself.
- Usually the study of subject areas—history, geography, and natural science—occurs with this stage. Ideas are introduced in these subjects that children can relate to beyond their direct experiences.

- Children read at this stage for factual information, for concept knowledge, and for a way to learn how to do things.
- Stage 4 might be subdivided into two phases:

  Phase A: Grades 4–6 (Ages 9–11)—Development of the ability to read content material and serious material of adult length.

  Phase B: Grades 7–9 (Ages 12–14)—Readers come close to being able to read on a general adult level, adult fiction, popular magazines, and newspapers. Readers grow in their ability to analyze and to react critically to different viewpoints they encounter.

Stage 5: Multiple Viewpoints: High School, Ages 14–18

The most essential aspect of reading in stage 5 is that it involves learning about topics from more than one point of view. In contrast with stage 4, in which children study history from one textbook and one point of view, stage 5 texts offer greater depth of topic treatments and reading from a variety of viewpoints:

- Students deal with layers of facts and concepts connected to those encountered in earlier learning.
- Students increase learning through multiple viewpoints by accomplishing their school textbook assignments, using original sources and reference works, reading more mature fiction, and enjoying liberal use of books, newspapers, and magazines.
- Generally, students at this level are engaged in the higher level thought processes of analysis and synthesis. They analyze different sources and viewpoints on a topic and then synthesize the information to be able to understand it, talk about it, and write about it.

Stage 6: Construction and Reconstruction—A World View, Age 18 and Older

College students and adults in this stage are able to read selectively about topics and knowledge areas in which they are most interested. Readers weigh information that is central to their own concerns and add it to their knowledge bank. The reading here is basically constructive, as the reader reconstructs the printed ideas of others to fit with his or her own beliefs. The mental processes here are analysis, synthesis, and evaluation:

- The reader judges what to read, how much to read, to what depth, and at what pace.

- The reader balances the understanding of what is read by analyzing and evaluating the ideas' compatibility with personal beliefs.

- Readers' familiarity with topics and ideas make the reading rapid and fluent, whereas unfamiliar subjects require slower, study-skills type of reading. (Chall's discussion of how to approach the reading of any new or unfamiliar text might be considered a metacognitive decision by the reader.)

- In summary, readers at stage 6 level of development have the ability to construct knowledge on a high level of abstraction and generality and can enhance their understanding from the beliefs of others.

Emergent Literacy: A New Perspective

Another perspective on how children acquire and develop written language is called **emergent literacy.** Marie Clay (1991) first coined the term, and the concept presently has widespread use and acceptance in schools, especially those embracing the constructivist view. Other researchers have traced the theoretical and educational viewpoints of what is meant by emergent literacy. Basically, emergent literacy represents a paradigm shift in how children become literate. From a concept of being ready or developing in stages determined by age or grade level, the shift is to a belief that children naturally flourish in literacy. The "bottom-up" notions such as letter naming and development of visual and auditory discrimination skills, formerly seem as central to reading acquisition, are now seen as peripheral, and invented spelling, once regarded as dysfunctional, is now viewed as critical (Lancy 1994; Smith, 1998; Teale & Sulzby, 1986).

James Moffett (1994) indicates that emergent literacy grew out of standard "folk practices" and is just a renaming of long-established learning activities for young children. He agrees, however, that the term legitimizes the unacknowledged and unfavored practices of how to help children learn to read and write. He implies that many educators and commercial producers of reading instruction materials have had powerful reasons to deny the naturalness of the concept of emerging into literacy. This concept, along with that of the whole-language philosophy, unsettled many in the educational-industrial complex because their implementation doesn't necessarily require trained professionals. Any literate person can induce the emergence of another person's literacy. All that is needed for successful literacy implementation is people, trade books, and paper, and not commercially prepared worksheets and skill building packages according to Moffett.

William Teale (1994) has contrasted the concepts of emergent literacy (EL) and reading readiness (RR) for us in five major ways:

- EL holds that for almost all children in a literate society, literacy development starts very early in life, whereas RR maintains that learning to read starts after prerequisite perceptual and prereading skills have been mastered.
- Within EL, reading and writing develop together and are interrelated, whereas for RR, reading is the central area of concern.
- EL focuses on meaningful and functional uses of reading and writing with the teaching of skills arising out of holistic contexts, whereas RR emphasizes skills isolation and their teaching as separate parts of a holistic context;
- EL embraces both broad and specific areas of language and literacy, such as concepts about print, story and informational text structures, and concepts about phonemic awareness and letter-sound relationships, whereas RR stresses skill work in visual and auditory perception and learning letters and sounds.
- With EL young children naturally emerge into reading and writing at their own rates and in different ways, whereas for RR, children scale the same sequence of skill-based hurdles at the same time before reading occurs.

You can see that the whole precedes the parts in an emergent literacy framework. Children hear and see a message or story told or written by the teacher. That message has a whole meaningful context. The words, letters, and sounds are embedded functionally within that whole context. Children construct their knowledge about words and the letters and sounds that make up words by being curious and actively involved with print (see the discussion on invented spelling in chapter 3).

In the emergent literacy view, learning to read is considered a natural process, similar to learning to speak and to understand the oral language. Writing is also part of the learning-to-read process. Children write words and their own sentences and stories, which are read by other children, the teacher, and the parents. In such an environment, written-literacy learning takes place in a friendly environment in which language serves a function and is used for practical purposes. Lester Laminack (2000) suggests that teachers need to capitalize on children's intense interest in print by providing consistent and supportive modeling and guidance to help them realize their expectations in using print.

An emergent-literacy classroom becomes a natural extension of children's encounters with print in home and community environments. Yetta Goodman (1986) has postulated that environmental print is a strong contributor to children's success with literacy; it is more accessible and pervasive for many young children than are books and other reading materials. Children see and respond to the print announcing their favorite fast-food restaurants, to the labels on foods and games, to the signs on streets and buildings, to the names of cars and trucks, and to the written words in the ads on television. Preschool and kindergarten teachers often label known objects in the classroom (as in Figure 5-2), continuing the outside connection of print with meaning. Carol Seefeldt (2001) believes that teachers of young children need to get beyond the mere labeling and use print in more functional ways. She suggests that teachers construct signs, posters, and charts that inform children of schedules, that welcome newcomers to the classroom, that publish news stories, and that explain what to think about, observe, and do.

Figure 5-2. Labeling the Known

Emergent-Literacy Classroom Practices

The practices of the emergent-literacy classroom extend children's curiosity about reading and writing into ways for them to be successful in their later literacy experiences. The following are literary and literacy-related activities that are found in such classrooms:

- The teacher conducts group storybook reading (reading aloud) with the whole class, small groups, or with individuals on a daily basis. Quality children's literature is read, and discussion ensues between teacher and children. Reading aloud reveals that teachers value the reading act and shows that they achieve knowledge and gain enjoyment during reading.

- Children engage in "pretend reading" of books that have been read to them. They also have access to literature in the classroom-installed library, also a place where they can engage in book reading. In a library center children's writing can be displayed for classmates to read. Some may wish to question the author.

- A **print-rich environment** is created to expose the world of print in functional, purposeful ways. Signs and labels are posted on common objects, routines and charts are printed, written notes are exchanged, children's written products are displayed, and tools of writing (pencils, pens, markers, paper, and computers) are visibly available. The classroom is a stage of words and children's print.

- As part of the print-rich environment, an interactive word wall is set up. This is a wall in a section of the room on which children can systematically alphabetize words that have been written on index cards. The word wall is not just a major display but also a major tool in building children's sight vocabulary. The words come from any number of sources, such as books read aloud and big books produced by children.

- Children respond to literature readings and discussion by using other literacy forms. Besides writing, children engage in artwork, flannel boards, music activities, or a dramatic reenactment of a story read to them. With modern-day software possibilities, children can create a computer-generated retelling of a story if computers are available for their use.

- Writing is part of the daily classroom "diet"; writing and reading are connected. The teacher can show the process of writing by writing a daily message on the chalkboard or chart paper while reading the message aloud. Then the teacher encourages the children to help her along with the reading as she moves her fingers or hand underneath the words.

- Phonemic awareness is fostered through such activities as nursery rhymes, poetry, songs, and oral language games. Children can be asked to focus on particular sounds so that they can discriminate individual phonemes that occur in our language.

- Connected with phonemic awareness is letter association. Through many of the writing and print activities children engage in, they learn the letters of the alphabet and the sounds associated with the letters. One way to achieve the connection is to set up an ABC center. In this center there can be magnetic letters and boards, individual chalkboards, and magic markers for children to use when they form letters and words. Old magazines can be cut up to remove letters to make whole words. Being able to manipulate letters with multisensory experiences about letters and words is key here.

- The natural connection of reading and writing to the oral language is demonstrated through the creation of written stories or messages and the retelling by children of those literacy events. When the teacher writes a story or message on chart paper or the chalkboard, he may be writing a piece that children are orally composing with him. He reads the piece several times with the children as he guides his hand and fingers along the words in the sentences. Next, the teacher may have the children retell what the message was by having them write it themselves. Depending on levels of literacy proficiency, some children may write and spell conventionally, some may use invented or creative spelling, some may use random letters, and some may scribble or draw. All of these hand-eye-mind activities are degrees of the process of writing, and each child's emergence into the world of print may be separated by levels of degree proficiency. To close this literacy event, the teacher should have children read what they wrote to others to achieve the oral and written connections of language once again.

Let Us Not Forget Artistic Representation

Artistic representations are based on humanity's desire to represent meaning in nonverbal, creative, and symbolic ways. This stage of human development is often an outgrowth of viewing and active experimentation with the environment, processes that give rise to nonverbal, representational thought. Many writers from various disciplines have believed that human learning occurs in a number of different ways of understanding, expression, and communication (Verriour, 1994). Furthermore, these various modes of thought and experiences cannot be contained within a model of leaning that focuses solely on a logical, sequential approach to describe how thought and language occur. By being attentive to nonverbal modes of learning, teachers will enhance and enrich children's ability to learn and communicate.

The young child's self-expression though pictures, clay, or dramatic play is a reconstruction of nonverbal experience without the immediate necessity for language. Vygotsky (1978, 1986) claimed that gesture is the child's developmental stepping stone in the process to written language. A child's earliest scribbles on paper are a form of gestural representation. These scribbles later become drawings of simple pictures and stick figures that represent the meaning of a child's thought. A major thinking breakthrough occurs when the child realizes that he or she can not only make pictures of representations in the visual environment but can also draw or make the figures that represent meanings expressed in the oral language.

The traditional language forms of listening, speaking, reading, and writing ask learners to process ideas through the spoken and written language. The arts, on the other hand, necessitate the use of other forms of representation that have their own language structure and communication style. Furthermore, music, dance, and the visual arts are forms of language that engage learners at their deepest and most essential levels (Weinberger, 1998).

Although art forms are unique in their own way to convey messages, they are often combined with oral and written words. Children do this most frequently in their early writing endeavors—the picture or other artwork with their name and their first words. In fact, noted Donald Graves (1979), when young children begin their first writing experiences, their drawings often become the driving force of the printed message. Such literacy combinations help to reinforce each other's meaning while sharing features with one another. Picture books and big books share illustrations and unique uses of words.

By realizing that children have different talents and inclinations, teachers can shape the learning of content and written literacy to maximize the children's talents. For instance, if the child likes to draw and is a fairly good artist, the learning of reading and writing can be preceded by or be done concurrently with the pictures, illustrations, and drawings the child produces. The learning of the words in pattern books or poetry can be done in harmony with song and musical rhythm. Creating a picture story board, a sequence of events on a poster, or using a flow chart or concept map are other ways to use visual design to organize thoughts and content before going to verbal delivery. One of the great powers of children's multimedia computer programs is that they allow children to combine verbal and nonverbal features such as artwork, photos, music, and movement (animation) to create unique, individual projects.

Building Word Reading—Naturally

Teachers need to keep several considerations in mind when they make that natural transition from talk language to print language without the explicit use of a sound-symbol approach as presented in chapter 3. Teachers should consider the following:

- Who are these word learners? Are they beginning, truly emergent learners possibly facing their first encounters with print? Or are they students along in the grades (even at the second-grade level) who haven't achieved in reading as well as their peers and are still having limited success with word reading?

- Whose words are going to be used? What is the source of the words?

- Why are you taking such a direct word-learning approach? Do you just want to show print and oral language connections for words, that a printed form represents something in talk? In this instance, a teacher of primary-grade children would label places and things in the classroom with just single words or a word phrase.

- Do you wish to build a firm sight or reading vocabulary for particular youngsters as rapidly as possible?

I have posed these questions because I have witnessed particularly good strategies and techniques used at various depths of purpose and success. For instance, many teachers believe that using a language experience chart is doing the language experience approach, which will be presented shortly. A chart may be fine and serve the purpose for one group of children, but it's not the same as using the approach for struggling readers to build fluency in reading. A retelling activity, noted earlier in the discussion of the emergent literacy classroom, asks children to do just that—to retell the events of a story or an episode in their lives. However, the retelling strategy could be pursued to a rather creative depth and could account for most of the displayed print and artistic work in a print-rich classroom environment.

So the issues of purpose (why) and audience (for what students) become important to consider when building word reading through a natural way. Some of the suggestions presented in this chapter could also very well appear in the next chapter, concerned with the learning of new vocabulary words. For instance, the retelling strategy could be used very well, as a means of acquiring new meanings of the words authors use in their works. A word wall could be amassed displaying newly read concept words learned from literary works, or another word wall could show basic, high-frequency words known in the oral language. A print-rich environment could be composed of word cards written by children to label places or materials in the classroom, or it could be composed of children's retellings, reports, and hard-copy, computer multimedia projects.

Finally, word attack and sound-symbol association connections can be made for troublesome words, but this route is not the primary focus of this chapter. With the natural way to printed word learning, the teacher is helping students to make meaning and print associations. Recall, however, from chapter 1 (see Fig. 1-2) that words share four properties. The teacher can and should bring in phonological, orthographic, and morphological properties to help the word learning process.

I often do this multiple process. A student has been consistently confusing *that* for *this* (or *this* for *that*). I step back and ask, "How do you know the word is *that*?" I try to motivate the child to study the word so that he or she consciously sees features and elements in the word to help pronounce it correctly. I'll say, "Put these parts on your mouth. What do you see and hear?" I'll be twitching my finger under the *th* and *at* elements. If the mouth movements and sounding are still not correct, I have to lead the child through the sound-symbol connections. I may have to trace the word and sound elements a few times. I'm also utilizing incidental or implicit phonics as a means to identify the word. The key here is for the child to tell *how* he or she knows it's that exact word and not any other word. Total convergence of thought is necessary to achieve correctness. Otherwise the confusion could persist for years. I've seen this happen for many children, and I'm not so sure it had to happen or if the particular special treatments or programs the children were in had achieved their goals.

When you say "How do you know . . . ?" and the child talks through the features or elements of a word, this process becomes **metacognitive**: The child has to tell you how and why he or she knows something. This process and attention to one child's persistent miscues takes time and patience, but it's worth it for that child to succeed in reading word building and subsequent literacy success. When teachers rush on to the next set of words to be offered according to some kind of curriculum or text plan, and previous words taught are not solidly anchored in children's minds, that's when a great many reading problems start.

Two of my favorite procedures for building word learning naturally are the language experience approach and the retelling strategy. They are different in their approach, as I will shortly point out, but complementary in that they focus on the whole. It would be a natural progression to begin with language experience and then turn to the use of retelling to enlarge children's literary landscapes and source of new words.

The Language Experience Approach

The **language experience approach** has a history and tradition in American education, according to Ronald Cramer (1994a) and Steven Stahl (1999). Both authors note that the major proponents of the approach were Roach Van Allen (1976), Mary Ann Hall (1980), and Russell Stauffer (1970), who presented the philosophical rationale and wrote the books on how to implement the approach. Cramer credits Sylvia Ashton-Warner (1959/1985, 1964/1986) as being the first to describe a language experience methodology in teaching reading in her books, published a decade or so before the approach took hold in the 1960s and 1970s. Both Cramer and Stahl credit the language experience approach as being the forerunner to whole language, and Stahl provides a review of the history and similarities of both movements.

There is a methodology to the language experience approach, and it proceeds from whole to part in word learning. The words children learn are those in their oral language vocabulary. They tell the teacher the words in talk language, and the teacher transcribes the children's words to print language. This is why the method is called language experience, because the language the children learn to read is based on their own experiences.

Let's track the method through in its logical progression of steps as a potential reading methodology. I am presenting this approach as a major vehicle of whole-word learning in a natural way with the child in control of the language.

Talking Through the Experience

First, for each printed narrative you wish to obtain, you need to focus on one experience. The printed narrative will soon appear as a language experience chart, and the oral narrative can come from one child, a group of children, or a whole class. Whole-class charts are often prepared with children in the primary grades as they discuss the seasons of the year, holidays, birthdays, and special events.

Kindergarten and primary-grade teachers use language experience as a continual mainstay in the literacy "diet" of their classrooms. Teachers will often create a story or chart before and after a class trip. Prior to the trip, all or some of the children hadn't had the experience yet. However, they will be predicting and visualizing the experience, such as what might they see or wish to see at the city zoo or special museum exhibit. Teachers write down the children's predictions, wishes, concerns, and questions. They read these, and off they all go on the trip. When the trip is completed and they are back in the classroom, the narrative of the experience is collected. Some of the same language that was offered before the trip may emerge in the second version. More often than not, because of the actual experiences lived and witnessed by the children, this second version—much more a story or narrative of the total experience—will be its own unique version.

For some years I worked in an elementary school as its reading specialist. During the second term of one year, the principal, at the request of the first-grade teachers, asked me to work with a group of "problem" readers. Soon I had two groups of 11, bright-eyed boys; no girls. Much to the dismay of the principal, I would periodically take the beginning part of one of our reading periods and engage in a universal experience. With the help of the gym teacher, we played basketball, softball, and soccer each time I needed to collect new stories. The play before the reading enabled me to be sure that these children had the same language for the same experience. In 20 to 25 minutes, they would hear and use the words *pass*, *dribble*, *shoot*, *net*, *basket*, *player* as they engaged in the basketball experience. Later, back in the reading room, they would tell me the words and language of their experience, and there were no unfamiliar words.

For my first individual clinical experience, I had a bit of luck. I was assigned to work with fourth-grader Richard, who had been retained in the grade and was still a struggling reader. In those days our label for students who had a meager sight vocabulary and couldn't read any text with understanding because of word reading inaccuracies was "nonreader." The lucky part was that Richard was a blossoming athlete and played football for a local community team. When I presented the suggestion that we could do stories of his favorite experiences, he became animated and excited about the project and immediately focused on football. Our very first language experience story was titled "The Job of Quarterback." Then in the fall we moved on to "The Center," "The Punter," "The Offensive Line Man," "The Defensive Line Man," and "The Super Bowl." The stories contained a great deal of word redundancy so that each story's words would reinforce the learning of previous written words.

Writing It Down

The teacher's job here is to write down or transcribe what the children say. The teacher becomes secretary and editor, but editing should be kept to a minimum. Although editing may be necessary to achieve correct syntax, sequence of events, and exactness of meaning, the teacher doesn't want to stray too much from the children's words. For instance, I wrestled a bit with changing Richard's words for his telling of the position of center. He said, "You got to hike the ball." I was tempted to write, "You have to hike the ball," thinking that the latter is more appropriate in spoken and written formal English.

When the teacher begins to write down what the children say to aquire the text that will become the language experience story, the teacher needs to realize that the story production is a process, just like the writing process. Rather than standing at the chalkboard or alongside chart paper to take the children's dictation as a final draft, the teacher should collect the children's words and sentences on regular notebook paper. The teacher may need to probe and question to achieve elaboration and more text for the story. "Tell me more about the center's job," you might say, or "What do you mean by the offensive lineman hitting the other guy? Who is the other guy?"

When the teacher is collecting a text from a group of children or the whole class, he or she will need to be especially mindful of the correct story sequence. As different children offer comments and narrative, the events will come helter-skelter, and the teacher needs a bit of reflective time to construct the story in the appropriate sequential order. The wise teacher of primary-grade children may begin to focus on the narrative discourse structure. The teacher may wish to include such "signal" words as *first, second, next, then,* or *finally* at the beginning of the sentences in the children's story. Some of the children may have actually used such time-ordering, signal words, and others may have thought them. Now the teacher is displaying them in print on the written narrative and is modeling a way that authors write to tell stories and relate events that happened.

After the initial drafts are collected and the teacher has made the ordering and editing decisions, he or she produces a traditional language experience story on a large piece of chart paper, poster board, or the chalkboard. A large amount of text is not required. Generally, a completed story could range from four to seven sentences. Think about how many words are contained in one sentence. Let's say the average is five or six words. For five sentences, the teacher would have 25 to 30 words. There will be redundancy with some words because function words are needed to produce sentences, but the function words are also high-frequency words and basic sight words. Thus the repetition of words is good. Remember that the objective of this procedure is to transfer the words children say to their reading and, quite often, to their writing vocabularies.

When working with one student, I number the sentences. When using the approach with a group of children, I place their first names in the margin before the sentence begins. For a whole-class collection of a story, the teacher may want to give each group of children a fun name associated with the experience of the event. That name would then appear in the margin. For example, for the zoo trip story, the "tiger" group said this, and the "monkey" group said that.

Besides providing the large rendition of the language experience story for the whole group to view and read, the teacher should consider preparing other formats. A second copy can be produced on poster board or on old manila folders, to be cut into sentence strips or single words. A third can be typed on a computer with large font and a number of copies printed, one for each child. I prepared a separate manila folder for each child, into which they clipped or bound each of their stories. Each child could name and decorate the cover (and back) of the folder. Now the teacher has a number of "texts" from which to launch into the reading event.

Getting It Read

Learning to read the words of each language experience story is the "bread and butter" step of the approach. Some children will have committed the words to long-term memory after several exposures and readings of the large chart-paper story. Many others will need a number of repetitions of the words, delivered in different formats and guises. A few will need many, many repetitions with the words through a great deal of drill and practice and with inclusion of modalities other than seeing and saying. The teacher must be committed to the process. The objective, stated at the outset, is to use the language experience stories as the vehicle of reading instruction.

I accomplished the process in various degrees of print intensity for individual children, small groups, and whole-class situations in much the same way. You'll notice, in the progression of steps that follow, that there is a movement from the larger whole to smaller and smaller parts and then a return to a secondary whole that comes from a number of parts. Each story is also prepared in a number of different formats so that these can provide practice outside class and can be brought back to the next session. Flash cards should be prepared for writing down individual words. Once again, cutting up old manila folders or durable construction paper works just fine.

First the teacher displays the large story chart and reminds the group that this was the story they told the day or hours before. If some time has intervened before the print display and the oral telling of the story, the teacher may wish to review what the children said. Most of the time, a teacher-pupil read-along, possibly repeated a few times, will be enough. Each child can have a turn at reading the whole story aloud. Then the teacher points to individual sentences to be read. They don't have to be read in sequential order because many children will have memorized the oral story by now.

Point to the numbered or designated sentence to be read. For the small group, say "Robert, please read Jay's sentence" or "Jay, read Christopher's sentence." For the larger group you would say, "Who in the monkey group will read the tiger group's sentence?" Once again, you want all children to do some reading. You want also to vary the order of the sentences so children concentrate on the individual words of the sentences.

Next you point to individual words on the chart to be read. The interesting behavior to watch for here is how many of the children will approach the reading. If you point to an unfamiliar word in the middle or ending part of a sentence, they will mouth all the words of the sentence until they get to the designated word. The context will tell them how to "call" the word. This is good reading behavior, but in this case we wish the word to be learned instantaneously as soon as it appears in the visual field. So on we go with the word learning.

At this point, the teacher can use the second copy of the story, cut up into sentence strips. Display the separate, mixed-up sentence strips and have children put them back in correct order. Some teachers erroneously think they are teaching the skill of sequencing with this procedure. The children already know the sequence of the experience; they have lived it and talked about it. The teacher is merely having children practice sequential ordering. The main focus of the activity is the children's concentration on the printed word forms as they read each sentence, understand it in the printed version, and place it correctly in the sequence of the larger story.

Next, we go to the flash-card stacks. When I was the teacher, I placed each word for every sentence on a separate, small flash card, cut from an old manila folder. Then I put a rubber band around that sentence flash-card stack. There were as many flash-card stacks as there were sentences in a story. If a group had five or six children, I would try to generate an equal number of sentences, one contributed from each child. Then I would arrange the children's desks in a circle in which I could move around quite easily in the middle.

On each child's desk, I would place a stack and name the sentence to be constructed. In the beginning I had to show some children how to make a sentence with printed words—like looking for the word with a capital letter, looking for the end mark of punctuation, and beginning the sentence with the first word placed on the top left of the desk. Each child would take the stack of word cards, shuffle the cards as they read the words, and eventually make the sentence on the desktop. Each child would read the sentence aloud to me when finished. Then the stack would be scooped up, the word cards shuffled, the stack rebanded and passed on to the next child.

This process would go on until each child was constructing the sentences rather well without help or reading assistance.

At the next sitting, we would duplicate the circle seating arrangement. The sentence card stacks would be ready. This time I said, "Make this sentence." Very often in the beginning children would say, "What sentence?" I'd say, "You figure out the sentence. You can read the words now. You tell me the sentence you made." Initially the word cards for the sentences were the same words that were contained in the sentences of an original language experience story. However, soon I substituted a word from one sentence into another sentence. These were usually nouns or verbs. Instead of "You got to *hike* the ball," I would substitute *throw* one time and *quarterback down* another time. The words *quarterback down* came from a subsequent story but were not learned in the context of the earlier words, *hike* and *throw*. At this point, I could sense that the students were actually reading the words they had used in the oral language and not saying them from memorization of the sentence sequences.

Figure 5-3 shows the steps of the "Getting It Read" portion of the language experience approach.

Figure 5-3. Learning to Read the Words of the Language Experience Story

Extending the Print Experience

There are a number of ways to extend the print experience through reading and writing the words used in the language experience stories. These extensions can range from a detailed analysis and study of troublesome words for one student to a creative adoption of ways to use the story for other children's reading pleasure. Figure 5-4 shows that two children have written and illustrated their combined stories to appear in a movie or television viewing format. After cutting a window out of a cardboard box, and attaching their rolled-up story sheets to a wooden dowel (a wooden broom handle works well), the children can roll their story through the viewing screen to the delight of others.

Figure 5-4. Children Scrolling Their Language Experience or Retold Stories in a Movie Format for Their Classmates to Read and Enjoy

The more labor-intensive activities that may have to be accomplished with particular children will be presented in the next section. What follows is a list of other activities that may be accomplished to engage children in the automatic reading of the language experience words and their use in writing contexts:

1. Be sure to prepare a separate manila folder-type booklet for each child so that he can "own" his collection of stories. The booklet is bound with a fastener to hold the stories the teacher has typed on standard-size paper. The additional pages that are produced for stories can be inserted at appropriate places as well. Children like to draw and illustrate the pages of their booklets, which soon become each child's very own "storybook."

2. Undoubtedly with verbal input from the children, you have titled each of the language experience stories. For this storybook rendition of their stories, you may ask children, on a designated spot near the top or bottom of the page, to write their own title for each story. In this way, you are asking them to rethink the whole meaning to arrive at their own conceptually conceived main idea.

3. You can use the **cloze** technique with separate stories or with a cluster story. In this technique, a word is omitted from the text and the child has to supply (close in) the correct word. The way this is usually done is to prepare a "word bank" near the top of the page. The bank will contain the words that were omitted from the story. In some instances you would focus on major content, meaning-bearing words; in other instances, with a separately prepared cloze selection, you might focus on children's use of function words. Remember that the words in the word bank need to come from just one story or a collection of stories.

4. In a separate section of their individual booklets, children can prepare their own word dictionaries or picture-word dictionaries. With major, meaning-bearing words to which a picture could be applied, either drawn or cut out of magazines or papers, children can alphabetize their newly learned words.

5. You might like to prepare a page called "Mix-Ups and Fix-Ups." Children really like doing this activity. In the left-hand column of a page, you would present a noun phrase or a sentence beginning. In the second column, you would show the verb phrase or the concluding part of a language experience story sentence. Each column is in mixed-up order. Children have to connect the right subject part to the correct predicate part. While the objective is correct meaning, the fun is the merriment of the silly sentences children compose, like "The yellow lion put water in his trunk."

With one student, Richard, I prepared a page called "Jobs" after five language experience stories were completed. At the top of the page were the subject beginnings, "A center . . . ," "The defensive lineman . . . ," "The quarterback . . . ." At the bottom of the page was the list of appropriate predicates. He had to write the correct predicate completion next to the appropriate football position. This task required reading and writing the words on his own with full understanding.

6. Probably the most rewarding activity from a fluent reading point of view is the preparation of a **cluster story**. This is composed of the words from two or more stories, but it is a separate story. What happens is that the child is reading previously encountered words in a new context, so you can tell if word recognition and fluency is being achieved. With Richard, I prepared "A Football Story" after three team positions were covered in individual stories, and I prepared a selection called "The Super Bowl" when that event occurred. I recently witnessed a teacher working with a second-grade girl who had a high interest in animals. They completed stories on dogs, cats, horses, and birds and then did a cluster story with some of the words from all four stories.

7. To achieve some writing practice with students, don't forget to prepare pages where you pose questions. You may have to teach the traditional words we use to ask questions: *who, what, where, when, why,* and *how.* Then pose the questions in writing, using the same words as are found in the children's stories. When the children write the words in full sentences, they are practicing and visualizing the words again.

8. When a fair number of words have been presented in several stories, students can be asked to group or sort words according to different categories. They should be asked to think of ways that the words have something in common. Once they sort a group of words a certain way, they can be asked to name the group. From this activity a word chart or word wall can be constructed that lists the category name on top and shows all the words in that category below. Because some words have multiple meanings, they can appear in two columns.

9. More creative aspects of writing can occur when you ask children to write their own stories. They will look at words learned from previous stories and add their own words. Now you are helping the children's composing and word-retrieval processes. With your help they can produce their own self-realized stories and package them in a way such as the TV-format presentation.

10. A modern-day adaptation to integrate with the stories is the use of stickers, which can be found at your local variety store. Stickers are available for the seasons, holidays, and various themes. Six-year-old Ricardo had passed through the garbage truck, the firefighter, the dinosaur, and the snake stages and had recently emerged into the wonders of the age of chivalry. His two favorite books during this time were *Prince Bear* and *May I Bring a Friend?* These told him about kings, queens, and castles and stirred his imagination. While looking at a sheet of stickers relating to the medieval period, he composed his first two stories over subsequent days. You can note in the photo that the stickers selected served as appropri-

ate story illustrations. The words he underlined were the words he wanted to learn to read first. Finally, the R placed in the lower right corner announces the authenticity of the author.

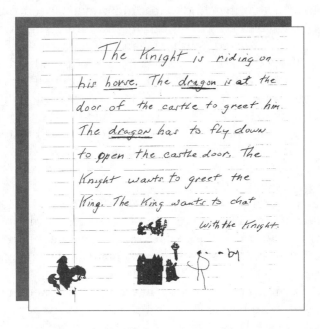

The language experience story approach to natural reading and writing encounters is a tried-and-true method of helping children achieve rapid word recognition and reading fluency. Understanding content is generally not a problem because the "story stuff" comes from the children themselves. They have lived and explained it. Children want to read what the teacher has written for them because they are the "authors" of the story.

When the Visual and Auditory Routes to Word Reading Are Not Enough

There will be times when looking at and saying certain words will not be enough for some children. Now is the time to bring in other modalities and converge viewing, saying, movement, and touch with the learning of particularly troublesome words. These may be words that a child constantly confuses for another, such as *from* for *for*; has trouble remembering, possibly because of difficult sound elements, such as *through* or *again*; or has trouble writing correctly, such as *gril* for *girl* or *saw* for *was*.

A technique used to help children read and spell troublesome words is known as the Fernald Technique, the **VAKT approach**, or the multisensory approach to word learning. Grace Fernald (1943) wrote about this approach, which incorporates a multisensory procedure in the learning of words for youngsters with severe reading problems. It became known as VAKT for its visual (V), auditory (A), kinesthetic (K), and tactile (T) components. This procedure is a great backup for learning difficult-to-read words in language experience and other stories. It is also good to use with those types of deep-rooted spelling problems discussed in chapter 3.

Basically, I've implemented the procedure in a series of "threes" in the following ways:

1. We trace the word three times, hand on hand.
2. The student writes the word from memory three times on paper. This could be done in the air, on the chalkboard, or with a box of kosher crystal salt.
3. Often I have the student write the word a few times in sentences he or she composes. Here it's important to focus just on the target word and not on other misspelled words.
4. Finally, each student must receive three check marks for correctness on his or her flash card over three successive days in order to have the word card placed in a secure word bank.

Now you can see why I mentioned earlier that this was a labor-intensive procedure. We're talking about the learning of one word here! For troublesome words it's wise not to do too many using the VAKT approach in one day. Initially, do two to five words per session in which the configurations are different. Remember, the student has great difficulty learning these words; they are not registering correctly in long-term memory. You're helping the memory process and building up the student's self-esteem when these words are finally learned correctly.

The materials needed for the VAKT approach are teacher generated, as they were for the language experience approach. I've relied on basic, unlined copy paper, $8\,^1/_2$ x 11 inches; a dark-colored crayon (black, purple, green, or red); 3 x 5 inch index cards; and a storage container for the cards. The teacher can purchase letters that have different qualities of "feel." However, I don't believe that touching different substances (the T) is the strongest part of the VAKT approach. The real strength lies with the K, the **kinesthetic movement** in the tracing of the letters of the word. The student gets the "feel" of the word in kinesthetic memory as he or she is looking at (the V) and saying (the A) the word.

Here's how I would recommend that you implement the VAKT approach once you've completed the language experience approach routine with one or several stories and have begun to witness troublesome words for any one student:

1. Take the blank copy paper and cut it lengthwise down the middle, leaving a small stack of 4 x 11^1/$_2$ inch sheets. The student sits alongside you, and you talk about the language experience approach words that he or she is having difficulty with, keeps confusing, and can't pronounce correctly. You try to elicit the words and convey a sense of the importance of learning them correctly. Then you write one of those words in big letters or script down the length of one 4 x 11^1/$_2$ inch sheet of paper. If the child is using **cursive writing** (rather than printing) in school, it's best to use that style when word writing. With cursive writing the strokes of the letters are joined within the word and, therefore, during the tracing, the child's fingers don't leave the word.

Next, you reach over and gently hold two or three fingers of the writing hand of the student and say, "Let's read and write this word." You guide the child's hand to trace the letters of the word as you both say the word. Saying the word as you trace it is important because you focus on the phonemic properties while the student is looking at the visual aspects of the word.

Let's say a troublesome word is *was* (as it is for many children, or its reversal, *saw*). As you trace, you both say "was" (you can stretch out the saying a bit as the fingers reach the letters). If you have the child pronounce the letters (spell), as I've seen some teachers do, the child will say "*w-a-s*." The focus on the spelling aspect is on the names of the letters, which are often different from their phoneme equivalents in the word. The gap widens between pronunciation and spelling with even more troublesome words such as *been*, *again*, *through*, or *though*. I hope you get the idea, to say the word's name to achieve the full visual, auditory, kinesthetic, and tactile input into the learning of the single word.

The reason I prefer the good old-fashioned crayon is that a smudge is created as we trace the word. The smudge is a noticeable trace of our having engaged in the features of the word and represents that kinesthetic feel. Once we have traced and pronounced the word three times together, I've often had the student "write" the word in the air a few times while making large arm strokes. If this particular word has been a spelling problem for the child, you may have the child close his or her eyes during the performing

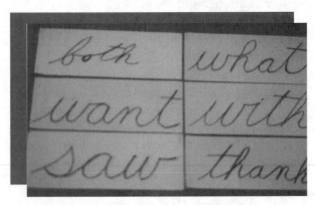

and saying of the word. With the eyes closed and the arm moving in the air to stroke the word, the child is visualizing the word with a full concentrative effort.

2. The next step involves writing the word on paper from memory. The just-completed arm movement "writing" in the air is a nice, natural forerunner to this step. Take the second sheet of 4 x 11 1/2 paper and ask the student to write the word from memory near the top. After the word is written, you can have the student compare his or her spelled word with the original traced word. If they match in correctness, you can proceed. If they don't match, you need to go back to the tracing step. The student doesn't yet have the feel of the word to write it correctly from memory.

Fold the paper down a bit so that the student can't see the word written on the top. Ask the student to write the word again from memory. Proceed by folding the page down each time so that the student writes the word correctly at least three times.

Next you might ask the student to use the word in a sentence, written on the next clean space on the writing page. Here you're establishing the meaning connection (remember the four properties of words) and also seeing if the word used naturally in a self-composed sentence will be written correctly. Don't focus on the other misspelled words in the sentence. This is a potential disaster; it pulls the student off track. Just make a notation of other badly spelled words that you may want to focus on in future lessons.

Once all the writings are complete, you've finished your intensive word work with the child for that day. Essentially what you've done is worked on short-term memory in learning the word. Intervening time is now needed to see if the word will be committed to long-term memory. You might want to use a recording or notation system to indicate the labor that went into learning the word. I use a slash mark (/) to indicate each successful trace. If unsuccessful, you can cross it out with an X. A check mark (√) is used to indicate each successful writing attempt. Then I add the date next to the notations. This detailed recording will come in quite handy when you need to consult with the parents or the "higher-ups" in your educational system. Many times, they don't understand the process and the effort it takes for some children to learn troublesome words.

Before the child leaves for the day, you might want to make the transition to long-term memory learning. The words for the day would be placed on flash cards. You shuffle the cards, lay them on the desk or table, and ask the student to read them. In preparing the flash-card words, most teachers now use block letters to portray the word as it appears in book print. Most of the time the child will correctly name most of the words practiced for that day, but there may be one or two that are stumbled over. You'll have to see if these words will need to be redone next time. Some words have taken me three sittings to be learned correctly.

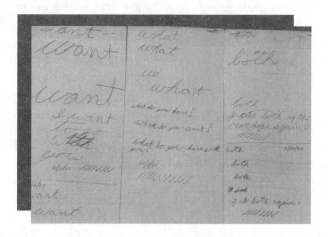

3. The final step involves calling the word correctly over at least three separate days as the word is flashed on the card. When the student is met for the next word learning session, the teacher should flash the words that underwent the VAKT approach in the previous session(s). Holding the stack of word cards, the teacher flashes the word by twisting the wrist. The flash should be rapid, with about a second or so exposure of the word. If the child calls the word correctly, the check mark and date recorded on the back. If not called correctly, the teacher knows that the word is still not committed to long-term memory and probably needs to undergo the VAKT approach once again.

Many educators, both verbally and in their writings, tell us that the context will help students figure out the troublesome words. Much as I am a believer in the use of context to unlock word meanings and identities (this will be covered in the next chapter), I don't believe that this is the correct strategy for students who have been confusing the identities of basic words. Remember from chapter 4 all the context cues and clues that can impinge upon a reader's processing at any given time, and recall that many words contain multiple meanings of their own. Although understanding the context is undoubtedly the major goal of reading, the words in the contextual array have to be perceived accurately to convey the meaning intended by the author.

Following the "threes" principle, the student needs three checks (with dates recorded alongside) in order to show that the word has been mastered. Sometimes it has not been fully mastered as another word from another story is being taught and learned. The second word has a similar configuration to the initially learned word and this visual aspect causes the student to misread or miscue, creating uncomfortable word confusion once again. The teacher may have to use the VAKT approach for both words as the distinctive differences between the words are brought out. Examples are *though, thought,* and *through; bought* and *brought;* and *those* and *these.*

What also happens, because three check marks are required over three intervening days, is that the stack of word cards has grown. More words from more recent stories have been added to the stack, and the cards range from no check marks to a number of check marks. Some words have more than three check marks if a student admits that more practice is needed. Thus achieving the three check marks is a fairly good test of long-term word reading. The next procedure involves investing the student's words for safekeeping into the student's word bank.

Banking One's Word Capital

Banking one's collection of learned words simply involves getting the word cards into some kind of container. The reason I suggested 3 x 5 index cards is that they fit nicely into most recipe-size file boxes or even shoeboxes, which young children like to decorate. The words can be alphabetized and separated by using alphabet dividers of the same size. The alphabetizing provides another great long-term memory activity. When many words began to accumulate for a particular letter, I would say, "Let's display your *b* or *m* words on the table (or desk or floor). I want you to read each word in any order and give it to me as fast as you can." As the children's eyes alight on different words, they pick them up, calling out each name in turn. There will be a few near the end of their instantaneous word calling whereby they will employ sounding out. Then there may be a few they can't remember or have confused. These may have to go back to the three check marks procedure.

The box format and the alphabet cards provide a nice, easily maintained management system for keeping track of all the words learned as well as a way of showing each student that his or her word capital is growing behind each alphabet card. Keeping the word banks has been, in my experience, one of the most motivating and rewarding ways to keep the student who has had word difficulty in the word learning business. One fifth-grade student reading well below level proudly yelled out when he was asked how many words he had in his word bank, "I have 93 words so far and still going upwards!"

The word banks provide an easy-to-understand form of assessment as well. When someone asks, "How's so-and-so doing?" the teacher can produce the box of words. What's inserted in the box wasn't there before. The words in the box show growth, and the checks and dates recorded on the backs of the cards show the evaluative procedures the teacher used as the child grew in word learning.

The words that go into the word banks don't just come from language experience stories; they can come from any source. They can be words learned through phonics or word family systems, or new meaning vocabulary words learned from content topics or themes. Ronald Cramer (1994b) agrees that word banks play an important role in the development of sight vocabulary even as they have been identified with the language experience approach and whole-language beliefs to literacy instruction. Burns et al. (1999) suggest that as a general rule word banks have been used in the primary grades, whereas word or vocabulary notebooks are used in the intermediate grades and above.

There's one more intermediary step you should use between the word card collection and the word bank storage. You might be thinking, "What do I do with all those word cards that haven't earned the three check marks yet?" Just procure two large envelopes to use with each child. Being the "non-artist" that I am, I drew a happy face on one envelope and a sad face on the second envelope. Into the latter went the words that didn't have three check marks. The happy-face envelope held, for a short while, the

mastered words requiring one more flash before they went into the word bank. Creative teachers have adapted the envelopes to be called "friends" or "acquaintances," "goals" or "penalty box," "yes" or "no," or have decorated them with cheerful and not-so-cheerful scenes. Use of word cards, manila envelopes or paper bags, and the word banks are sure, natural ways to invest word reading and word knowledge mastery for each and every child you teach.

The Retelling Strategy

The **retelling strategy** is a highly motivational, effective, and versatile way to build both word reading and vocabulary development for all levels of students. It is versatile because the language of instruction comes from authors. Children's literature and sometimes information books are the vehicles of instruction. Retelling is a more child-oriented way to say "reconstructing." Retellings, therefore, become verbal, artistic, and written reconstructions of author's stories and information in the children's own words and imagery. When children verbally retell an author's story, they reconstruct the story in their minds using their own language. As these retold stories are written down, they become the basis of the children's reading and writing experiences.

Because the volume of children's literary and informational selections is quite rich today, connected to all ages and grade levels as well as to the themes and topics children cover in school, retellings can be integrated quite nicely into the language arts curriculum while providing a fun way to do reading and writing. Moreover, when the teacher connects the sheer volume of children's literature to the number of ways to accomplish the retelling activity, the literacy possibilities become enormous. Retellings become highly natural ways to either build sight vocabulary for those children who need to do so or increase meaning vocabulary for these children who are already reading but need to enlarge their wealth of word meanings. Sequencing events in order is a natural, intrinsic part of the process.

The Process of Retelling to Build Word Reading

The words that children use in retelling an author's story become the basis of their sight vocabularies. Here's how the teacher could proceed with the process.

1. The teacher talks to the children in a general way about a book or literary piece. Curiosity is aroused about the title, the author, and the artwork. Predictive questions about the piece are asked, and the children's background experiences about the topic are ac-

cessed. Interaction and ownership of the topic are encouraged by verbal interchanges.

2. In most cases the children cannot profitably read the piece for enjoyment and understanding, so the teacher reads the piece. The teacher may stop at previously selected points in the story to ask retrospective questions about what has been happening and why. The teacher asks new predictive questions about what is coming next. New words may be clarified in context by a rereading. Children are encouraged to talk using the language of the piece. Rereadings are done to emphasize a particular point, to help children visualize a section better, or to help them learn the words of the story.

3. The book or literary piece can be read again in a number of different ways. Sometimes the teacher models and students follow aloud. Shared reading is done, with the teacher and designated students changing sections. Choral reading is done to achieve smooth fluency of the language of the author.

4. Now we're at the step in which children are asked to re-create the story and use their own written words. To do this, you could prepare a "story map." I've taken a larger sheet of copy paper, the $8\,{}^1/{}_2$ x 14 inch size, and divided it down the middle. Leave room on top of the page for children's names, the title and author of the book they are retelling, and any other information you require. With 2 or 3 inches used for this, you are left with the rest of the paper to make picture and writing panels. Take a ruler and measure off about four sections down the page and draw lines across. You then have a page layout with four panels to the left of the line drawn down the page and four panels to the right side—eight panels in all.

The next step is your call, whether you would like the children to plan their artwork first or attempt to do their writing first. I like going with the artwork first because it helps children to visualize the story events to which their writing will be connected. One side of four panels will be for children's artwork, and the other side will be for their written retellings. Please don't limit children just the four combined panels; some children take two pages or six or seven panels to retell the author's story.

5. Children are asked to retell the story through the creation of picture panels. You will probably need to lead them initially through this thinking by asking, "How do you see the events of this story? What do you see happening first?" After they tell you what they perceive as the first major event, you could say, "How would you draw that here in this first box [panel]?" Then you would say, "What happens next? How would you draw that?" You would proceed this way until the story has been reimagined in each child's mind's eye.

Students draw key episodes of the plot by revisualizing the story or by looking at the artist's illustrations. The number of picture panels produced by a student depends on the richness of the student's imagination, his or her ability to draw, and the teacher's purpose in having the student re-create the story in depth. The point is that for each picture panel generated, there will be an accompanying text provided by each student in retelling the story. The writing panels are prepared on the other side of the divided page.

6. Next, each student retells the story in writing by matching the ideas reflected in the picture panels. Many emergent and problem readers, who are yet uncognizant of correct English spellings, will use invented or creative spelling when writing their story. Others will ask the teacher to help them spell particular words correctly. The teacher often rewrites the child's invented spelling of the text by using self-stick notes of paper affixed alongside the child's version. The child then reads the teacher's rewritten version.

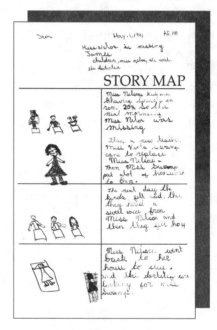

With all these combinations, teachers use the written retellings as the basis for building the children's sight and/or meaning vocabularies.

Some teachers create an icon to represent the selection the children will retell. The icon of an apple drawn in the left and right columns of a standard 8 1/2 by 11 inch sheet of paper, represents the story of Johnny Appleseed. One student needed a second page, or six more "apples," to write and draw his retold story.

Between the apple figures the teachercould place a figure into which students put those important function words that direct the forward movement of the narrative. These words, which signal the movement of time and help to sequence ideas and sentences in the students' retold narrative, could be posted on one chart in a section of the classroom. Another chart could show spatial-oriented function words, such as *up, down, beside, under,* and *away from,* whereas another could contain comparison-and-contrast function words, such as *and, also, but, however, both, together,* and *too,* to help children think and write when using other discourse styles.

If the teacher wishes to exploit the fun and story writing achieved by students completing the story maps, he or she should consider the six-step process described above as a first-draft procedure. In other words, the best is yet to come. Use the story maps, run off on a copy machine with standard paper, as a way to collect the students' first draft. Also, downplay the energy and creativity the children often put into their artwork; tell them to make simple drawings using stick figures and just a little coloring.

Making Retold Books

You can then have children enter the fun and creative world of making **retold books** in all kinds of shapes, patterns, and styles. Below is a simple list of these retelling activities. Appendix B describes how to construct each one. Pictures are provided there as well to show how teachers and students have used the retelling strategy to make children's books. In most cases, the illustrative artwork and written text appear on the same panel.

> **Retold Books**
> Accordion Book
> Character Development Book
> Circle Story Book
> Create-a-Book
> Finger-Puppet Book
> Flip Book
> Flip-Flop Book
> Fold-a-Book
> Mobile Book
> Pop-Up Book
> Scroll Story Book
> Shape Book

The Power of Retelling

The retelling procedure provides a means for strategic literacy development in three major ways. First, children naturally create their own print-rich environment. When the story maps and various children-constructed books are displayed in the classroom, one has a sense that the environment is vibrant, alive with the written words and illustrations of children. The literary work should spill out of the classroom to highlight the hallways, entranceways, auditorium, and lunchroom of the school. In this way, the print-rich environment celebrated by the school society serves in a pragmatic,

cultural way to positively influence children in the importance of print acquisition. Some researchers have noted that print-oriented societies have a strong input into how young children learn literacy (Goodman, 1994).

Second, and without formal teaching, children are immersed in the writing process. The children are authors in apprentice. Thus the concepts of retelling and retold books are important ones. The notation on the cover page of each self-made booklet should contain the original author(s), illustrator(s), the title of the book, and the apprentice's byline, "Retold by [the child's name]. The "retold by" means that a child was engaged in the process of telling a story.

Children of all ages will want to become involved in this process. After they have finished their first drafts with their single-page story maps, they enjoy reading and showing their artistic panels to their teachers and peers. At this point, they listen to revisions and editing suggestions because they want to show their best work in the retold book. When they prepare the illustrations and writing panels for the retold book, their efforts are usually quite concentrated and exacting because they have to plan and execute the writing and illustrations on the same panels for others to read and enjoy.

When you do an initial lesson using one of the retold-book procedures, you have several options. You'll note that each retold book requires specific materials and a "know-how" procedure. If you want to emphasize the composing and meaning process in the initial lesson, as you might want to do, you should have the props ready. For instance, for the Circle Story Book, you will have assembled the two cardboard circles or paper plates and connected them together in the middle with a fastener. You would have accomplished the cutout on the top circle to reveal the space where children will write and draw underneath. However, when you wish the children to learn the Circle Story Book construction procedure and the others on the list so that they can independently apply these on their own when retelling future readings, then you would teach children the steps of the construction procedure. At the same time, another major objective may be to help them learn some major principles of arithmetic. For instance, with the Circle Story Book, you will be showing them how to accomplish a quarter, a fifth, or a sixth of a whole circle, depending on how many panels their retold stories take to tell.

The third major benefit derived from the collection of children's retold books is that you have a natural children's library. They truly enjoy reading each other's books. So not only does the print-rich environment visually display the children's literacy efforts to the larger school community, but the books themselves are a source of the children's independent reading materials. As one child reads a colleague's book, the words of the original author are reinforced. However, the author's new vocabulary words may be used by the apprentice author in a slightly different way and in a different written context than the child who is reading the retold book. Reading the retold books is such a pleasurable way to increase children's fluency while instilling a high motivation to read.

In short, retelling is an effective strategy to use with both emergent and problem readers because having a sense of the whole allows them to predict the words in their own retold stories as well as the retold stories of others. The repeated readings accomplished through the class collection of retold books helps readers predict a text's vocabulary. Furthermore, the children's own written context helps them to visualize the words that enter the reading visual field.

The power of the retelling strategy lies in the way it fuses the verbal with the nonverbal and the in-the-head factors with the new. Children use visual art to help initiate the written words they wish to use in their story sequence, and they use the unusual words of the author to tell about events and characters in the story. Children write, revise, and edit to complete the apprenticeship work. Other children read what the apprentice author wrote. Thus, we can see that a total literacy event has occurred. The art and revisualizing propels the writing, and the writing becomes a source of the reading—all in an affective climate of high motivation and pleasure. The retelling strategy applied in the elementary and intermediate grades creates a win-win literacy situation.

Summary

This chapter presented natural ways that children learn about print and about the reading and writing of words. "Natural," in this context, means that a progression occurred from knowing words in the oral language to being able to recognize words in the written language. The progression occurred without taking the words apart to analyze the letter or sound equivalents. We noted that book language is different from talk language, and reading aloud to children expands their knowledge of words, grammatical relationships, visions, and background knowledge. Therefore, reading aloud at home and in school environments becomes a natural bridge to learning to read on one's own.

Three major practices were presented whereby children are nurtured in print language and brought to it in a natural way. First, we looked at the construct of emergent literacy and how the practices of emerging into literacy capitalize on concepts such as environmental print, print-rich environments, and writing-artwork connectedness. Second, the language experience approach revealed that the oral language of children could become the basis of their initial sight vocabularies. For those difficult-to-learn words or words often confused, the VAKT approach served as a good multisensory backup to language experience words. Third, the retelling strategy showed us a number of guises by which children can learn the rich and diverse vocabulary of authors.

A **word structure map**, based on the work of Robert Schwartz and Taffy Raphael (1985) also known as a *concept word map* and a *structure of a word map* and, can be used by teachers throughout the grades when a key concept word, such as *explorers, pioneers, migration,* or *communities*," is developed. Three questions are posed about the concept word:

What is it?

What is it like?

What are some examples?

The questions lead students (and teachers) through the critical thinking of classifying. When students tell or write about what the concept word is, they are establishing the class and category to which the word belongs. For instance, if the concept word was *nomads*, students might write something like "a kind of people who wander and travel to search for food or care for their animals." Students will give the attributes, characteristics, and features of the concept word with words such as *hardy, courageous, brave, determined, lonely,* and *resourceful*. They provide examples of the concept word, and in this case it could be *Mongols, Lapps,* and *Eskimos*.

This chapter presented some major concepts for teachers. At least four come to mind, and each separate concept word would be placed in a center concept box. Thus four separate word structure maps would be developed for these concept terms: emergent literacy, the language experience approach, the retelling strategy, and the VAKT approach. Other concept terms could be considered as well, such as invented spelling, print-rich environment, or reading aloud. Notice that each concept word is defined in a particular way, has its own features, and is represented by different examples. For instance, features of the language experience approach would be "language derived from children," "child centered," or "children's oral language basis of initial reading words," and an example would be "used with one child, a group of children, or whole class to build sight vocabulary."

Concept Words and Terms

cloze   print-rich environment
cluster story   reading aloud
cursive writing   reading readiness
emergent literacy   retelling strategy
kinesthetic movement   retold book
language experience approach   stage model
metacognitive   VAKT approach
                                    word structure map

Word Challenge for Teachers: The Word Structure Map

This activity requires more divergent thinking from students. When attempting to build the map from concept words suggested, the student needs to search the text and think of the ideas that the reading offered. Some ideas may be explicitly stated, but others may need to be inferred, especially when describing the features or characteristics of the concept word. For VAKT, I used "labor-intensive" as a way to describe the focused effort that goes into the learning of each word. However, you may have inferred that "time-consuming" was another attribute of the VAKT approach.

Don't be bound by a three- or four-box format. Many times students will come up with many more attributes and examples, so boxes can be added to house their ideas. Other types of thinking can be addressed as well. For instance, for the concept topic "Explorers," some teachers have their students arrange their example boxes in a time-line format. Students write down the names of the various explorers with the dates and places of exploration in a left-to-right chronological sequence. Once the map is complete, a good concluding activity would be to write a good paragraph or two about the key concept word.

The map outline is available for you with suggested concept terms to place in the center. There is no answer key for this activity.

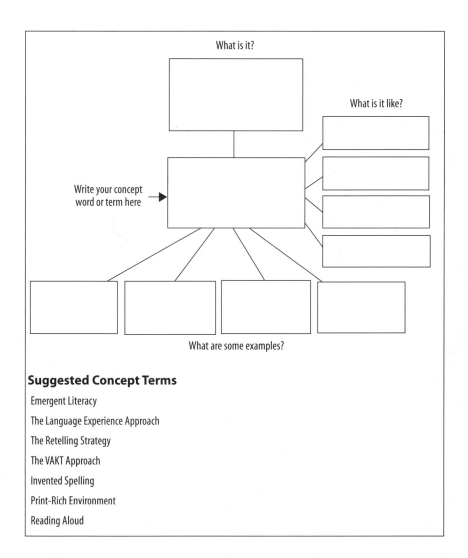

Suggested Concept Terms

Emergent Literacy

The Language Experience Approach

The Retelling Strategy

The VAKT Approach

Invented Spelling

Print-Rich Environment

Reading Aloud

6

Building a Meaning Vocabulary

Focus Questions

1. How do wide and divergent experiences help build vocabulary knowledge?

2. What procedures can the teacher use to help students learn the new vocabulary of authors?

3. Why are concept maps good tools to use to help students apply the new vocabulary of topics and themes?

4. How can children's understanding and use of word parts, known as prefixes, roots, and suffixes, help them grow in vocabulary development and cognitive development?

5. How does knowledge of how to use the context help readers during free and independent reading?

Vocabulary development is a critical aspect of schooling, especially today, when the words used on prime-time television are less challenging than the words found in most children's books (Cunningham & Stanovich, 1998). Vocabulary not only reflects one's knowledge (Hirsch, 2000) but is also an excellent predictor of how one comprehends written text. To reaffirm this belief, the National Reading Panel (2000) recently reported that the more robust a person's oral or reading vocabulary, the easier it will be to understand a text. For many children in the elementary and intermediate grades, a new reading word is also a new vocabulary or a new concept word (see chapter 1). This presents an ever recurring challenge for the teacher in developing children's meaning and reading vocabularies.

Vocabulary Development
in the Classroom Context

Here's one major way that vocabulary development occurs in the classroom. Fifty percent of the children in your classroom might know the meaning of *hibernate* in the oral language but can't read it yet. (Many other words, such as *tadpole, migrate, nomad,* and *pasture,* could be used in this illustration as well). Another 50% may not know what "hibernate" means, and yet they will be facing the word for the first time when it appears in their reading on bears and other animals that hibernate. These children have to do double duty: they have to learn the word's meaning as they simultaneously do the word reading. Of course, knowledgeable teachers will discuss the meanings of new words before visual encounters to establish prior knowledge in the children's minds.

As far as the teacher is concerned, he or she is presenting the word for the first time in a visual and auditory reading experience to 100% of the children. The children are involved with visual recognition of the word, breaking the word into three separate parts, putting the parts back together to reconstruct the whole word, and any other word-play activities the teacher unfolds. The lesson and the reading ends. *Hibernate* and all the other new words introduced in the reading, and all the other new words with new experiences presented to the children that day, are now scattered like unconnected threads across their minds as they leave school to return the next day. Now memory, particularly long-term memory, becomes a factor.

When *hibernate* is exposed to the children on a subsequent day, 25% of the children in the group that knew the word's meaning beforehand will be able to read the word at sight, and the other 75% will struggle with the word's identity. From the other group, those who didn't know what *hibernate* meant, 85% will have mastered reading that word. How can this be, the teacher laments? One would think that if the meaning was known, then visual recognition of the word would be easy, like matching a visual template onto a known concept. That's the mystery of successful word recognition and vocabulary understanding for particular children at particular times in particular contexts. Children from both groups will need more visual and meaning encounters with the word before it becomes learned in long-term visual memory. Frank May (1998) suggests that direct teaching of new vocabulary will work when the teacher takes the time to develop depth of knowledge about each word.

With another word, the percentage of rapid word identifiers may change. The challenge for the teacher is to help all children acquire new reading words to add to their growing sight vocabularies as efficiently and solidly as possible. To assist this process from a visual and meaning perspective, the teacher should show and have children use each new word in written contexts, such as sentences, paragraphs, letters, and reports.

Acquiring new words enriches children's understanding of each new topic and the concepts associated with that topic. New words open up children's horizons to allow for the inclusion of more new words. When teachers are about to engage their students in a new topic experience through a textbook reading, such as might occur with topics like *amphibians, metamorphosis, the water cycle,* and *immigration,* teachers need to consider the depth of students' prior knowledge with that experience and whether they understand the vocabulary used by the text authors to understand that experience. The basic rule is this: Because vocabulary represents concepts and information, the richer one's vocabulary for a topic, the better chance one has of success in dealing with that topic.

What happens with children who don't have rich language exposure and who enter school with low vocabulary backgrounds? When provided with the same lesson, the low-vocabulary child will predictably learn less than the high-vocabulary child (Hart & Risley, 1995). This is because the low-vocabulary child is operating on "overload." When confronted with so many words that aren't read efficiently, the low-vocabulary child doesn't integrate well the new concept vocabulary with that previously covered in other topics and subjects. This meaning overload was revealed recently in a study involving 66 kindergartners who listened to a single reading of a storybook narrative. The children with higher vocabulary knowledge learned significantly more words than did children with lower vocabulary knowledge. When children were more actively involved in storybook participation, they learned significantly more words than their peers placed in a more passive situation (Ewers & Brownson, 1999).

How can new word learning be accomplished? How can teachers help students gain knowledge of these 44,000 or so words that constitute 99% of written text? Do they teach new words directly every day in their classrooms, do they show students ways to figure out new word meanings, or do they just provide dictionaries when students ask for help? These questions have puzzled educators for years (May, 1998), and research has yielded unbalanced, conflicting results (Baumann et al., 2002; Kuhn & Stahl, 1998; National Reading Panel, 2000).

Yet common sense and knowing the enjoyment of introducing new language to children impels us to think that there is wisdom in teaching ways to word meanings. I've attempted to sort out a schema for doing just this. It is shown in Figure 6-1.

You can see that I've separated vocabulary development into three broad but mutually reinforcing categories: (a) what the teacher does explicitly in the classroom to teach new words directly through projects, strategies, and activities; (b) what the teacher does as reading and thinking behavior so that students have the skills required to figure out new words when they're encountered in new readings; and (c) what students do as independent listeners, readers, and writers engaged in recreational, personal, or purposeful activity in which literacy is done. These three categories are reciprocal and mutually reinforcing in that what happens in the classroom may influence the understanding of words faced incidentally in a literary reading, while the words understood in a literature selection read independently may help the student's understanding in the classroom. Moreover, while morphemic analysis and strategies for how to use the context (the middle column) will initially be taught in explicit lessons (the left column), the goal of such lessons is for students to have tools to unlock word meanings in independent reading when unknown words appear (the right column).

Classroom Instruction in the Understanding and Use of New Vocabulary

The five major procedures listed in Figure 6-1 do not complete the wealth of techniques teachers can bring to the classroom to help students learn new words. However, the five may be considered to be comprehensive in that they embed many of the traditional ideas and activity suggestions found in teachers' manuals, skill books, reading and literacy textbooks used in college coursework. For instance, the one concept-level relation of "classification" on the Taxonomy of Concept-Level Comprehension (Pearson & Johnson, 1978), promotes the thinking processes necessary when engaged in most cognitive or semantic map use, semantic feature analysis, word structure maps, and word sorts.

Experience Language

Experience language is the counterpart of language experience. In the latter procedure, the oral language comes freely from chil-

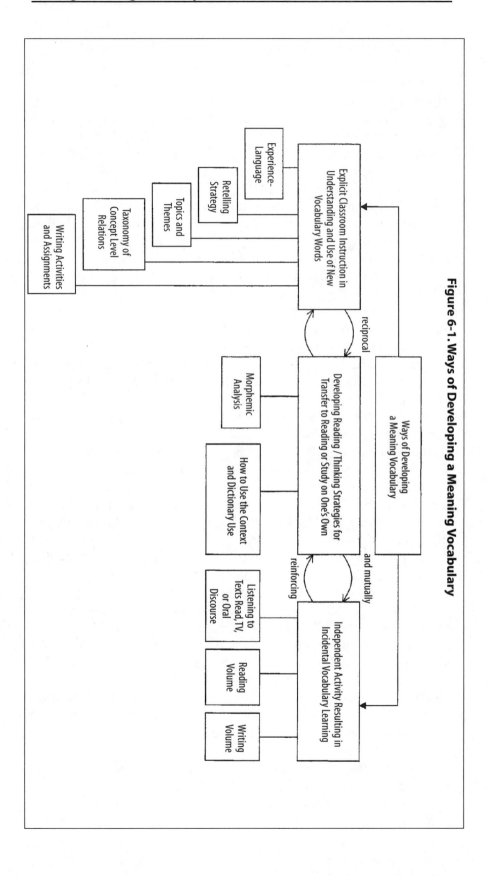

Figure 6-1. Ways of Developing a Meaning Vocabulary

dren, and language becomes the basis of their word reading. Because the words were familiar, there was no problem with understanding. With experience language, the teacher provides a new experience with the explicit purpose of using the vocabulary associated with that experience to allow students to make experiential and language growth connections. It's the same natural order of things when parents immerse their children in life's wonderful experiences. They take their children shopping, to museums, to zoos, and to other points of interest; they involve them in arts activities and athletics and go on trips to near and far destinations. Each of these life experiences has its own vocabulary, and parents and other adults naturally use the words of the experience as it is unfolding. This learning context is that of the natural environment.

During the regular school year, with scheduled periods of instruction occurring at fixed intervals during the day to cover state- and district-mandated subjects, schools have a difficult time achieving such natural learning contexts. They do this best when they send their students "off campus" for summer and weekend educational programs, field trips, and cultural events. In one such program, seven outdoor activities provided the natural context for the introduction and learning of 175 vocabulary words (Sinatra, 1991). For instance, in the activity of field mathematics, inner-city children demonstrated *pace, pivot,* the 3-foot *stride,* and *intervals* in order to calculate distances between buildings. Based on these calculations, they could do area and perimeter calculation work.

Teachers do accomplish experiential, hands-on learning situations when they involve their students in science experiments; math problem-solving activities in which the tools of measuring, weighing, and calculating have to be used; and computer-generated projects. The key for teachers is to structure an experience in which children are involved in action as the words of the experience are being used and woven into the experience by the teachers. Just thinking of the ways that action-oriented activities occur in school settings makes one recall such rapidly disappearing school subjects as gym, music, shop, home economics, health, and the visual, graphic, and fine arts. Possibly the most shameful concept prevalent in education today is doing away with the real thinking and literacy builders named above (because they're considered "frills") and doubling up periods on the so-called "basics" of math and reading instruction. More of the same being delivered in the same old way doesn't provide ways to use literacy in purposeful and meaningful ways. Connecting literacy to experience-language activities, with new learning, new concepts, and new vocabulary, does. The many different fields of the arts alone provide a variety of forms of representation, language that is necessary to understand and express those forms, and the sensory-motor experiences that provide the imaginative mind with new ideas, perspectives, and ways to use language.

Edgar Dale (1969) has provided a rather unique model, called the **Cone of Experience**, based on the premise that the learning of new concepts precedes from the concrete to the abstract. Because so much of new word learning includes learning new concepts as well, teachers can use the model to help students learn new vocabulary. Visualize a cone with its base sitting on a plate. The base, supported by the plate, represents the concrete foundation of experience. Proceeding upward toward the point are three major types of activity levels: action, observation, and abstract representation. **Activities of action** involve the mental and physical energy of the whole child, with all or most of the senses coming into play. During **observation**, viewing and listening are the primary modes of learning as children see demonstrations, exhibits, film, and pictures. The **abstract representation** level at the top of the cone has two important groups for teachers: visual symbols and verbal symbols. These appear at the pinnacle.

Visual symbols, as presented by Dale, include those conceptual frameworks that present information and data in nonverbal ways. During the activity of action, students experience concrete activities in which many physical senses are involved. Then they are asked to conceptualize and express the experience in such visual forms and structures as illustrations, drawings, diagrams, picture maps, graphs, charts, flow charts, and time lines. Today we would certainly add concept and semantic maps to this visual grouping. Students can be shown how to use a visual or graphic representation that best communicates the meaning of the original experience. For instance, a simple illustration can show the workings of a balance scale, a bar graph can show the increasing length of the plant stem when measured over days and weeks, and a flow chart can show the cycle of a butterfly's life.

The **verbal symbols** can be experienced by any number of literacy activities. Here students engage in reading, writing, and oral presentation work using the new vocabulary of the experience. Students can simply retell the lived experience while the teacher helps them with the vocabulary connections during the oral recitation. Then the retelling is written down in much the same way as the language experience narrative. Students read the new experience, with the new vocabulary appearing and reappearing in its natural context. At this point, many teachers reprint the written selection with the key vocabulary omitted. Students have to insert the vocabulary words as they make sense in the textual reading. Many activities from the Concept-Level Relations Taxonomy, which will be presented shortly, could aptly allow students to apply the new words in unique and challenging ways.

In Table 6-1, selected concept topics are presented by discipline area and general grade-level range. I've indicated the activity materials and settings required to provide the experiential base to activate the lesson. The new vocabulary words that were taught through the lesson are indicated in the last column. Would you concur that these words were predictably appropriate to learn at these grade levels and for these topics?

Taable 6-1. Vocabulary Taught Through Classroom Lessons Having an Experiential Base

Discipline and Grade Level	Concept Topic	Concrete Activity Materials and/or Settings	New Vocabulary
Science—Primary	The Five Senses	Common objects and materials to see, hear, smell, taste, and touch	Sense(s), sight, eyes, vision, touch, feel, fingers, ears, hear, listen, nose, smell, scent, tongue, taste, bitter, sweet
Science—Intermediate	How a Thermometer Works	Long sheet of oak-tag, markers, zipper, ruler	Measure, degree, temperature, thermometer, liquid, mercury, Fahrenheit, Celsius, ruler, scale
Science—Intermediate	Muscle Cells: How They Work	Chicken feet obtained from butcher. End of foot trimmed to expose ends of tendons.	Tissue, muscles, nerve(s), ligaments, tendons, cartilage, cells, fibers, joints, flexible, contrast, relax
Social Studies—Intermediate	How the Archaeologist and Anthropologist Work	A large tank or basin filled with soil or sand. Different-colored soil would indicate strata. Into soil are placed artifacts such as coins, pottery pieces, jewels, and bones. Children have brushes, spoons, tweezers, strainers, and magnifying glasses.	Anthropologist, archaeologist, artifacts, primitive, excavate, hypothesis, civilized, strata, composition, conclusions
Social Studies—Junior High	Reenacting the Constitutional Convention of 1789	Arranging the classroom to portray how the delegates representing the original colonies were seated at the Constitutional Convention of 1789.	Constitution, convention, delegate, independence, founding fathers, federal system, compromise, clarify, representatives, branches, quorum, unanimous
Arithmetic—Primary	The Balance Scale	Begin with seesaw on school playground and continue with balance scale use in the classroom.	Balance, scale, weigh, equal, unequal, amount, compare, light, heavy, predict, add, subtract, items
Arithmetic—Intermediate	Making Estimates, Proportional Comparisons, and Using Statistics	A small box of raisins for each child	Predictions, recorded, estimate, actual, average, mean, median, mode, data, calculate, plot, graph, represent

Revisiting Retellings

Recall that the retelling strategy was highlighted in chapter 5 as a major way to build word reading in a natural way. In that use of the strategy, children retell literary selections in written story maps and retold books as a means of learning a sight vocabulary. Now I'm revisiting the retelling strategy for an equally important reason, to help students use the new vocabulary words of authors. The procedure is basically the same as before, but the teacher needs to reshape it a bit by providing a way for students to see the new words. Teachers can do this by preparing a word wall pertaining to that selection on the chalkboard, on chart paper, or by mounting cards on a wall. Students need to refresh their memories of the new words used by the author so that when they prepare the pages of their retold books, they can use the words appropriately in their own contexts.

Notice in the picture one sixth-grade girl wrote her version of *The Winged Cat*, told in the form of a shape book. Cleverly she put fold-down wings on the shape of her cat. She has correctly used the newly learned word *amulet* in the first page of her retold narrative. Also notice in the upper left-hand corner a stack of word cards. The teacher has provided her students with a ring binder so that each student can keep his or her collection of new words together, ready for use for reading and writing activities prompted by the teacher.

Some years ago as a visiting classroom teacher, I had a very enjoyable lesson with a third-grade class that was reported to be a little reluctant about engaging in the writing process. We had completed reading A. A. Milne's wonderful story "In Which Pooh Goes Visiting and Gets Into a Tight Place." In that story, Pooh Bear consumes just a little

too much of rabbit's honey and condensed milk (the larder was cleaned out) and gets stuck in rabbit's entranceway to his house. So Pooh's head is emerging out of the ground, and his backside and legs are dangling down in rabbit's living room.

I thought that the visual picture of Pooh stuck in the hole provided a wonderful opportunity to use the accordion book format for a retold book. So I prepared long strips of paper about 4 inches wide. The strips were cut from chart paper, and 10 folded sections were made with an icon of a bear's head pasted on the first panel and an icon of the bear's backside and dangling legs pasted on the last panel. The folded-up effect showed a complete bear profile, and the stretched-out effect revealed eight blank 4-inch squares. When I held up one such prepared accordion book in front of the class and said, "Who wants to write the story of Pooh Bear on this book?", I had 100% commitment.

However, before we began we orally composed our first draft and focused on the new vocabulary of the author. I asked, "How do you see Pooh if you were going to draw and write about him on the first panel of the book?" Children agreed that he was in his house doing his exercises and humming a little song. "What kind of exercises was Pooh doing? Let's look back in the story," I said. Children found the word *stoutness*. After discussion of that word and why and how Pooh would want to be *stout*, we continued revisualizing the story.

I continued to focus on the predictable new vocabulary words as we discussed the unfolding narrative. I would pause to interject the author's words, and we would orally reread the context in which the words were used. I placed these words on the chalkboard, not in a list arrangement but in a spaced-out way on the board to accommodate the way children visualized the retelling. Some words, such as *stoutness*, *scuffling*, and *whiskers*, were written separately, whereas *condensed*, *excited*, *greedy*, *convenient*, and *towels* appeared in small groups on the chalkboard. Children experienced great mirth when they understood Rabbit's words to Pooh, stuck in the entranceway hole: "And I say, old fellow, you're taking up a good deal of room in my house—do you mind if I use your back legs as a towel-horse? Because, I mean, there they are—doing nothing—and it would be very convenient just to hang the towels on them" (Milne, 1996, p. 28).

I hope the reader can sense that the retelling strategy works, once again, in a natural way to enlarge word understanding. Not only are children using the new words appropriately in their own contexts, they are also involved in the writing process. While engaged in a whole-class modeling lesson as illustrated above, the children's retold books were similar in format, yet there was sentence and paragraph variability among individual children. Writing the new vocabulary words in their own sentences is a highly successful way for children to take personal, meaningful ownership of the words.

Topics and Themes

Teachers accomplish many of their classroom lessons through topics and themes. Indeed, state and district content standards for the various disciplines list many discrete content topics that students are expected to cover through the grades. Units of instruction accomplished through topics and themes bring many facets of knowledge to students and the specific vocabularies both define and make the units understandable.

A topic focus generally occurs within a separate discipline such as science, social studies, the English language arts, or mathematics. For instance, in science a traditional topic unit would be our solar system or the planets. Just consider some of the specific vocabulary that students could be confronting for the first time in either the oral or written language besides the specific names of the heavenly bodies. Students would undoubtedly learn words such as *revolution, rotation, axis, position, light years, universe, rings, satellites, inhospitable, inhabited, barren,* and *canals,* as well as the names of the gases in the atmosphere.

A thematic unit usually occurs when one or several teachers design an instructional unit to integrate two or more content disciplines over a certain period of time, generally 2 to 6 weeks. Although the theme acts as a central organizer, each separate discipline contributes its own content and specific vocabulary to the overall conceptualization of the theme. This could have easily occurred with the study of the solar system example above. Mathematics and the English language arts could have been brought into play to make an enriching theme experience for students. Problem solving involved with distances between the planets and their satellites and literary readings of space voyages would be naturally woven into the theme.

An enticing thematic unit at the junior high level is often a study of the Middle Ages and feudalism. The feudal system of medieval Europe creates imagery and wonder for students (and adults as well), and teachers can get to the underlying economic, social, and political organization of the system by focusing on the concept of land ownership. Who owned the land, who wanted to occupy a neighbor's land, and who served whom in the system of servitude gave rise to a form of life of allegiance, loyalty, oaths, vassals, knights, and foot soldiers. The land was held by lords and barons who gave military service as vassals to higher leaders (often queens and kings), and the land was worked by serfs or peasants (also the foot soldiers), who were bonded to the land for life.

The concepts above are generally covered by the social studies teacher, who presents the topic through the regular curriculum plan.

The English teacher, on the other hand, has to locate and plan readings on "The Age of Chivalry" and "Knighthood" and plan written assignments and reports. The science teacher focuses on plant life and covers the major crops of wheat, rye, barley, peas, oats, and beans and how these were processed on the lord's estate. The mathematics teacher takes the information from the science and social studies coursework and has students design the fields for crop rotation.

The economics of the system called for an annual three-field plan in which two were planted and one remained fallow. One field of a number of acres, usually containing wheat or rye, may have been next to a fallow field of so many acres. Creating fields of so much acreage within the three-field system of thirds gives the mathematics teacher the opportunity to provide many types of word problems involving mathematical calculations. One of the culminating activities of the project created by students was a styrofoam board replica of the manor showing the position of the dwellings and the fields. The fields showed the acres of specific crops within the three-field system.

From such topics and themes arise a great deal of new vocabulary and the concepts that the vocabulary embraces. Teachers can use the ideas of experience language to assist students with physical involvement and visualization of the new vocabulary (such as with the styrofoam board replica) or they can use many of the activities in the Concept-Level Relations Taxonomy that follows in helping students practice and manipulate the words in different thinking contexts.

Another way to show the concepts and major vocabulary of a theme or topic is in the form of a concept, cognitive, or semantic map. A **concept map** is a visual, graphic array using such figures as boxes, rectangles, and circles to house words and phrases. The figures of the map, with the words written therein, are arranged and linked in ways that express a concept idea to show the relation of the whole to its parts and the parts to the whole. A logic of organization and meaning is therefore expressed. Because the information presented with the Middle Ages topic was descriptive in nature, I used a Topic Development Map to present the concepts and information rather than another map format (see Sinatra, 2000, for a full discussion of concept maps and how they are used to present different organizational and thinking plans).

I like to "build" the map with students. Whole-class participation promotes a very interactive lesson in which students have to consistently refer to their text and informational sources to help the map "grow." In a whole-class modeling lesson of how to use a map to organize text information, I suggest that the teacher write the concept word or topic on the chalkboard (or use the overhead projector) and box it or circle it. The teacher formulates the first key question to achieve the organizational structure of the logic of the map. In this case, the question would be "Who were the different peoples who had distinct life styles in the Middle Ages?" With this question, the teacher should be able to elicit the five levels of society and lifestyles during feudal times that were presented in the textual readings. With the five major terms placed on the map and connected to the central circle, the teacher can take the time to cover each category or subconcept, in as much depth as the information and concepts require.

Most often, my goal as a classroom teacher in using a detailed concept map, such as the one presented in Figure 6-2, is for students to translate the information on the map into a written essay or report. To make the map, they have to read and reconstruct the information in their readings. Furthermore, they have to read whole texts; they need to have a sense of the whole so that they can analyze the parts. Very often the information is scattered about under different subheads in one or several textual readings. For instance, a subhead might read "Life on the Manor." The text following that head might present information relating to the lifestyles of the rulers and the serfs. Yet later other subheads might read: "Royalty" and "Serfs: The Laboring Class." In short, reading begets mapping, mapping begets writing, and writing begets an organized report or essay that shows use of the new vocabulary in generally appropriate ways. Revision allows for good interaction to occur between student and teacher regarding word usage, sentence sense, and style.

The teacher needs to be skillful with concept map construction. It's not good practice to just place words willy-nilly around the targeted concept word. The teacher should think ahead about where he or she is going with this particular concept and what is offered in the textual readings or information resources that add to the children's knowledge base. The teacher wants to arrange the concepts, subconcepts, and related details in the most logical, cohesive way. Teachers must engage their students in *how* the map should be constructed. Doing this will involve them in the higher order thinking processes of categorizing, organizing, and making judgments.

More and more words and subparts can be linked by arrows and figures to an ever growing conceptual map. For instance, for the topic "Animal Life" there could be the subtopic "Different Habitats." To "Different Habitats" could be linked *tundra*, *tropical waters*, and *forest*. To these words could be linked *musk ox*, *manatee*, and *wolf* and all other appropriate animals. In this way, low-vocabulary students see all the words arranged in a conceptual way.

It would be a wise move for the teacher to call on students to provide an oral recitation of a subtopic to see if such students can

Figure 6-2. A Concept Map Showing the Major Vocabulary Used to Describe the People and Customs of Feudal Times, or the Middle Ages

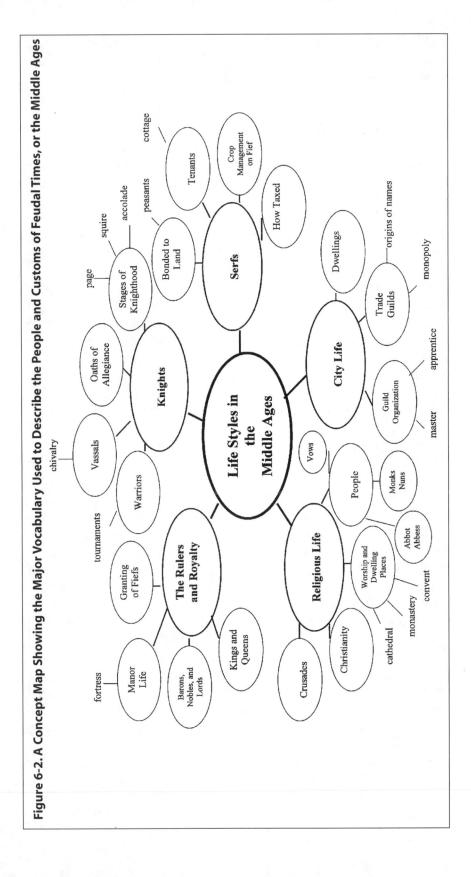

use the words appropriately in their own language. For instance, while pointing to "Different Habitats" and "Mammals," the teacher could say, "Who can connect these ideas to build a paragraph?" Once a sentence is offered, a new sentence using related concept words would be added, and so on. An entire written piece can be accomplished later by children who use the new words in appropriate contexts as shaped by the teacher. The resulting selection can be read and reread to assist low-vocabulary performing students in particular.

Taxonomy of Concept-Level Relations

P. David Pearson and Dale Johnson have presented us with an insightful **taxonomy** or classification system of word relationships, in two companion books, *Teaching Reading Comprehension* (1978) and *Teaching Reading Vocabulary* (1984). The taxonomy is as useful now as it was then. What the authors did was present a categorical system of nine word relations in the following order: synonym, antonym, association, classification, analogy, connotation and denotation, multiple meaning, homograph, and homophone. From the category of synonym to that of connotative-denotative relationships, the higher level word-concept relation subsumes the thinking of the lower. For instance, when doing the thinking required of classifying, the thinking of association and the understanding of synonyms and antonyms occurs as well. Note the student accomplishing classification through word sorts below. He's placing words of association under heading topics that he himself has named.

Although Pearson and Johnson presented tasks and activities that teachers could use in a general way with students to help them with the thinking of each word-concept level, I have adapted their classification system to be used with a specific topic vocabulary. I suggest that teachers take the new vocabulary that ac-  companies each subject topic and present activities by beginning at the synonym level and working the words upward in different thinking-level activities. Very often, however, words at the homograph and homophone level do not occur with specific topics. With some topics, they do. For instance, in the topic of "Landforms" would be homophones like *boulder* (*bolder*), *plain* (*plane*), and *bare* (*bear*). In the topic of "Road to Revolution" could be the homographs *rebel, subject, convert*, and *refuse.*

In Appendix C I have arranged the nine concept-level relations in hierarchical order and have indicated a range of activities that can be accomplished for each relation. The chart will allow teachers to make a quick visual inspection to select the specific activities that they believe to be appropriate for student practice and application with a new group of words. Although a few of the activities are duplicated, such as the "matching columns" listed under both synonym and antonym, the teacher can see that much variation is offered for students to use words in different thinking contexts.

Appendix D gives an array of specific activities to elicit thinking at different concept levels. This array complements the "Middle Ages" theme that was discussed previously. Many of the activities were conceived by Maureen Walsh, who prepared them for actual student use in her school, P.S. 56 in Queens, New York City. In this way the teacher can see how the vocabulary of the theme forms the basis of the content for each concept-level relations activity. Thus, not only are students learning the new vocabulary words of a topic or theme, they are also engaged in different levels of thinking that should sharpen their perspective on how words are related to each other.

Writing Activities and Assignments

Many regard writing as a complex language activity in which time, practice, and thinking involvement serve to enhance the development of the writer. By its very nature, writing is a constructive process. Writers construct meaning as they tell about themselves, what is happening or has happened in their readings, and the imaginative scenarios they are formulating in their minds. By its very nature, writing requires work and a sense of discipline. Work is required to think through a piece and decide what are the best words to use in particular syntactic arrangements. Discipline is required to learn the conventions and forms of written language so that one can be understood successfully when one's written work is read. One author team notes that writing requires the thinking skills necessary for analyzing, inferencing, evaluating, problem solving, and using the understandings derived from reading (Burns et al., 1999).

The reader has undoubtedly noted that throughout this book I have urged teachers to promote the use of writing while learning new reading and vocabulary words. You have seen that I am a big advocate of the retelling strategy because the task itself requires the work and discipline of writing, especially if one follows the two-draft procedure. I'm also a strong advocate of the reading to mapping to writing process, as indicated in the discussion of topics and themes. Such activity, along with others in which children are experimenting with their new words, requires them to make meaning connections at the syntactic, semantic, and pragmatic levels. What occurs through writing exploration and experimentation, enhanced with evolving writing and reading experiences at home and in school, is the elaboration and refinement of old forms and the emergence of new writing forms (Kamberelis, 1999).

When children begin to use their new vocabulary words in their own self-constructed sentences, they are taking ownership of the words. They may need different opportunities to use new vocabulary in different contexts so that the mind can call up words more automatically when appropriate writing contexts occur. When they use vocabulary flash cards or vocabulary notebooks, not only should the new word and its meaning be listed, the student should also be asked to write each new word in a novel sentence. In the novel sentence, the writer should be asked to show a prospective reader that the writer is signaling the meaning of the word. For instance, for the new word *reluctant*, the sentence "The girl was reluctant to go swimming" doesn't show why she didn't want to go. By the addition of "because the water was too dirty," the student shows why the girl was reluctant.

You'll recall from Figure 6-2 that there was a great deal of new vocabulary displayed to describe the people and lifestyles of the Middle Ages. I've learned through trial and error as a teacher that once the basic structure of a map is laid out with the major subtopics displayed on the chalkboard or chart paper, it's better to pursue each subtopic in depth through discussion and text analysis and write a first-draft paragraph on that subtopic. If you develop a whole map and tell intermediate and junior high youngsters that they're going to write an essay or report on the whole topic, you'll not only hear the moans and groans, you'll probably get a slipshod effort because of their perception of the enormity of the task. Thus I've learned to develop each subtopic of the whole from a discussion, reading, and writing perspective.

This perspective allows students to implicitly focus on the **macrostructure**, or organization of the whole. The macrostructure organization of the map shown in Figure 6-2 cries out to the logical mind about to engage in the writing process that at least five paragraphs are needed to explain the topic. Many, many more paragraphs are needed to do the topic well, and one can see that the new words *Crusades* and *Christianity* are not elaborated at all. Thus the good writer can do more, and most language arts teachers will likely require more. They'll add the introductory and concluding paragraphs to the minimum five-paragraph body to achieve a cohesive work and to satisfy the traditional format standard of the three-part essay formula.

Because my major focus has been for students to use the new content vocabulary as they engage in the mental, constructive process of writing, I have been content to go paragraph by paragraph with **revising** and **editing**. The wise teacher will circulate among the students as they are writing and offer individual suggestions for new word use by pointing to the map and to the words a student has written. For instance, Hector, a junior high student in an inner-city school in Brooklyn, New York City, began his paragraph on "Knights" the following way: "Knights were one part of the feudal system of government. Knights have to protect their own leader." I could see that Hector may have had the concepts of *vassal* and *oaths of allegiance* in mind because he had written "their own leader." I said to Hector, "What did the knight do before to show that he would protect his leader?" He pointed to one of the circles and interjected, "Knights have to protect their own leader because he made an oath of allegiance." Through the act of writing, a problem arises with the use of pronouns and antecedent relations and correcting that problem may take a great deal of teaching and practice. Next Hector wrote the following:

> Knights are brave warriors that go into battle when the leader says. The knights use different weapons to protect the leader and in war. They use armor, lance, swords, shields, and they use horses to travel when they go to war.

The reader can see that Hector has some rather concrete imagery of the knight and that all of the concept words have not been integrated into his written paragraph. Hector, we can safely surmise, is still emerging at the **microstructure** level of writing in that word choice, sentence variety, and **conventions** have to be more robust and mastery oriented. Such is writing for all levels of people. Hector does have an organized paragraph even without my one interjection. In fact, it is so well organized at the macrostructure level that with a bit of coaching and mentoring, Hector could nicely integrate the other concepts and vocabulary into his thought process.

Another way to help your students have immediate visual access to words so that they can use them in their writing is the use of the word wall technique discussed earlier. The words amassed on the word wall can come from multiple sources: books read or retold in class, experiences of trips or excursions, visitors telling or sharing unusual life stories, and so forth. The word wall also serves as a focal point for the discussion of words. Words are discussed, defined, and used in oral sentences before they are written and placed on the wall. Students may borrow words from the word wall to take to their desks or centers if an opportunity arises for them to use that word in one of their own written stories or reports. A manila pocket envelope can also be hanging on the word wall for children to return the words they borrowed. Since each word has been written on a large index card, the teacher can help an individual child learn a particularly troublesome word by tracing the word with the child's fingers and then telling the child to look away and trace the word in the "sky."

For the past six years I have been the project director of a summer program called Inner City Games CAMP-US, held for housing development children bused to the university campus from the five boroughs of New York City. The New York City Housing Authority is the prime financial supporter of the project, and according to its most recent resident characteristics, a total of 175,184 families with an average gross income of $13,304 were housed at its 115 borough sites. The goal of the Inner City Games CAMP-US program is to provide a quality academic and athletic program for the residents' children, who would not normally experience a university-based program, who would be exposed to inner-city risk factors (Office of Juvenile Justice and Delinquency Prevention, 1998), and who would predictably lose educational ground during the summer months (Borman, 2000). The program addressed the three broad-based themes of the dangers of substance abuse (say no to drugs, alcohol, and cigarettes), strong character development (be of good character at home, at school, and on the playing field), and respect for the environment and community (don't litter and pollute). The messages of these themes were supported in the children's readings and writings in literacy classes, in their computer projects, in the experiments in science labs, and in the coach's words on their athletic field.

The picture shows a colorful word wall of new vocabulary words that arose from the children's readings and discussions. The words are, as yet, purposefully mixed up according to the three themes so that the children will review the words themselves as they write a paper or discuss a topic related to one of the three themes. Later a category "sort" will occur in which children group the words under one of the three theme names. As new words arose from other readings, they were listed on the chalkboard.

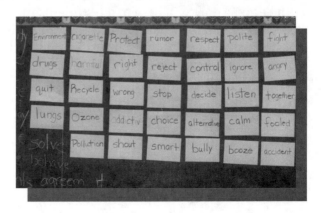

The word *litter* was a new reading word for many and was used in the context of respect for different environments. Note the use of the word *litter* in the following paper written by 8-year-old Lyanne, who just completed second grade. Not only has she shown mastery of the word concept, she also uses the word syntactically in a number of grammatical ways: as a noun gerund, subject of a sentence ("Littering causes a lot of trouble"); as a verb ("If you litter"); as a verb participle ("You should never do littering"); as a direct object noun ("Do not make litter").

> Littering causes a lot of trouble. If you litter you would get in trouble because a police might be thair [sic] and [you] might get a ticket. You should never do littering again because littering is bad. Do not throw anything in the ocean at all. Do not make litter.

While Lyanne changes voice and shows miscues with some word use (*police*) and spelling conventions (*thair*), she does hold some rather strong beliefs about littering. These beliefs could be nurtured to achieve more elaboration of content ideas from Lyanne. Yet, remarkably, her syntactic levels of meaning allow her to use word parts to transform a word correctly into appropriate sentence use. I'm sure she doesn't know what gerunds and participles are, but her use of them is being applied correctly in this context.

Developing Reading and Thinking Strategies for Student Transfer

Two major strategies, regarding the understanding and use of morphemes and how to use the context, present two concerns for the teacher. The first is that the teacher has to show students "how to." This means that there will be some direct teaching and/or modeling, as occurred with the activities of explicit classroom instruction. The second concern is the major goal of the teacher. Once students have been shown "how to," the teacher hopes that students will invest the mental energy to use the strategies on their own because they will help make students more successful readers and writers. Thus, the teacher presents these strategies as potential vocabulary builders without the focus on words directly but on the ways that word meanings can be unlocked.

Morphemes and Meaning

Now is a good time to return to the discussion of morphemes and the linguistic science of morphology (see Fig. 1-1 and 1-2). Teachers, parents, and children conceive of the world of words as "words," whereas many linguistic experts and other educators think of the world of words as "morphemes." A morpheme, we saw earlier, is defined as the smallest meaningful unit in the English language. For instance, the word *squirrel* is a morpheme (unit), but what happens when we say "squirrels" or the "squirrel's food"? In each of the latter cases, the meaning has changed, and meaningful units have been added to the free morpheme word *squirrel*. To the free morpheme have been added two examples of bound morphemes, one that makes a case for pluralization and one that indicates possession. Notice also that in the sentence just written, we had to use many bound morphemes, such as *-ed*, *-s*, *-ize*, and *-tion*, to convey exact meaning.

The internal structure of words is analyzed in the science of morphology to determine which parts can transmit meaning. Word parts that convey meaning are called morphemes; word parts that can also be formed but have no meaning are called syllables. Syllables are units of pronunciation; they do not contain meaning by themselves. The word *plural* is composed of two rather clear syllables, but the root word is *plural* itself. What happens with *pluralization*? To the free morpheme *plural* we added *-ize* and *-ation*, two bound morphemes whose meanings change the overall structure of the base word as it will be used in a sentence. The base word *plural*, originally an adjective, becomes a verb as *pluralize*, which becomes a noun as *pluralization*. The reader is no doubt aware that if we were able to put *de-*, *in-*, or *im-* in front of the word *pluralization*, we would not only change the structure of the base word, we would alter the meaning to be contrary to the original meaning.

Where has all this heady discussion on morphemes led, and why is this discussion important for the teacher responsible for students' language and vocabulary development? Recall the information we learned from the word frequency studies and counts. The Dale and Chall (1948) list of 3,000 words contained a core vocabulary to sustain children to approximately a fourth-grade reading level, and the Carroll et al., (1971) study revealed that 5,000 words occur with 89% frequency in texts, whereas 43,831 words make up 99% of words in running text. What is it about words that 3,000 to 5,000 are basic to accommodate some measure of reading success, but mastery of another 40,000 words would ensure that the reader has familiarity with 99% of the words in all texts? The answer is morphemes.

Approximately two-thirds of the words less frequently used in English are derived from other languages and are characterized by being multisyllabic with identifiable morphemic elements (Coady, 1994a). Furthermore, high-frequency words are characterized by few syllables and identifiable parts. The value of understanding morphology and its relationship to vocabulary development should be becoming increasingly clear to teachers. They may need to consider the use of more classroom time in the systematic learning of morphemes (Arnoff, 1994). Once children have left the early elementary grades, the words they will encounter in school texts and literary reading will have morphological parts joined to familiar words. Readers who have a strong intuitive understanding of morphology are usually able to understand new words encountered in context with little effort. Mark Arnoff used the word *reacceleration* as an example in a piece written about space flight. The reader should have little difficulty understanding the meaning of that word if the morphological part *re-* is intuitively realized.

Manipulating Dinosaur Parts

A rather motivating activity in the area of morphemic analysis is to use a topic that captivates the attention of most children: dinosaurs. Through a presentation of the names of the dinosaurs, how they came by their names, and what their names mean, the teacher can skillfully engage children in the understanding of the word parts of prefixes, suffixes, and roots. I've seen this done with a whole class of fourth graders, and there was no holding them back with their creativity in manipulating the dinosaur parts (the word parts, of course!).

To begin, the teacher should acquaint the children with how dinosaurs came to be named. Many dinosaurs are named because of a noticeable or interesting body feature. Scientists and discoverers generally used a combination of two or more Greek or Latin words or word parts to name a dinosaur. Many of these Greek and Latin word-part meanings still exist with us today, and we can find them embedded in modern-day words. However, not all dinosaurs were named after a characteristic body trait; some were named by the name of the person who discovered the fossil remains, or they were named after the locale in which they were discovered. For example, the dinosaur Vulcanodon, meaning "Vulcan tooth," was named for the Roman god of fire because the fossilized teeth of a predator believed to be feeding on Vulcanodon were found in volcanic rock. The fossilized remains of the dinosaur Muttaburrasaurus were found in Muttaburra, Queensland, Australia, whereas the remains of Alxasaurus were discovered in Alxa, a desert region of Inner Mongolia.

With this introduction, the teacher could present the information in Table 6-2 to students. The chart shows the scientific name of some well-known dinosaurs, the meaning of the word parts in their names from the Greek and Latin, and the special characteristics that made paleontologists and others use those words to name the creatures. With the general knowledge that *-saurus* means "lizard," children can see how the dinosaurs got their names. For instance, if *cerato* means "horn," then Ceratosaurus was aptly named because it had a horn on its snout. Pachycephalosaurus was so named because *pachy* means "thick" and *cephalo* means "head," and this dinosaur had a rounded, domed skull that was about 10 inches thick. Other word parts that are not listed that children might know from names of dinosaurs are the following:

compo	=	pretty
dactyl	=	finger
dino	=	terrible
para	=	similar
pale	=	old

Now we can see the derivation of the word "dinosaur" itself. It means "Terrible Lizard."

Once your initial lesson is completed, you can turn your children loose for dinosaur-naming creativity. The children will come up with great names of their "own" dinosaurs, and I've even seen them bring in knowledge of their native languages, particularly with counting words. *Uno*, many realize, means "one," and the number "four" begins as *quat* in many languages. Now is a good time to form the children into small groups with chart paper and crayons and/or magic markers. They will come up with clever names of their dinosaurs, and their artwork is directed to capture the characteristic traits of the dinosaur noted in its naming. You will get creatures like Quattrodactylankylosauraus, meaning "four-toed jointed lizard."

Although the paleontogists might shudder at the naming process, you have successfully intrigued your students with the manipulation and joining of word parts, morphemes, and prefixes, suffixes, and roots. If you wish to do more exploration with other dinosaurs and their naming process, you may want to go to these Web sites: http://www.enchantedlearning.com/subjects/dinosaurs, http://www.childrensmuseum.org/kinetosaur, http://www.zoomdinosaurs.com/subjects/dinosaurs, and http://pubs.usgs.gov/gip/dinosaurs.

Using Word Parts to Identify Words

The natural segue from learning the meanings of dinosaur names is to learn the meanings of and how to use modern-day English word parts, called **prefixes**, **suffixes**, and **roots**. Appendix E lists many currently used prefixes, suffixes, and roots with their meanings or, in the case of suffixes, the purpose of their being affixed to words or free morphemes. The word examples provided show how the morphemic part influences the word meaning. Although prefixes often change the meaning of the root word, suffixes are added

Table 6-2. How Did Dinosaurs Get Their Names?

Scientific Name of Dinosaurs	Word Parts and Meaning	Characteristics That Contributed to Animal's Name
	Saurus = Lizard	
Ankylosaurus	Ankylos = hooked, jointed	This was a huge, armored dinosaur with thick, oval plates as part of its tough skin.
Ceratosaurus	Cerato = horn	This was a meat-eating dinosaur with a short horn on its snout.
Oviraptor	Ovi = egg Raptor = plunderer	This dinosaur was believed to be an egg eater because its fossil remains were found on top of some eggs. Its name means "egg stealer."
Protoceratops	Proto = first, Cerato = horn Ops =eyes or face	A bony neck frill made this dinosaur's face look very large.
Pteranodon	Ptero = wing, feather Odon = tooth	This was a "toothless flying lizard." "Nodon" meant "no teeth."
Stegoceras	Stegos = roof or cover Ceratos or Keras = horn	This dinosaur had a large head with a domed, thick skull. The skull had a ridge of horny knobs along its rear.
Stegosaurus	Stegos = roof or cover	Stegosaurus had two rows of horny plates that ran along its back from head to tail. So it looked like a "covered" or "roof lizard."
Supersaurus	Super = super, large, powerful	This was a huge plant-eating dinosaur with a long neck and a long whiplike tail. It was about 140 feet long.
Triceratops	Tri = three, Cerato = horn Ops = eyes or face	This "three-horned face" dinosaur had three horns projecting from its face. The horns may have served to protect this plant eater's eyes from meat eaters.

to a root word to achieve both meaning and syntactic correctness. Suffixes change a word's use from one part of speech to another, depending on how the root word is used in a sentence. For instance, in the sentence beginning, "Unlikely as it may seem," the prefix *un-* changes the meaning to "not likely," whereas the suffix *-ly* changes the preposition *like* to the adverb "likely." The addition of the two bound morphemes alter the meaning and the way the root word will comply with the grammatical rules of sentence construction.

Roots can be recognizable words ranging from one syllable to a number of syllables, or they may have originated from Greek or Latin. Words such as *wind, pay,* and *count* are roots, or free morphemes of one syllable. The root words *agree, honor,* and *human* have two syllables, whereas *platypus* is a root word with three syllables. Students can be asked to look for a recognizable word, which we know to be the free morpheme, to which affixes such as prefixes and suffixes can be appended. On the chalkboard or chart paper, the teacher can model how recognizable words are changed by the addition of prefixes and suffixes. For instance, with the little word *use* written for children to see, the teacher can introduce *re-* in front, discuss the meaning change, and then add *-able* at the end. Next the teacher can show *mis-* in front, discuss that meaning, and add *d* or *-ing* at the end. The teacher can continue adding and dropping prefixes and suffixes to see if other "real" words can be made. It would be wise to have dictionaries available so that students can practice their dictionary skills as they confirm word identities.

Appendix E shows many common roots passed down through the centuries from Latin and Greek. Many of these root parts are embedded in larger words, and it may take more work by the teacher and practice by the students to learn the parts well before transferring the skill to reading and writing activities. Some of these roots exist as recognizable, complete words such as *corps* and *port,* and others may be made easy to understand because of common words known by most in the oral language. So the *dyn* meaning of "power," in the word *dynamite,* the *photo* meaning of "light" in *photograph,* and the *scrib* meaning of "write" in *scribble* may help students learn other words with those parts. It has been confirmed that knowledge of the Greek and Latin roots are highly effective in building word understanding, and students who have such knowledge need less guidance from teachers in understanding English words (Fox, 2000).

Appendix F provides models for you to use to help students build words using the meanings of prefixes, roots, and suffixes. Each figure shows an activity in a different way and can be used by the teacher as is, but they are intended to suggest ongoing procedures for the teacher. For instance, with Figure F-1, "Pack-a-Word," the teacher can place, one at a time, the common roots *ject, mis, mit, rupt*, and *vis* instead of *port* in the child's backpack and engage children in additional word discovery. With a new root inserted in the center, the prefixes and suffixes may need to be altered a bit as well. Teachers may wish to conceptualize a new figure to express the meaning of a particular root word.

Using the Context

A teacher asks a student who has encountered an unknown word to use the context as a word identification strategy rather than sounding it out. The teacher predicts that a clue within the immediate sentence or the surrounding sentences will help the child to figure out the word's meaning. In essence, the teacher is asking the child to think—to read on and form interpretations so that the meaning of the unknown word can be intelligently predicted. Use of context clues not only facilitates word recognition but also strategically points the way to word meaning (Juel, 1994).

The strategy of using the context should be taught in an explicit way by the teacher during initial lessons so that students have the mental tools to use the strategy in an implicit way during general reading. With direct teaching students can also learn the function of grammar. Grammar functions to clarify meaning. Because many aspects of grammar signal the meaning identity of words, teachers should have a clear strategy whereby the study of grammar can be integrated within the natural contexts of reading and writing. For instance, when the teacher discusses the use of relative pronouns (*that*, *which*, *who*) and their use with subordinate clauses, teachers show students that writers use this clause structure to identify something just named. There is, therefore, a thinking connection between a key word, probably a noun, in the main part of the sentence and the meaning of the words in the relative clause.

For readers, the meaning of a particular unknown word may be clarified by the grammatical relationship between the words in a sentence or the structural arrangement of sentences in a longer passage. Moreover, syntactic and semantic conventions are mutually dependent, in that grammar identifies meaning associations for readers. For instance, the appearance of the words *the*, *an*, and *a* in a sentence immediately indicate in written English that a noun must follow. If an adjective follows the article and the reader knows the meaning of the adjective but not the noun, the reader at least knows that a person, place, or thing is being described.

However, the meaning of many new words encountered in contextual reading have to be inferred from a sentence or the surrounding sentences. This type of thinking is often called "reading between the lines." To make these meaning inferences, the reader takes note of the important vocabulary and relates grammatical and semantic clues to their own prior experiences and knowledge. Inferential thinking is involved because readers must make implied meaning relationships between the unknown word and the surrounding context while connecting their background knowledge of the topic with their understanding of written English conventions. To illustrate, look at the word *sterile* and the relationship of the two following sentences: "All instruments used during an operation need to be sterile. They have to be free of germs so that none are introduced into the patient's body." The word *sterile* is defined in the second sentence, with the assistance of the pronoun *they*, which refers to *instruments*. The comprehension process is that of inferential thinking, because the reader has to make the implicit connection between *they* and *instruments* and possibly use his or her background knowledge of the importance of cleanliness in a hospital. The word *sterile* is not explicitly defined by the grammar and has to be understood by reading between the lines.

Thus, one major outcome of teaching and showing students how to use context clues is the general improvement of reading comprehension. Not only does inferential thinking often occur when students make connections between sentences and sentence parts, but students are also involved in "deep processing" the text. **Deep processing** refers to making more meaning connections between known and new information as well as contributing a high degree of mental effort to learn. John McNeil (1987) has indicated that the deeper one processes text through the thinking processes of elaboration of content and understanding of the author's organizational framework, the greater and more effective will be the comprehension. Steven Stahl (1986) has added that strategies that help students think more deeply about a word and its relationships are likely to be beneficial.

In 1991, with Cornelia Dowd, I reviewed a number of textbooks and journal articles to determine how other literacy authors viewed the topic of context clues. Although most textbook authors devoted a chapter to context clues, there was little agreement about the types of clues, and there was no clear distinction made between those clues that were grammar related and those that required inferential and deep processing to figure out a word's meaning. In short, we came up with a framework—a taxonomy of sorts—of 15 types of context clues, 6 of which helped readers to figure out new words through grammatical structures found within single sentence construction. The other 9 context clues helped readers to figure out word meanings by interpreting relationships within and between sentences.

Authors, particularly of informational texts, often use the grammar to help readers achieve explicit or literal understanding of a new word. For instance, authors know that by use of the coordinating conjunction *or* with commas, they are presenting a choice or alternative meaning to the reader. Authors provide the new word's alternative meaning on one side of the conjunction because they predict that the reader knows a familiar meaning to make the direct connection to the new word. For instance, in the sentence "The settlers became the proprietors, or owners, of land in the west" the alternative choice *owners* directly renames *proprietors* through the little conjunction *or*.

The Intelligent Guess Strategy

Another tried and true method that has worked for me over my teaching years is the **intelligent guess strategy**. The idea for the technique came from a vintage textbook from the chapter entitled, "Understanding the Meaning Intended" (McKee, 1948). The "intelligent guess strategy" can be used as a prereading or postreading tool. Either way, it involves students in thinking about words and how the context works to identify meaning. Students have to think deeply about grammar and inferential clues to figure out word meanings. Moreover, it's a terrific way to integrate the use of dictionaries.

Here's how the strategy works. Simply have students divide a page into five columns. The first three columns will be done as one activity, either before or after reading a selection with a fair amount of new vocabulary words. The fourth and fifth columns can be completed after the topic or reading unit is completed. The first column would have the head "Vocabulary Word," the second column "Intelligent Guess," the third column "Clues to Help Make Guess," the fourth column "Dictionary Entry," and the fifth "Original Sentences." The teacher makes a prediction about the new meaning words and actually displays the words on a chart or on the chalkboard with the appropriate page number for each word. An example page for the topic of "Large Sea Animals" is shown in Table 6-3.

Table 6-3. Making Intelligent Guesses About Words

Vocabulary Word	Intelligent Guess	Clues to Help Make Guess	Dictionary Entry	Original Sentences
beak p. 3				
tentacles p. 3				
breach p. 4				
baleen p. 4				
dorsal p. 5				

This is generally an enjoyable activity for students because they're "puzzling out" the meaning of the text. In the intelligent-guess column, they write down what they think the word means in a particular sentence context. In the clues column, they have to write down what specific words or phrases in the same sentence or surrounding sentences helped them to make their intelligent guess. This is important because they are thinking about the meaning relationships and trying to figure out intuitively how the grammar works. You can see that I have placed the context of dictionary use (a favorite in a traditional way to understand word meanings) within the context of how to use the context. This column is done on another day, with classroom dictionaries allowing students to use this important tool in a constructive way. They have to figure out the entry meaning that best fits the use of the word in this particular context.

After discussion about students' entries in the various columns and praise by the teacher for their thinking skills, the fifth column, or notebook entry, can be accomplished. The final rewarding task would be to ask the students to use each new word in their own sentence or sentences. The key here is to show students how to use a new word in a sentence so that the reader can figure out the word's meaning. So instead of writing, "The squid has long tentacles," the student should be encouraged to write in his or her "Original Sentence" column, "The squid has long tentacles to grab other sea animals to eat, just as people use fingers to eat." This fifth activity is highly important in the constructive process of learning new words because the learner applies the word in his or her own original context, therefore showing that ownership of the word is occurring.

Independent Activity Resulting in Incidental Vocabulary Learning

The reader can see in Figure 6-1 that three activities are shown whereby people can learn new vocabulary meanings on their own just by being engaged in listening, reading, and writing. To be sure, children of all ages, as well as adults, can learn new words by hearing texts read to them. We noted the effectiveness of reading aloud to young children in an earlier chapter. Listening to narrators and commentators on TV shows can increase vocabulary as well, and many of the animal, documentary, and scientific shows children watch certainly increase their conceptual development and enlarge their background experiences.

Being engaged in consistent writing activity serves to increase vocabulary usage as well. When one writes, one searches for the right word to use in the right context. Words learned in school in one context of a topic or theme covered in a particular subject area may be transferred to another context as the student writes for another purpose. "What was that word we learned in science when we studied the tropics?" the writer thinks while at his or her desk or computer at home. "Oh, yes, it was *perspiration*; I can use that word to show what's happening to my character as he becomes more and more scared." Most research on vocabulary development and activity outside school has focused on reading involvement, however.

Reading Volume

The discussion of the intelligent guess strategy revealed a way that teachers can intentionally activate an engaging activity to help students learn new words in classroom settings. What happens when students just read on their own outside school? In other words, instead of children watching hours of television or playing video games, what would happen if they read just 5, 10, or 15 minutes each day?

It would seem reasonable to expect that if teachers showed students ways to figure out new words from the context, as in the strategy discussed above, then when students read on their own, they would have a mental skill to transfer to their own pleasurable and informational reading. Indeed, learning how to use context clues provides students with thinking tools to deal with the wide range of texts and literary materials they will encounter in a lifetime. Because many writers use the conventions of syntax and semantics to present meaning clues to readers, they predict that the conventions selected are comprehensible to their reading audience. Therefore, many new vocabulary words can be learned as students are encouraged to read and as they engage in quiet and natural reading in and out of school (Kuhn & Stahl, 1998; Leu & Kinzer, 1999).

In recent research reports, this condition of natural reading done mostly out of school has been called **reading volume**, **casual word learning,** and, more recently, **incidental word learning**. Incidental word learning is contrasted with intentional word learning, which is instituted by a teacher or student who purposefully sets out conditions for how to learn the meanings of new words. This purposeful activity conducted by the teacher has been the basis of most of this chapter. Now we're examining the act of reading pursued on its own merit.

One research team found from the analysis of 20 experiments conducted on students accomplishing reading as a pleasurable activity that the average probability of learning unknown words from context is about 15%. This means that without a teacher, parent, or friend around to tell them what an unknown word means, students can spontaneously derive and learn the meaning of about 15 words of every 100 unknown words they read in context (Swanborn & deGlopper, 1999). What an important statistic! It suggests that students think while they're reading, because so many words in context are not intentionally defined by authors, requiring students to accomplish implicit, interpretative comprehension.

Anne Cunningham and Keith Stanovich (1998) have researched and written extensively on the topic of reading volume and how it contributes to children's growth in verbal skills, vocabulary learning, and overall cognitive development. They report that if children read just under 5 minutes a day, they will encounter 282,000 words in print in one year. The child who reads just under 15 minutes a day would read 1,146,000 words during the year. Compare the volume of these words encountered in print, some of which have to be new words, with the potential consequences of not reading in out-of-school settings.

These researchers also investigated the question of whether the speed of beginning reading competence at the first-grade level would predict continued engagement in reading at the high school level. They found that students who are early successful readers are likely to continue reading through the years. Even more astounding was the finding that reading engagement helps children to develop cognitive ability by increasing their vocabulary and general knowledge. These authors maintain that students who read a great deal increase their verbal intelligence—or, stated another way, reading in itself can make children smarter.

Another author reported on recent research in vocabulary and how it relates to the achievement gap between social classes and ethnic and racial groups (Hirsch, 2000). Hirsch maintains that educators and others who wish to narrow achievement, or "digital divide," gaps between groups need to focus on vocabulary development. Vocabulary is the largest academic gap between groups, and, as noted earlier, the gap gets wider as children maintain their reading habits in school and outside school. Hirsch concludes that it's difficult for anyone to use the Internet or a reference source if vocabulary understanding precludes them from making sense out of what they're looking up.

Causal Connections With Word Mastery

The evidence suggests that a causal relationship exists among the ability to achieve early fluency in reading, the ability to learn and use new words in readings in and out of school, and a transfer process to increased language and cognitive development. This causal relationship is indicated in Figure 6-3.

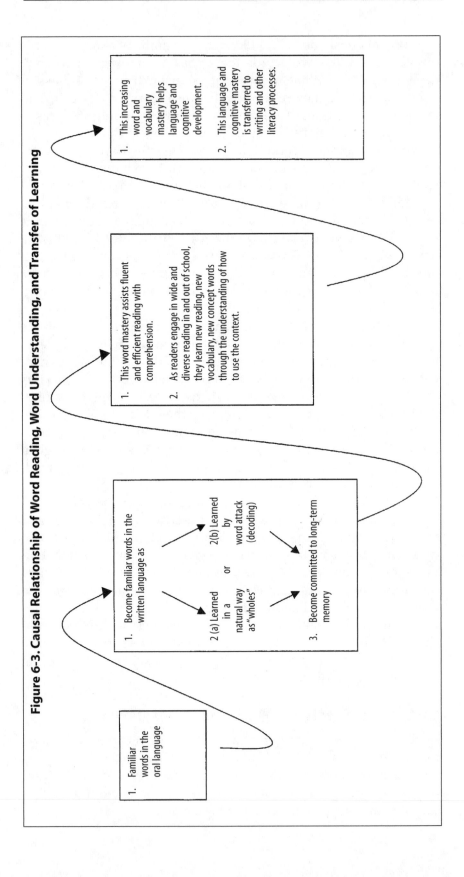

Figure 6-3. Causal Relationship of Word Reading, Word Understanding, and Transfer of Learning

Familiar words in the oral language can become familiar words in the written language through the act of reading. The familiar reading words are either learned as wholes by sight or through a word-attack route, which is usually called phonics. In either case, the words learned have to become committed to children's long-term memories, and these words become known as sight words. Establishing sight reading of words allows children to read with fluency. As they become fluent, they may be more inclined to engage in wide and diverse reading. As we all know, having a talent or skill doesn't necessarily mean that one will use that talent. Motivation and will are also strong factors in achievement. When children do read naturally, they will encounter new vocabulary in various contextual situations, requiring them to mentally manipulate the context to figure out unknown words. As they learn more vocabulary and information through reading, they will be able to transfer their knowledge when they write, work on computers, and read about new topics. The thinking required to call up unique words to fit contextual applications during writing or computer work helps learners to develop their versatility as writers and manifests their use of a wide and diverse vocabulary.

Summary and Conclusion

This chapter has discussed both broad methods and specific activities to help students through the grades develop their meaning vocabularies. Strategies and specific activities were presented in the context of three broad but mutually reinforcing types of procedures that engage students and teachers. These procedures were characterized by what the teacher explicitly does in the classroom to directly teach vocabulary, what the teacher does to help students learn how to transfer knowledge to unlock word meanings, and what students do on their own to broaden their vocabulary knowledge.

To conclude, the reflective teacher is the one who has to work through the world of words and vocabulary development. The teacher has to use his or her own common sense about how reading and writing work for young, maturing, and problem readers. The teacher has to know a bit about how the English written system works and what cues are transmitted to readers through the world of print. Moreover, the teacher should be able to communicate this knowledge of how print works to parents in a meaningful and constructive way.

Regardless of the systems approach or methodology used by a school, district, or state, the teacher knows that a primary goal of

reading instruction is to rapidly increase children's sight vocabularies. Figure 6-3 shows us that the information contained in this
book helps teachers connect learning encounters in a causal way to
each learner's literacy and cognitive development. Each child's sight
vocabulary provides a way for that child to be fluent in reading so
that comprehension can proceed smoothly and without halts to figure out or decode unknown words. Fluency also allows children to
maximize reading energy of known words so that when unknown
words or new meaning words are encountered in print, the child
can devote his or her mental effort in using the context to think.
Once children begin manipulating the contextual sources of words,
they should be encouraged to read more to add additional vocabulary fuel to their powers of mind.

Concept Words and Terms

abstract representation
activities of action
casual word learning
concept map
Cone of Experience
convention
deep processing
editing
experience language
incidental word learning
intelligent guess strategy

macrostructure
microstructure
observation
prefix
reading volume
revising
root
suffix
syllable
taxonomy
verbal symbol
visual symbol

Word Challenge for Teachers: Semantic Feature Analysis

This activity is in the form of a semantic feature analysis grid. In
the "Concept Terms" column you'll see listed most of the major procedures discussed in the chapter. Across the top, you'll note features and characteristics of the procedures. Although I've attempted
to elicit a plus-sign response for the way the information was presented in the chapter, there's no doubt that a check-off for a feature
could match up with another concept term. For instance, for the
feature "Using authors' vocabulary words," the presentation in the
chapter discussed this technique in the context of "Retellings." However, a plus sign could match up with "Writing" as well. Recall,
however, that features are characteristics and attributes of something so features can be part of a number of experiences and topics.
An answer key is found in Appendix A.

Directions:
Look at the concept terms discussed in this chapter and which are arranged in the left column. Then look at the "feature" words across the top column. These words tell about, are a characteristic of, or are associated with a concept term. Place a plus sign or a check mark in the box to show that a meaning match has been made.

Features:

Concept Terms	Reading Volume	Cone of Experience	Writing	Taxonomy of Concept Relations	Experience Language	Retellings	Topics and Themes Using the Context	Using the Context	Morphemic Analysis
Three main levels of activities									
Off-campus learning									
Making retold books									
Classification system of word relationships									
Introductory, body, and concluding sections									
Ways to arrange subject-matter information									
Reading on one's own									
The intelligent guess strategy									
Study of word parts									
Visual and verbal symbols									
Revising and editing									
Prefixes, roots, and suffixes									
Incidental word learning									
Direct experience as the basis of word learning									
Using authors' vocabulary words									
Connect dictionary usage									
Use of concept maps to represent information									
Nine levels of word relationships									

Appendix A
Answer Keys

Word Challenge for Teachers:
Word Search Answer Key

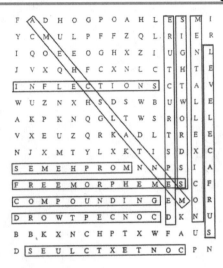

Word Challenge for Teachers:
Crossword Puzzle Answer Key

Word Challenge for Teachers:
Tic-Tac-Toe Answer Key

Game 1

Phonogram	Perceptual Conditioning	Vowel Patterns
Encoding	Word Family	Kinesthetic
Diphthong	Pattern Book	Spelling Pattern

Game 2

Systematic Word Attack	Inductive Word Attack	Transfer Word Attack
Implicit Word Attack	Mastery Word Attack	Pattern Book Word Attack
Incidental Word Attack	Analogy Word Attack	Word Wall Attack

Game 3

Rimes	Kinesthetic	Writing a Word in the Air
Synthetic Phonics Instruction	Encoding	Transfer
Spelling	Perceptual Conditioning	Onsets

Word Challenge for Teachers:
The Classification Concept Map Answer Key

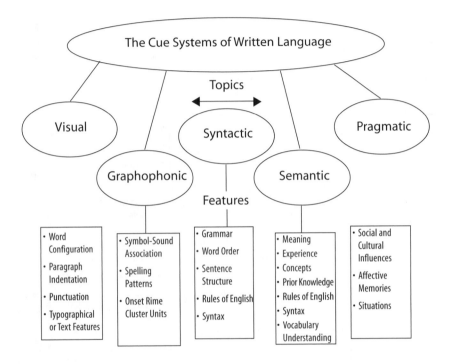

Word Challenge for Teachers: Semantic Features Analysis Answer Key

Directions: Look at the concept terms discussed in this chapter and which are arranged in the left column. Then look at the "feature" words across the top column. These words tell about, are a characteristic of, or are associated with a concept term. Place a plus sign or a check mark in the box to show that a meaning match has been made.

Features:

Morphemic Analysis	Using the Context	Topics and Themes Using the Context	Retellings	Experience Language	Taxonomy of Concept Relations	Writing	Cone of Experience	Reading Volume	Concept Terms
							X		Three main levels of activities
				X					Off-campus learning
			X						Making retold books
					X				Classification system of word relationships
						X			Introductory, body, and concluding sections
		X							Ways to arrange subject-matter information
								X	Reading on one's own
	X								The intelligent guess strategy
X									Study of word parts
							X		Visual and verbal symbols
						X			Revising and editing
X									Prefixes, roots, and suffixes
								X	Incidental word learning
				X					Direct experience as the basis of word learning
			X						Using authors' vocabulary words
									Connect dictionary usage
		X							Use of concept maps to represent information
					X				Nine levels of word relationships

Appendix B

Retold Books

Figure B-1. Accordion Book

Materials:

Index cards or large strip of paper, writing tools, crayons or magic markers, and tape (with cards)

Directions:

1. You can make the accordion book in two ways, as shown in the two pictures. You can cut a long strip of paper about 4 inches wide from chart or construction paper, or you can take index cards and tape them together to make a fold. You fold the long strip into separate, equal-size folds.

2. Students put their writing and artwork on each panel of the accordion book, retelling the story in sequential order.

3. A "head" and a "tail" can be placed on the first and last fold of the accordion book, so that when the book is folded the "whole" of the image appears intact.

Figure B-2. Character Development Book

Materials:

Piece of regular copy paper or construction paper, pencil or magic marker, writing tools

Directions:

Children trace the outline of one of their hands as seen in the illustration below. They then respond to the question prompts that may have been written on a chart or the chalkboard. The answer to the questions are written in the finger spaces. The children then do a written piece about the character in the hand section.

Figure B-3. Circle Story Book

Materials:

Two paper plates (not plastic coated), paper fasteners, pencil, magic marker, and scissors

Directions:

Divide one paper plate into fourths, fifths, or sixths with a pencil or magic marker. This paper plate is cut so that only one event can be seen on the second plate at one time. After the cutout is made on the top plate, the second plate is placed underneath. The cutout section is traced on the second plate. On the four, five, or six panels of the second plate are drawn and written the episodes of the story. Episodes should be numbered so readers know the sequence. The two plates are attached with a paper fastener through the center.

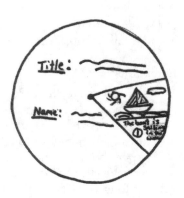

Figure B-4. Create-a-Book

Materials:

Small notebook, index cards, or sheets of paper. The cards and paper will be stapled together.

Directions:

1. Use a small notebook, or staple together index cards or small sheets of paper.
2. Print the title and author of your book on the cover. Be sure to indicate that you are the retelling author.
3. Retell the story and color pictures on each page to represent a book you've read.
4. Staple the pages together to make a flip-type book.

Figure B-5. Finger Puppet Stories

Materials: Standard copy paper, construction paper, crayons or markers, scissors, and glue or paste.

Directions:

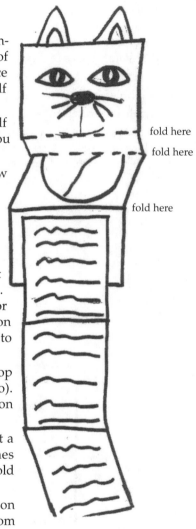

1. First we'll make the head of the finger puppet. Use a standard piece of 8 $^1/_2$ x 11 inch copy paper or a piece of construction paper. Fold it in half lengthwise.

2. Open the paper and fold each half toward the center crease. (Now you have four equal long parts.)

3. Fold once more so that there is now one strip.

4. Fold the strip in half from bottom to top. Fold each open side of the strip in half, one **over** and one **under** in the same direction.

5. You should now have a puppet head that measures 3 x 2 $^1/_4$ inches. Show children how to insert two or three fingers in the upper portion and a thumb in the lower portion to open the puppet's mouth.

6. Draw the puppet's eyes on the top of the head (where the fingers go). Draw the puppet's tongue inside on the lower portion.

7. From a second piece of paper, cut a strip 2 inches wide and 11 inches long. Have children accordion or fold the strip into 3 inch sections.

8. Children lay out the story strip on their desks and retell the story from top to bottom on the folded sections. Children design their own stories by alternating pictures with sentences as they retell on the strip. The text and illustration can also appear on the same small panel. If they desire, children can add additional sections with another pasted strip.

9. Paste the top panel under the puppet section where the thumb goes. (When the puppet open its mouth, the whole story pops out).

   The whole retold story can be folded back up to be inserted into the puppet's mouth to open again for the next reader.

Figure B-6. Flip Book

Materials: Crayons or marker, hole puncher and yarn, construction or drawing paper or regular copy paper, either 8 1/2 x 11 inches or 8 x 14 inches.

Directions:
1. Take several pieces of construction or drawing paper.
2. Cut each page 1 to 2 inches shorter than the previous page.
3. Punch holes and tie yarn at the top of the book.
4. Illustrate and retell the story on each page in sequential order.
5. An easy variation of this procedure is to take three or four sheets of regular copy paper (see sizes above). Lay the copy paper on a flat surface and offset each page about 1 1/2 inches. Then fold the pages downward so you see the offsets. Staple the corners of the fold, and you have a flip book.

Figure B-7. Flip-Flop Book

Materials: Standard-size 8 ¹/2 x 11 inch paper or construction paper and crayons or magic markers.

Directions: Follow the numbers of the pictures.

Fold the piece of paper in half.

Fold once again in the same direction as before.

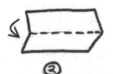

Now fold crosswise.

When you open up the whole piece of paper, you should have a folder outline of eight panels.

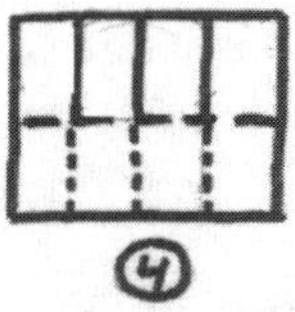

Cut in between the top four folds so that the top panels can fold down. Fold the top cut pieces down at the center fold. Press tightly.

Students retell story on four panels underneath the folded-down panels. Art work can be done on top (folded down) panel, and writing can be underneath (when top is flipped up) or vice versa. A little cutout can also be made in the shape of a diamond, circle, or square to make a "peek" into the artwork below. Underneath the artwork would be the writing on the same panel.

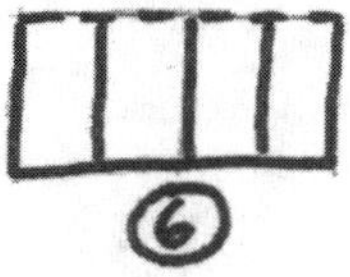

Figure B-8. Fold-a-Book

Materials: Standard-size paper, scissors, and glue, paste, or tape.

Directions: Follow the numbers of the pictures.

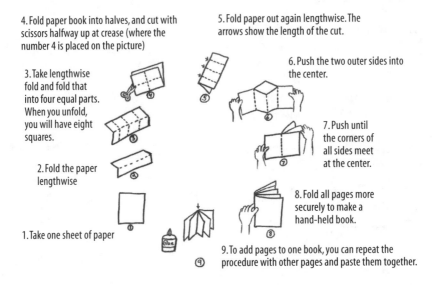

4. Fold paper book into halves, and cut with scissors halfway up at crease (where the number 4 is placed on the picture)

5. Fold paper out again lengthwise. The arrows show the length of the cut.

3. Take lengthwise fold and fold that into four equal parts. When you unfold, you will have eight squares.

6. Push the two outer sides into the center.

7. Push until the corners of all sides meet at the center.

2. Fold the paper lengthwise

8. Fold all pages more securely to make a hand-held book.

1. Take one sheet of paper

9. To add pages to one book, you can repeat the procedure with other pages and paste them together.

Figure B-9. Mobile Book

Materials: Metal or plastic hangers, string or yarn of various lengths, old manila folders or oak tag to cut up, or index cards, and hole puncher.

Directions:

1. Cut small rectangles from sturdy paper or use 3 x 5 inch index cards. Each student needs enough panels to retell story.
2. Draw picture and write text to go with each illustration.
3. Punch holes on the top of each panel.
4. Thread a piece of string or colored yarn through the hole and knot it.
5. Tie the other end of the string to the bottom of the hanger. The hanger can be wrapped by ribbon or yarn.
6. To indicate sequence of events, attach the first picture to the hanger with the shortest string. For each event that occurs in the story, the length of the string is increased. The last event should be attached with the longest string. Here's a good time to have the "time order" function words available.

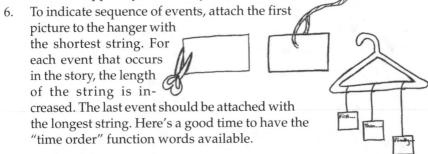

Figure B-10. Pop-Up Book

Materials: Construction paper (standard size works well), various shapes related to the story, scissors, glue or paste, and writing paper.

Directions:
1. Fold a piece of construction paper in half.
2. From the folded side of the paper, cut two slits. Space the slits about 2 $^1/_2$ to 3 inches apart.
3. Open and reverse the cutout fold. Push the fold out to make a box, as shown in the middle picture.
4. Put glue or paste on the X, as shown in the illustration.
5. Paste down the shape on the area marked by the X. Students may have drawn shapes beforehand to have them ready.
6. Add the written paper to the area below the pop-up figure.
7. Repeat steps 1 to 6 to add more pages to the pop-up book. There can be different figures to represent the meaning of the story.
8. Glue each page to the preceding one so that figures will pop up on turning the pages.

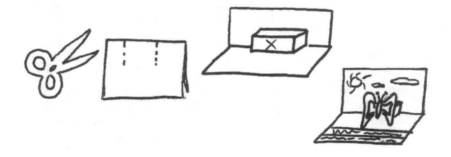

Figure B-11. Scroll Story Books (2)

Materials: Paper, pencils, crayons, markers, and yarn

Directions:
1. First plan a story with illustrations and text on scrap paper.
2. On long strips of chart paper, copy the edited and revised story.
3. Be sure to leave room for illustrations, and space them around your text.
4. Roll up the paper and tie yarn around it.
5. On the outside of the scroll, write the title and the author's and illustrator's names. Be sure to indicate that you are the author of the retold book.

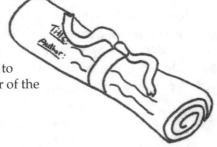

Materials: Two sheets of lined writing paper, glue or tape, pencils, crayons, markers, empty paper towel roll, and two paper clips

Directions:
1. Tape or glue two sheets of lined paper end to end.
2. Write your retold book on the paper, leaving room at the top (about 2 inches) so you can tape your paper to the towel roll.

3. You can illustrate this retold story by placing your pictures off to the sides of the paper.
4. Tape your story sheet to the towel roll.
5. Roll up your story sheet on the towel roll.
6. Hold it in place with a paper clip at each end.
7. Be sure to include the author and illustrator credits and note that you are the retelling author.
8. Your classmates will enjoy unrolling your story to read it.

Figure B-12. Shape Book

Materials: Oak tag or construction paper, crayons or markers, white lined paper, paper punch, yarn, pencil, and scissors

Directions:
1. Decide on a shape for your book. The shape can represent a character or theme of a story (see below).
2. Draw the shape on a piece of construction paper or oak tag that has been folded in half.
3. Cut the drawn shape so that you have a front cover and a back cover.
4. Use crayons or markers to decorate the covers.
5. Lay one cover on the writing papers and trace around it. Cut out the shape drawn on the separate pages.
6. Write and illustrate the separate pages to create the retold book in sequential order. It's best to have both retold text and artwork on the same panel page.
7. Punch holes in your covers and paper so that the book can be tied together with yarn.
8. Write the title of your book and the name of the author and illustrator on the front cover. Be sure to include that the book was retold by you.

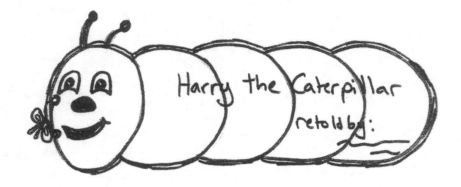

Appendix C

Concept-Level Relations Taxonomy;
Nine Levels

Chart C-1. Use of Concept-Level Relation Taxonomy to Apply New Vocabulary of Topics and Themes

Concept-Level Relation	Meaning	Activities
Synonym	A word that means the same as another	1. Matching columns of new word and its synonym or meaning 2. Sentence completion by filling in new word from word bank or group of words 3. Cloze-deleted selection in which new words have to be inserted correctly in context. Synonym needs to be provided near or under blank space. 4. Word search (see chapter 1) 5. Crossword puzzle (see chapter 2) 6. Tic-tac-toe synonym (see chapter 3) 7. "Go fish," in which a fish shape is drawn. On the top half of the fish figure is the new word. In the "fish bowl" are meanings or synonyms. Students reach into bowl and make a match.
Antonym	A word that means the opposite or nearly the opposite or is a counterpart of another, like *polar region* and *tropics* or *discovery* and *concealment*	1. Matching columns of words that are opposites 2. Replacing underlined word in a sentence with a word in the word bank or word group that means the opposite or nearly the opposite of the underlined word. 3. Writing on a blank line whether two words matched side by side are antonyms (A) or synonyms (S). 4. An antonym-synonym maze activity in which the student enters the maze at "start" with pen or pencil and finds words that match clues provided such as "What word means the same as *apparel*?" or "What's the opposite of *dryness*?" 5. "So what's the difference?" activity in which the student writes on a line provided under a pair of words why the two words are opposites, such as *liberty* and *tyranny*. 6. A "continuum ladder" activity in which the rungs of a ladder are drawn onto the two sides of a standing ladder. Below the bottom rung appears one word of an opposing or contrary word pair such as *germinate* or *opaque*. Above the top rung, the opposing concept word is placed, such as *die* or *transparent*. From a word bank, students place words in the intervening rungs according to the interpretation of meanings of the two target words. Thus, *generate* and *sprout* would be close to *germinate* and *wither* and *expire* would be close to *die*. 7. A "diamanté poem" contrasts two words using the shape of a diamond. At the top of the diamond is written one word, such as *lord*, and at the bottom of the diamond is written the counterpart person, or *serf*. Then clues appear to the left or right of the diamond with appropriate blanks in the diamond. On two lines closest to the target words, students answer the clue and write two adjectives describing the two types of people. Across the middle of the diamond are drawn five lines. Students have to write five words that tell about the culture or time period. Between the middle and adjective line, students write three words describing the actions of the two types of people. Then students read their works as poems.

cont.

		8. Antonym task cards in which two words with contradictory meanings are written on two ends of oaktag or a flash card. Different jagged cutouts are made near the center of the card. Students shuffle the cutout card ends and have to match the meaning and cut-out edges.
		9. A "bunch of words" activities in which a bunch of grapes on a vine are drawn. The grapes where synonyms appear, the student colors green, and the grapes where antonyms appear, students color purple.
Association	Words are often bonded or linked together because of the way they are used in the culture. They "go together" because of meaning associations. For example, *patriot* would be linked to *Americans* and *Tory* to *England*.	1. A circle map in which a concept word, such as *plant* or *nomad*, is written in the middle of a circle on the chalkboard. Around the circled word is arranged through brainstorming all the other words students associate with the concept word. A circle is then drawn around the brainstormed words. In the outer circle that's left, students tell the "in-the-head factors" that made them use certain words. They provide their background knowledge experiences for the brainstormed words. For plants it could be that a student has grown some and knows that they need sunlight, water, and air to survive.
		2. A grid format showing at the top the four heads: words meaning the same, words meaning the opposite, words that go together, and words that are not related. In the left column are pairs of words from your topic or theme. The student checks off the correct relationship.
		3. A "link-a-sentence" activity in which the teacher has set up three columns of sentence parts with new vocabulary words embedded in the parts. In column 1 are the subject phrases, in column 2 are the verb phrases, and in column 3 are the direct object phrases. However, the three sentence parts are arranged in mixed-up order in each column. Students have to locate the correct meaning relationship to fix up the sentence, and they write the correct sentence below.
		4. A "shape poem" activity in which students create an outline shape of a person, animal, plant, or object. featured in the topic. For instance, for "The Arctic Region" topic, students might draw the animal outlines for a polar bear, musk ox, caribou, seal, or narwhal. Around the shape of the animal, students write phrase statements about the creature. New words used to describe, or that are associated with, the animal are used with the phrases. Students read off their encircling statements as a poem. For *narwhal* could be "the ocean unicorn; breathes through blowholes; hunted by Eskimos for oil, meat, and ivory; long spiral tusk part of male's jaw; tusk extending out of the sea like a lance."
Classifi-cation	Classifying, also known as categorizing, grouping, and sorting, is based on class, attribute, and example relationships. The major class often has subclasses such as in the category topic "Kinds of Rock on Earth." This topic in then classified into sedimentary, metamor-phic, and igneous. Each of these subclasses has specific types (examples) of rock, and each of these	1. A classifying concept map which "grows" from the top down. Class, subclass, attribute, and example levels of words are linked by arrows and concept "nodes" (boxes or circles which house the concepts). See chapter 4.
		2. A semantic feature analysis grid which links topic, type or class features in the vertical left column with attribute, characteristic, or feature qualities across the horizontal top. If the concept term in the left column contains that feature noted in the top column, the student places a "plus" or a "check" mark. So for the "narwhal" listed on the left along with "polar bear, musk ox," and others, check marks would appear when the feature terms of "has a long tusk, is an ocean mammal, hunted for ivory," etc. See chapter 6.

cont.

Classification cont.	specific rocks (slate, granite, lava) has its own attributes, characteristics, or features.	3. A word concept or a word structure map in which the structural form arises as three questions are answered, "What is it? What is it like? What are some examples?" See chapter 5.
		4. A "find the impostor" activity in which four concept words related to a topic are written across a line. Students have to locate one word that doesn't belong with the other three and cross it out. On a blank line below, they have to tell why the crossed-out word, didn't belong. For instance, in the topic of _____ with _____ the four words, *worms*, *insects*, *birds*, and *sponges*, the word "birds" does not belong because it is a vertebrate.
		5. An activity called "which category" involves traditional word sorting. Present your major class concept terms at the top of the columns. Leave blank spaces under each head for students to write features or examples of that category word. For instance, for the "Types of Rock" topic, you would place the concept names for the three types on top. From a word box, students would write terms and words such as *limestone, formed by volcanoes, pressure changes rock structure, lava,* and *formed by deposit of sand and rocks*" under the appropriate category name. Some teachers use an icon, such as a box or a paper bag, and tell students to "box" or "bag" the words into the container.
		6. A "what's in common" activity in which three words or terms appear on a line. Students have to write on a blank space at the end of the line what the three words have in common. For instance, for the three words associated with the topic of Light are written *prism, diamond, rainbow*. On the blank to the right we expect wording such as, "they all refract or bend the light waves."
		7. "Jeopardy," in which the features or some examples are given as the answers and students have to come up with the questions. For instance, for the feature phrase, "exoskeletons of sea animals," the question "What is sedimentary rock?" would be appropriate.
Analogy	With this type of thinking, students are making comparisons and seeing relationships with concept words found in other thinking categories in this taxonomy. Visualizing and understanding the many meanings of words are important mental processes stimulated with the use of analogy activities. The Miller Analogies Test, taken by adults, indicates that the following types of thinking often occur with pairs of concept words offered on the test: similarity, contrast, describing, classifying, completing, seeing part-whole and whole-part relationships, and seeing sound, letter, and word associations. It's important to teach students these relationships so they know what to look for in analogous comparisons.	1. Set up an analogy comparison by leaving a blank space for one of the words in the relationship, such as "*Mammal* is to *vertebrate* as *insect* is to _____."
		2. Use punctuation marks instead of words in the example above. Also provide a choice of words to complete the analogy, with one word being the correct one. The structure would appear the following way: odyssey: trip; labyrinth: _____ (puzzle, voyage, cave, basement); (the relationship is synonym).
		3. On top of an oak-tag ice cream cone is placed a "scoop" of "ice cream." Inside the scoop is written an analogous relationship that students have to figure out. Suppose one of your new words placed in a word box was *minuscule*. In the scoop could be written the word puzzle "A flea is like a fly, only more _____." On the next scoop, would be this puzzle: "A _____ is like a pebble, only more _____." From the word box, students would select *boulder* and *gigantic*. The scoops continue to build as teachers and students conceive of analogous word-puzzle relationships with new vocabulary words.
		4. A chart completion activity in which students have to select appropriate words from a word box to complete relationships. The chart would be divided into two sections with concept headers on top to describe the dual relationship. For instance, such headers could be: "Animal—Name of Home," "Titles of People—Roles in Society," or "Types of Governments—Characteristics." Students would fill in spaces on the chart with some words of the relationship being offered to provide thinking clues.

cont.

Connotation-Denotation	The thinking involved with this relationship is supported by the number of meanings one has accrued in one's mental dictionary for words in general. The mind sorts words into shades of meaning to capture the most expressive meaning. For instance, when would one use *saunter*, or *amble*, or just *walk* to tell about the same experience? Connotative-denotative relations, therefore, are linked to synonym relationships. However, one's understanding of when to use and best express a word in a particular way comes into play. The denotative use of a word is its direct, explicit meaning. The connotative use of a word bears the word's associative use in the culture or its emotional overtones besides the explicit, denotative meaning.	1. An activity called "Why do you think so?" in which one sentence contains two words that are synonymous, with one of the words being a new meaning word. The student has to answer the question prompt about the meaning expressed by the two words and also tell why he or she thinks so. For instance, with this question based on the vocabulary from the "Volcano" topic, "Which is more violent, a scream or an eruption?" the student has to tell what is more violent and why.
		
		 2. A "choose your words" activity to make two sentences. Here the teacher writes one sentence with two word choices. From that initial sentence, the student chooses words from the word pair that seem to go together best. Here are sentences the student could rewrite into two sentences using some of the "Volcano" topic vocabulary: "The (scream, eruption) was (violent, noisy)" and "The (liquid, molten) substance (oozed, ran) off the table."
		
		 3. An activity called "create-a-sentence" is which two words, rather close in meaning to one another, are arranged as a word pair. The student has to create one sentence using both words appropriately. Here are some examples:
		    outburst – eruption
		    molten – melted
		    magma – lava
		
		 4. In "the thinking detective" activity the teacher makes interesting statements about a topic that may have a one-sided point of view. The student reads the statement, which contains some of the new vocabulary of the topic, and answers in writing why he or she thinks so. Here are a couple of statements using the vocabulary of the Revolutionary War era. "A loyalist viewed a patriot as a rebel. Why do you think so?" "If you were a peaceful British colonist living in the colonies and wished to obey the law, you would think that the Minutemen were dangerous traitors. Why do you think so?"

Multiple-meaning word	Many words have multiple meanings, and context use plays a large part in assigning a particular meaning to a word. A dictionary can be most helpful in assisting one to figure out if a word known to be used in one context can be used in another context.	1. A dictionary can help the teacher set up a traditional activity called "match the correct meaning." With the volcano topic, words such as *peak*, *crater*, and *eruption* have multiple meanings. The teacher can list the multiple meanings of the three words on an activity sheet or have students find the meanings in their dictionaries. The teacher, however, should write sentences in which the word is used in one way according to the context. Then the student matches the meaning of the word as it was used in the sentence with the dictionary entry. For instance, with the sentence, "She was at the peak of her career," the student should select the meaning of "a summit or top." For the sentence, "The peak kept the sun out of his eyes," the student should select the meaning of "the projecting front part of a cap, a visor." 2. In the "two of a kind" activity, the teacher writes three sentences, each containing the same new word. Two of the sentences use the new word in the same way; one sentence uses the word correctly but with an alternative meaning. The student selects the two sentences that share the same meaning for the new word. 3. An "add-a-sentence" activity in which the teacher writes two or three sentences using a multiple-meaning word in a particular way. The student has to write the next sentence using the new word in the same way.

cont.

Homograph	A word that is spelled like another but differs in meaning and pronunciation from it. Very often the accent changes to signal the intended meaning. For instance, look at the sentences with the word *rebel*. "She would often re-BEL when asked to do her chores." "He was a real REB-el when it came to homework." Notice the shift in accent coordinated with a shift from verb to noun usage.	1. The three activities listed above for multiple meanings could be used here as well. These are:"match the correct meaning," "two of a kind," and "add-a-sentence." 2. The homograph pair appears side by side. Students are asked to write one sentence using the homograph pair. Thus, they write one sentence using such words as *refuse, subject, convert,* and *project* in their verb and noun usages.
Homophone	A word that sounds like another but differs in meaning and spelling from it. Most of the time two words meet the criterion, such as *root* and *route*. Sometimes three words can apply, as with *cent, sent,* and *scent*.	1. The activities provided above for words of multiple meaning and homographic words could apply here as well. Thus, the teacher could use: Match the Correct "match the correct meaning," "two of a kind,""add-a-sentence," and Homophone Pair" (or threesome). 2. Children can be asked to draw or find a picture that represents each meaning. 3. Sentences can be written in which one spelling of the homophone pair is correct. The student would select the correct spelling and meaning word, such as for the sentence, "The parade followed a (*root* or *route*) through the city." 4. The teacher composes a short story in which the incorrect homophone words are used. From a word box of homophone pairs, students would select the correct homophone meaning and spelling and rewrite the story. Here's such a story:"Susie followed a walking root threw the woulds. She herd music. She said,"Eye like the music. Wear is it coming from? She followed the sounds and wanted to no more. Soon she could sea a band playing and a lot of cars parked on rodes nearby. She had come to a fare in the forest." 5. A more creative activity than the one indicated above would be to arrange the homophone pairs occurring with a particular topic in a word box. For instance with the study of "Landforms" were such words as *boulder, plain, herd, bear,* and *due*. With these words, their homophone counterpart, and other homonyms, the teacher asks students to write a creative story or tall tale about a landform. Students could tell how the landform was created, who or what lived there, and why it was useful. 6. A last activity might close the concept-level relations activity involvement. Teachers can create an activity called "Which is which?" whereby students have to place a large S next to word pairs that are synonyms and an *H* next to pairs which are homonyms. Thus, for the "Living organisms" topic, we could have word pairs such as *genes/jeans, nucleus/center, mussels/muscles, trait/ characteristic, cell/sell*.

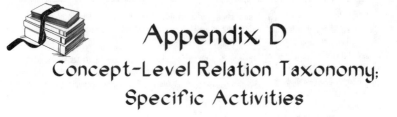

Appendix D
Concept-Level Relation Taxonomy:
Specific Activities

Antonym Activity: Task Cards

Directions: Working alone, or with a partner, shuffle the following antonym task cards. Then, try to connect and match the cards with each new
vocabulary word and a word with the opposite meaning. You will know
you have matched the correct pairs because the two pieces will fit together
like a puzzle. Good luck!

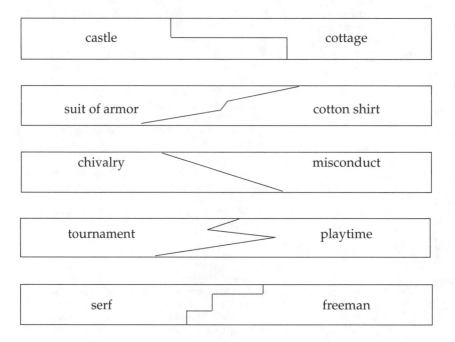

Antonym Activity: Diamanté Poem

Directions: Let's make a diamanté poem by contrasting the mighty rulers—the kings and queens—with the lowly serfs, or peasants. The shape of the poem is in the form of a diamond. Please read the clues to the right and fill in the blanks with some of your new vocabulary words.

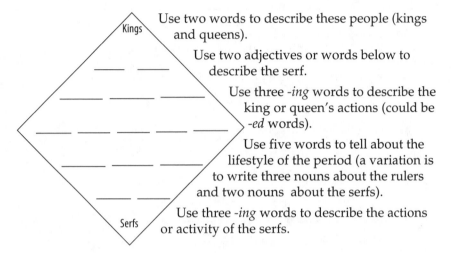

Use two words to describe these people (kings and queens).

Use two adjectives or words below to describe the serf.

Use three -*ing* words to describe the king or queen's actions (could be -*ed* words).

Use five words to tell about the lifestyle of the period (a variation is to write three nouns about the rulers and two nouns about the serfs).

Use three -*ing* words to describe the actions or activity of the serfs.

Association Activity: Choose the Relationship

Directions: Read the pair of words listed under the column "word pairs." Check the box that tells if the two words are the *same, different, go together,* or if they are *not related.* Not related means the words don't usually go together in any meaningful way.

Word pairs	Same	Different	Go together	Not related
tournament/ jousting contest	X			
manor accolade				X
royalty serf		X		
knight lance			X	
vows oaths of allegiance	X			
convent vassal				X
owner tenant		X		
page squire			X	

Association Activity: Link-a-Sentence

Directions: Look at the three columns below and read the sentence parts. Then connect the ideas in each of the three columns to make five good sentences that make sense. Write your sentences on the lines below.

Column 1	Column 2	Column 3
1. The serf	took oaths of allegiance	to the land for life.
2. A mighty fortress	often protected	from a master.
3. The apprentice	learned the trade	the royal family from harm.
4. Granting of fiefs	was the major means	of raising an army.
5. Vassals	was bonded	to protect the interests of the lord.

1. _____

2. _____

3. _____

4. _____

5. _____

Classification Activity:
Semantic Feature Analysis Grid

Directions: Look at the words placed in the column below under "Features." Match the feature words with the concept words in the left column by placing a check mark or a plus sign in the box.

Features

Concept Terms	Vassal	Monk	Guild	Bonded to land	Granted fiefs	Took oaths	Lived in cottages	Lived on manors	Apprentice
Knight									
Serf									
Royalty									
Religious People									
City Life									

Classification Activity:
What's in Common?

Directions: The pairs of words below are connected in some way. Read each pair of words and decide what they have in common. On the line below each pair, write a sentence or two explaining what they have in common.

knight and accolade

What's in common?

_____

tournament and lance

What's in common?

_____

guild and craftsman

What's in common?

_____

serf, manor, and fief

What's in common?

_____

monk and nun

What's in common?

_____

Analogy Activity: Chart Completion

Directions: Carefully look at each chart below. Decide how both columns of words are related and use your new terms and vocabulary words to fill in the blanks.

Word Box

Title of Position in Society	Role
noble	
	warrior
	own the manor
serf	

knight
works the fiefdom
ruler
royalty

Type of Event	Purpose
granting of fiefs	
	was a battle between knights
accolade	
pledging oaths of allegiance	

granted a squire knighthood
created a system of vassals
bonded serfs to land
tournament

Analogy Activity:
Scoops of Word Flavors

Directions: Read the statement making a comparison in each scoop of ice cream. From the word box, select the word or words that add the best meaning flavors to the scoop of ice cream. If you can make your own analogy comparison, add it to the next building scoop.

Add your own word flavors to the ice cream scoop.

An _____ is like a _____ but is learning the job and trade.

_____ are like vows but were spoken to _____ .

A _____ is like a _____ but in earlier stages of training.

A _____ is like a church but much bigger and magnificent.

Word Box

cathedral
squire
apprentice
royalty
knight
oaths of allegiance
master

Connotative-Denotative Shades-of-Meaning Activity: Create a Sentence

Directions: Read each pair of words below.
Think about their meanings and create a sentence using both words in the same sentence.

1. competition—tournament
    _____

2. accolade—ceremony
    _____

3. rules—chivalry
    _____

4. guild—association
    _____

5. fortress—manor
    _____

6. knight—vassal
    _____

Connotative-Denotative Shades-of-Meaning Activity: Choose Your Words

Directions: Read the sentences and word choices below. Make two sentences from the sets of words given in each sentence. Select the words that best express the meaning for each sentence. Can you explain why you chose the words you did?

1. The (knight, noble) dressed in new (clothes, armor) for his (accolade, ceremony).
    _____

2. (Knights, Athletes) compete in dangerous (competitions, tournaments) and learn (chivalry, rules).
    _____

3. The (servants, serfs) follow the directions and orders of the nobles, who ruled the (fiefs, manors).
    _____

4. The brave knight used his (weapon, lance) to defeat his opponent in the (joust, battle).
    _____

Multiple-Meaning-of-Words
Activity: Which Meaning

Directions: Read each sentence below. Think about the meaning of the italicized word. Match the meanings provided for the underlined word with the way the word is used in the sentence.

1. When the boy saw his dog after being away all weekend, he ran to it and gave it a warm accolade.
   Accolade means:
   - a. an expression of approval
   - b. ceremony for knighthood
   - c. an embrace of greeting

2. After mastering his skill, the blacksmith became a member of a famous guild.
   Guild means:
   - a. an association of people of the same trade
   - b. one of four groups of plants

3. The noble was in charge of and took care of the serfs who worked his land.
   Noble means:
   - a. not active
   - b. belonging to the royalty class
   - c. grand in appearance

Homonym Activity:
What Are the Right Words?

Directions: Read each sentence below. Figure out what's wrong in each sentence, circle it, and explain the problem on the line below it. Then, rewrite the sentence correctly.

1. The nobles collect tacks from the people on the manor.
   What's wrong? _____
   Corrected sentence: _____

2. At his accolade, the night was finally recognized as a warrior.
   What's wrong? _____
   Corrected sentence: _____

3. If you lived during the Middle Ages, would you like to be a craftsman or a surf?
   What's wrong? _____
   Corrected sentence: _____

4. A none made a vow to give up all her property and live in a convent.
   What's wrong? _____
   Corrected sentence: _____

Appendix E
Word Parts:
Prefixes, Roots, and Suffixes

Table E-1.
Common Prefixes and Their Meanings

Prefix	Meaning	Word Examples
a-, ab-, abs-	away from, without, removal of	abnormal, anemic, abduct, absolve
ante-	before	antecedent, antedate
anti-anta-	against, opposed to	antidote, antiseptic, antagonist
ambi-	more than one, both	ambivalent, ambidextrous
auto-	self	automatic, autocrat
bene-	good, well	benefactor, beneficial, benevolent
bi-	two	biannual, bipedal, bifocal
circ-	around	circumnavigate, circuitous, circumspect
co-, col-, con-, cor-	with, together	coexist, cohesion, concord, correlate, collaborate
de-	away from, down	depart, demote, dethrone, detract, depress
dis-	not, opposite of, apart	dislike, dismiss, disconnect, disapprove
dys-	bad	dysfunction, dyslexia, dystrophy
epi-	among, beside, on, over	epidemic, epigraph, epitaph, epicenter
eu-	good	eulogy, euphemism
ex-, exo-	out, off, out from, outside	export, excavate, explode, exit
extra-	beyond	extracurricular, extraterrestrial
fore-	ahead of	forefather, foreground, foreshadow, foresight
hyper-	excessive, beyond	hyperactive, hyperbole
im-, in-, il-, ir-	not	impair, immature, inept, inexpensive, illicit, irrational
in-	in, into	indoors, inject, invade, income
inter-	between	interject, intermission, interview, intervene
mal-	bad	malice, malady, malevolent, malign
mis-	wrong, error, hatred	mistake, mistrial, misanthrope, misdemeanor, misunderstood
mono-	one	monopoly, monarch, monologue
multi-	many	multiply, multilateral, multimedia, multiplex
per-	through	pervade, perform, persist, permeate, perforate
poly-	many	polygon, polyglot
post-	after	postwar, postscript, postmortem, posterior
pre-	before	preamble, precedent, precursor, predetermine, preview, predict
pro-	forward, before	prologue, prospectus, project, proceed, propel
re-, retro-	again, back	repay, retrace, repeat, recede, reclaim, revise, retroactive, retrospect
semi-	half, partly	semiskilled, semifinal, semiliterate
sub-	under, below	submarine, subdue, subject, subordinate, subvert
super-	above	supermarket, superfluous, superior, superintendent
trans-	across, beyond	transport, transmit, transaction, transgress, transpose
tri-	three	triangle, trinity, tricycle
un-	not, reversal	unhappy, unbeaten, uneven, untie
uni-	one	universal, uniform, unilateral

Table E-2.
Common Roots and Their Meanings

Root	Meaning	Word Examples
an	year, yearly	annual, semiannual, annuity, superannuate
arch	government	oligarchy, matriarch, patriarch, anarchy
bio	live	biology, symbiotic, biopsy
ced	yield	concede, antecedent, recede, precede
cide	kill	pesticide, genocide, homicide, herbicide
corps	body	corporal, incorporate, corpulence
cred	truth	incredible, credulous, credentials
dem	people	democracy, endemic, demographics
derm	skin	pachyderm, ectoderm, dermatology
dic	speech, talk	diction, edict, indict, verdict, valedictorian
dole	sad	doleful, doldrums, condolence
duc, duct	lead	aqueduct, induct, viaduct
dyn	power	dynasty, dynamo, dynamite
equa	balanced, fair	equitable, equal, equilateral, inequity
err	mistake	error, erroneous, erratic
fac	ease	facile, facilitate, benefactor
feder	league, treaty	federal, confederate, federation
gen	born	generate, progeny, congenital, engender
grat	please, favor	grateful, gratuity, congratulate, ingrate
gnos	knowledge	cognitive, recognition, diagnosis, agnostic
graph, gram	write, draw	graphic, telegram, monograph, grapheme, epigram
grat	move	migrate, immigrate, emigrate, transmigrate
greg	gather	congregate, aggregate, gregarious
habit	reside	habitat, inhabit, habitual
jac, ject	throw	eject, project, reject, ejaculate
log	word	monologue, prologue, travelogue, analogy
man	hand	manual, mansuscript, manipulate, manicure
meter	measure	odometer, chronometer, asymmetrical, parameter
mis, mit	send	missile, mission, emit, remit, remission
mort	death	mortal, immortal, mortuary, mortify
nova	new	novel, novelty, novice, innovate
oct	eight	octopus, octet, octocular
para	beside	paralegal, parasite, paraprofessional, parabola
ped	feet	quadruped, pedicure, expedite, impede
ped	child	pediatrician, pedant
pend	hang	append, depend, appendix, pendant, impending
phon	sound	phonics, phoneme, cacophony
phot	light	photography, photosynthesis
port	carry	import, export, deport, report, portfolio
prehend	to take hold of	apprehend, comprehend, reprehensible
rupt	break	rupture, disrupt, interrupt, eruption
sed, sid, set	settle	residue, subside, reside, sedate
spic, spic	see or view	spectacle, aspect, perspective, prospect, retrospect
stas, stat	rest, at rest	statue, static, statistic
temp	time	tempo, contemporary, temporal
therm	heat	thermal, thermometer
vac	empty	vacant, evacuate, vacuum
ven	come, to come to	circumvent, invention, convene
ver	truth	veracity, verdict, aversive, veritable
vers	against	diverse, versus, adverse, reverse
vis	sec	vision, visor, visionary, revise, invisible
viv	life	revive, vivid, vivacious
voc	voice	vocal, invoke, invocation, vociferous

Table E-3.
Common Suffixes and Their Meanings

Suffix	Meaning	Word Examples
-able, -ible	can be, worthy of	likable, lovable, audible
-al, -ial	process of, action of	personal, editorial, arrival, denial, sentimental
-iac	consisting of, pertaining to	maniac, cardiac
-ance, -ence	the state or quality of	resistance, abstinence, annoyance, absence
-ant, -ent	one who	mutant, servant, penitent
-ar, -er, -or	one who	liar, teacher, investor, professor, inspector
-cracy	government of	democracy, autocracy
-et, -ette	small	packet, dinette, booklet
-ful	full of	respectful, insightful, hopeful
-hood	quality or state of	adulthood, childhood, statehood
-ia	having to do with	mania, militia, paraphernalia, utopia
-ic	having to do with, characterized by	basic, skeptic, tragic, eccentric, angelic
-icle, -ucle	small	bicycle, particle, molecule, icicle
-ify	to make	amplify, rectify, simplify
-ine	resembling	feline, serpentine, valentine, bovine
-ish	like something named	smallish, brownish, foolish
-ism	condition or doctrine of	barbarism, heroism, communism, paganism
-ist	one who	socialist, populist
-itis	sickness or inflammation of	arthritis, bronchitis
-less	without	senseless, hopeless
-ling	young	yearling, duckling
-ly	in the way or manner	rapidly, harshly, slowly, earnestly
-ment	state or quality of	enjoyment, entertainment, interment
-ness	state or quality of	hopefulness, kindness, anxiousness, pleasantness
-ology	study of	paleontology, biology, zoology, criminology
-ous	having the characteristics of	famous, instantaneous, joyous, fatuous
-phobia	fear of	acrophobia, claustrophobia
-ship	art or skill or state of	statesmanship, friendship, courtship, censorship
-sion, -tion	state or quality of	pension, creation, attraction, tension
-ure	state or quality of	creature, failure, treasure
-ward	direction	westward, homeward
-y	full of	nosy, crabby, sleepy

Table E-4.
Suffixes That Identify Parts of Speech

Used to Identify Nouns		Used to Identify Adjectives		Used to Identify Verbs	
Suffix	**Word Example**	**Suffix**	**Word Example**	**Suffix**	**Word Example**
-acy	democracy	-aceous	crustaceous	-ate	decorate
-age	suffrage	-ar	stellar	-en	darken
-an	median	-ary	stationary	-fy	rectify
-ancy	buoyancy	-ate	ornate	-ise	surprise
-ard	coward	-ent	different	-ize	stabilize
-ary	(the) ordinary	-er	drier		
-ate	palate	-ern	western		

Inflectional Endings

-cy	dependency	-escent	fluorescent
-dom	freedom	-id	valid, rabid
-ee	referee	-ile	facile
-eer	racketeer	-like	birdlike
-ency	regency	-ory	satisfactory
-ent	(a) dependent	-ose	verbose
-ery	stationery	-some	lonesome
-ess	stewardess	-ulent	corpulent
-ice	cowardice	-wise	lengthwise
-ier	financier		
-ite	respite		
-ity	finality		
-ive	palliative		
-kin	bumpkin		
-let	piglet		
-mony	matrimony		
-ory	statutory		
-ster	trickster		
-teen	thirteen		
-tude	gratitude		
-ty	thirty		
-yer	lawyer		

Don't forget those inflectional endings and their purpose in English. Recall that there are only a few handful of these in the English language, and they are used repeatedly by speakers and writers. Here they are again, with the jobs they perform:

1. To make nouns plural
   -s   birds
   -es   churches

2. To change the tense of verbs
   -ed   littered
   -ing   littering
   -s   litters

3. To show comparisons
   -er   bigger
   -est   biggest

4. To indicate ownership or possession
   's   one bird's house
   s'   many birds' houses

Appendix F
Word Building Activities

Figure F-1. Pack-a-Word (Sample)

Directions: Read the root word or root part in the child's backpack. Look at the prefixes and suffixes arranged on the hiker's arms. Write the words you make and their meanings on the lower part of the backpack. Then try to use each word in a good sentence.

Figure F-2. Pack-a-Word (Blank)

Directions: Read the root word or root part in the child's backpack. Look at the prefixes and suffixes arranged on the hiker's arms. Write the words you make and their meanings on the lower part of the backpack. Then try to use each word in a good sentence.

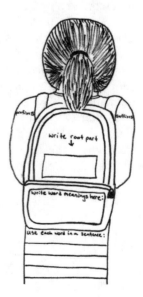

Figure F-3. A Handful of Words (Sample)

Directions: Place a root word or a root part (see Table E-2) in the center of a child's drawn hand. Place prefixes that work for the root selected in the finger nails and place suffixes that work in the sleeve part. Have children write the words formed in the finger areas.

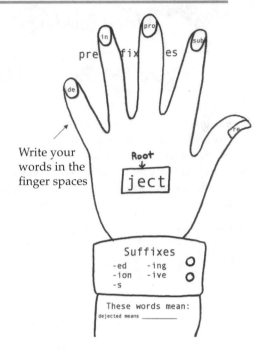

Figure F-4. A Handful of Words (Blank)

Directions: Place a root word or a root part (see Table E-2) in the center of a child's drawn hand. Place prefixes that work for the root selected in the finger nails and place suffixes that work in the sleeve part. Have children write the words formed in the finger areas.

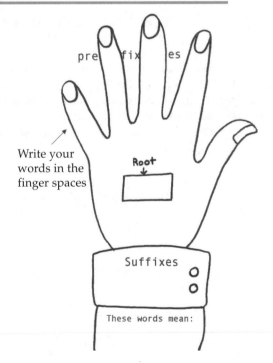

Figure F-5. Hinge-a-Word (Sample)

Directions: Using durable construction paper or oak tag, fashion a piece whereby a root part of a word can be written or mounted in the center. Leave a few inches on either side of the piece so that a flap can be folded down toward the center part. When the flaps are folded down, the backs of the flaps become aligned with the root part. On the backs of the flaps, prefixes, suffixes, or both can be written or taped down. You might consider making a horizontal cut in the flaps, so prefix and suffix cards can be inserted. This way the "Hinge-a-Word" construction folder can be used over and over again for new roots, prefixes, and suffixes. The illustration below shows the prefix and suffix part on the front of the flap for visual purposes. Remember to follow the arrows of the fold and place the affixes on the back of the fold.

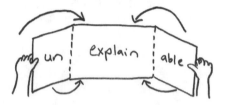

Figure F-6. Hinge-a-Word (Blank)

Directions: Using durable construction paper or oak tag, fashion a piece whereby a root part of a word can be written or mounted in the center. Leave a few inches on either side of the piece so that a flap can be folded down toward the center part. When the flaps are folded down, the backs of the flaps become aligned with the root part. On the backs of the flaps, prefixes, suffixes, or both can be written or taped down. You might consider making a horizontal cut in the flaps, so prefix and suffix cards can be inserted. This way the "Hinge-a-Word" construction folder can be used over and over again for new roots, prefixes, and suffixes. Remember to follow the arrows of the fold and place the affixes on the back of the fold.

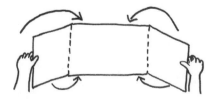

Figure F-7. Unlock-the-Word

Directions: For this activity, you place a key word with some or multiple word parts in the middle of the lock space. Students "unlock" the word by placing the prefix on the lock fastener on top, the root word or part on the padlock itself, and the suffix part in the keyhole. Then students write the meaning of the "unlocked" word in the key. Try this with words such as:

repayment

enclosure

prospector

unsuitable

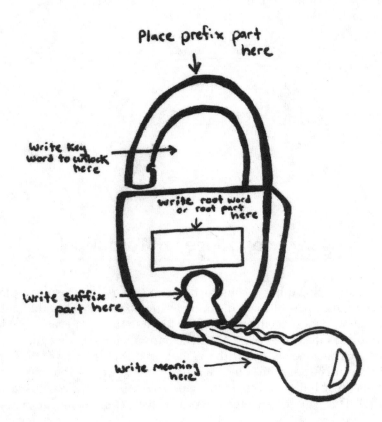

Figure F-8. Leaving Words (Sample)

Directions: You can use this tree figure or draw a tree on a large sheet of construction paper. To the roots of the tree, attach or tape root words (*tell*) or root parts (*vis*). The roots of the tree can be fashioned by small strips of cut-up oak tag or manila folders. The index cards can be slipped behind the tree roots waiting to be pulled off by children.

Prefixes and suffixes are written on other index cards or folder parts and placed face down in a pile. The prefixes and suffixes can also appear on the tree trunk as shown and children would select the affix parts to make words. Children pick up an index card containing a prefix or suffix and match with a root part. If a successful match is made, the word is "leafed" on the tree. A child can opt to take a second card to add another affix to the growing word (*truth-ful-ness*).

This is a great team game!

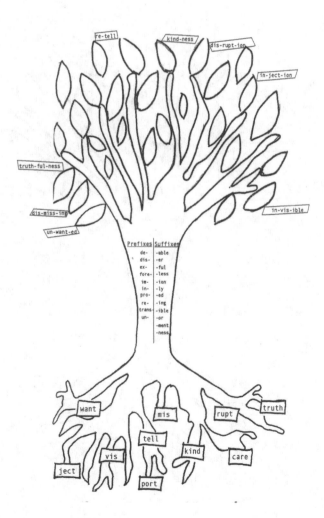

Figure F-9. Leaving Words (Blank)

Directions: You can use this tree figure or draw a tree on a large sheet of construction paper. To the roots of the tree, attach or tape root words (*tell*) or root parts (*vis*). The roots of the tree can be fashioned by small strips of cut-up oak tag or manila folders. The index cards can be slipped behind the tree roots waiting to be pulled off by children.

Prefixes and suffixes are written on other index cards or folder parts and placed face down in a pile. The prefixes and suffixes can also appear on the tree trunk as shown and children would select the affix parts to make words. Children pick up an index card containing a prefix or suffix and match with a root part. If a successful match is made, the word is "leafed" on the tree. A child can opt to take a second card to add another affix to the growing word (*truth-ful-ness*).

This is a great team game!

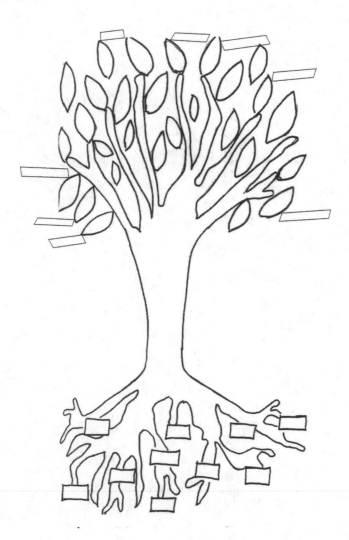

# References

Children's Literature Resources

Aardema, V., & Dillon, L. (1979). *Who's in Rabbit's house? A Masai tale.* New York: Penguin Putnam Books.

Allard, H., & Marshall, J. (1982). *Miss Nelson is back.* New York: Houghton-Mifflin.

Buckley, R. (1985). *The greedy python.* New York: Scholastic.

De Reginiers, B. S. (1999). *May I bring a friend?* New York: Econo-Clad Books.

Geisel, T. S. (Dr. Seuss). (1978). *I can read with my eyes shut!* New York: Beginner Books.

Heine, H. (1991). *Prince bear.* New York: Simon & Schuster.

Irving, W. (1966). *The legend of Sleepy Hollow & Rip Van Winkle.* Mineola, NY: Dover.

Lattimore, D. N. (1992). *The winged cat.* New York: HarperCollins.

Lindbergh, R. (1990). *The day the goose got loose.* New York: Dial Books.

Kroll, S. (1976). *The Tyrannosaurus game.* New York: Holiday House.

Martin, B. (1983). *Brown bear, brown bear, what do you see?* New York: Holt, Rinehart and Winston.

Meramec, C. (1995). *A fake snake tale: A step-by-step practice story.* New York: Open Court.

Milne, A. A. (1996). *The complete tales and poems of Winnie-the-Pooh.* New York: Dutton.

Mosel, A. (1989). *Tikki Tikki Tembo.* New York: Holt.

Slepian, J., & Seidler, A. (1967). *The hungry thing.* New York: Scholastic.

Snow, P., & Dunnington, T. (1984). *A pet for Pat.* New York: Children's Press.

References

Academy of Orton-Gillingham Practioners and Educators (1999). *Philosophy of the academy.* Amenia, NY: Author.

Adams, M. J., & Bruck, M. (1995). Resolving the great debate. *American Educator, 19,* 7, 10–11.

Adams, M. J., Foorman, B., Lundberg, I., & Beeler, T. (1998). The elusive phoneme. *American Educator, 22,* 18–29.

Allington, R. (1997). Overselling phonics. *Reading Today, 15,* 15–16.

Arnoff, M. (1994). Morphology. In A. C. Purves (Ed.), *Encyclopedia of English studies and language arts* (pp. 820–821). New York: Scholastic.

Ashton-Warner, S. (1985). *Teacher.* New York: Simon & Schuster. (Original work published 1959)

Ashton-Warner, S. (1986). *Spinster.* New York: Simon & Schuster. (Original work published 1964)

Atwell, N. (1998). *In the middle: A framework for literacy* (2nd ed.). Portsmouth, NH: Heinemann.

Barry, A. K. (2002). *English grammar: Language as human behavior* (2nd ed.). Upper Saddle River, NJ: Prentice-Hall.

Baumann, J. F., Edwards, E. C., Font, G., Tereshinski, C. A., Kameenui, E. J., & Olejnik, S. (2002). Teaching morphemic and contextual analysis to fifth-grade students. *Reading Research Quarterly, 37*, 150–176.

Bear, D., Invernizzi, M. Foorman, B., Lundberg, I., & Johnston, F. (2000). *Words their way: Word study for phonics, vocabulary, and spelling instruction* (2nd ed.). Upper Saddle River, NJ: Merrill.

Board of Education of the City of New York (1997). *Performance standards: English language arts.* New York City: Author.

Borman, G. (2000). Summers are for learning. *Principal, 80*, 26–29.

Burns, P., Roe, B., & Ross, E. (1999)."*Teaching reading in today's elementary schools* (7th ed.). New York: Houghton Mifflin.

Calkins, L. (1997). *Raising lifelong learners: A parent's guide.* Reading, MA: Addison-Wesley.

Carroll, J. B., Davies, P., & Richman, B. (1971). *Word frequency book.* Boston: Houghton Mifflin.

Cernek, K. (2000). *Exploring word families: Using word patterns to build beginning reading skills.* Huntington Beach, CA: Creative Teaching Press.

Chall, J. (1992). Research supports direct instructional models: Point/counterpoint, whole language versus direct instruction models. *Reading Today, 10*, 8–10.

Chall, J. (1996). *Stages of reading development* (2nd ed.). New York: Harcourt Brace College.

Chard, D. J., & Dickson, S. V. (1999). Phonological awareness: Instructional and assessment guidelines. *Intervention in School and Clinic, 34*, 268–270.

Clark, E. (1998). Morphology in language acquisition. In Spencer, A., & Zwicky, A. (Eds.), *The handbook of morphology* (pp. 374–389). Malden, MA: Blackwell.

Clay, M. (1985). *The early detection of reading difficulties* (3rd ed.). Portsmouth, NH: Heinemann.

Clay, M. (1991). *Becoming literate: The construction of inner control.* Portsmouth, NH: Heinemann.

Coady, J. (1994a). Lexicon/Vocabulary. In A. C. Purves (Ed.), *Encyclopedia of English studies and language arts* (pp. 736–737). New York: Scholastic.

Coady, J. (1994b). Word lists. In A. C. Purves (Ed.), *Encyclopedia of English studies and language arts* (pp. 1278–1279). New York: Scholastic.

Cramer, R. (1994a). Language experience approach to reading. In A. C. Purves (Ed.), *Encyclopedia of English studies and language arts* (pp. 703-705). New York: Scholastic.

Cramer, R. (1994b). Word banks. In A. C. Purves, (Ed.), *Encyclopedia of English studies and language arts* (pp. 1275–1277). New York: Scholastic.

Cunningham, A., & Stanovich, K. (1998). What reading does for the mind. *American Educator, 22,* 8–15.

Cunningham, P. (1994). Word families. In A. C. Purves (Ed.), *Encyclopedia of English studies and language arts* (pp. 1277–1278). New York: Scholastic.

Dahl, K., & Scharer, P. (2000). Phonics teaching and learning in whole language classrooms: New evidence from research. *The Reading Teacher, 53,* 584–594.

Dale, E. (1969). *Audio-visual methods in teaching.* New York: Holt, Rinehart and Winston.

Dale, E., & Chall, J. (1948). A formula for predicting readability. *Educational Research Bulletin, 27* and *28,* 11–20 and 37–45.

DeFord, D. (1994). Linguistic and context cues in reading. In A. C. Purves (Ed.), *Encyclopedia of English studies and language arts* (pp. 741–743). New York: Scholastic.

DeFord, D., Lyons, C., & Pinnell, G. S. (Eds.). (1995). *Bridges to literacy: Learning from Reading Recovery.* Portsmouth, NH: Heinneman.

Dixon-Krauss, L. (1996). *Vygotsky in the classroom: Mediated literacy instruction and assessment.* White Plains, NY: Longman.

Dolch, E. (1936). A basic sight vocabulary. *Elementary School Journal, 36,* 456–460.

Dolch, E. (1948). First thousand words in children's reading. In *Problems in Reading.* Champaign, IL: Garrard Press.

Ehri, L. (1997). Sight word learning in normal readers and dyslexics. In B. Blachman (Ed.), *Foundations of reading acquistion and dyslexia* (pp. 163-189). Mahwah, NJ: Erlbaum.

Elkind, D. (1975). We can teach reading better. *Today's Education 64,* 34–38.

Elley, W. B. (1989). Vocabulary acquisition from listening to stories. *Reading Research Quarterly, 24,* 174–187.

Estes, T. (1994). Readability. In A. C. Purves (Ed.), *Encyclopedia of English studies and language arts* (pp. 978–980). New York: Scholastic.

Ewers, C., & Brownson, S. (1999). Kindergarteners' vocabulary acquisition as a function of active vs. passive storybook reading, prior vocabulary, and working memory. *Journal of Reading Psychology, 20,* 11–29.

Fabb, N. (1998). Compounding. In Spencer, A., & Zwicky, A. (Eds.), *The handbook of morphology* (pp. 66–83). Malden, MA: Blackwell.

Fernald, G. (1943). *Remedial techniques in basic school subjects.* New York: McGraw-Hill.

Flood, J., & Lapp, D. (1986). Type of texts: The match between what students read in basals and what they encounter in tests. *Reading Research Quarterly, 21,* 284–297.

Fowler, D. (1998). Balanced reading instruction in practice. *Educational Leadership, 55,* 11–12.

Fox, B. (2000). *Word identification strategies: Phonics from a new perspective* (2nd ed.). Upper Saddle River, NJ: Merrill.

Franzen, A. M. (1994). Reading readiness. In A. C. Purves (Ed.), *Encyclopedia of English studies and language arts* (pp. 1010–1012). New York: Scholastic.

Freppon, P., & Dahl, K. (1998). Theory and research into practice: Balanced instruction—Insights and considerations. *Reading Research Quarterly, 33*, 338–358.

Fromkin, V., & Rodman, R. (1998). *An introduction to language* (6th ed.). New York: Harcourt Brace.

Fry, E. (1975). Developing a list for remedial reading. *Elementary English, 34*, 456–458.

Fry, E. (1998). The most common phonograms. *The Reading Teacher, 51*, 620–622.

Fry, E., Fountoukidis, D. L., & Polk, J. K. (1985). *The new reading teacher's book of lists.* Englewood Cliffs, NJ: Prentice-Hall.

Fry, E., Kress, J., & Fountoukidis, D.L. (1993). *The Reading Teachers' Book of Lists* (3rd ed.). Des Moines, IA: Order Processing Dept.

Gallagher, T. (1993). Language skill and development of social competence in school-age children. *Language, Speech, and Hearing Series in Schools, 24*, 199–205.

Gaskins, R. W., Gaskins, J. C., & Gaskins, I. W. (1991). A decoding program for poor readers and the rest of the class, too! *Language Arts, 68*, 213–225.

Gaskins, R. W., Gaskins, J. C., & Gaskins, I. W. (1992). Using what you know to figure out what you didn't know: An analogy approach to decoding. *Reading & Writing Quarterly, 8*, 197–221.

Glass, G. G., & Glass, E. W. (1976). *Glass-Analysis for decoding only.* Garden City, NY: Easier to Learn.

Goodman, D. (1999). *The reading detective.* Portsmouth NH: Heinemann.

Goodman, K.S. (1996). *Ken Goodman on reading: A common sense look at the nature of language and the science of reading.* Portmouth, NH: Heinemann.

Goodman, K. S., Shannon, P., Freeman, Y. S., & Murphy, S. (1988). *Report card on basal readers.* Katonah, N.Y: Owen.

Goodman, Y. (1986). Children coming to know literacy. In W. H. Teale & E. Sulzby (Eds.), *Emergent literacy: Writing and reading* (pp. 1–14). Norwood, NJ: Ablex.

Goodman, Y. (1994). Environmental print. In A. C. Purves (Ed.), *Encyclopedia of English studies and language arts* (pp. 443–444). New York: Scholastic.

Goswami, U. (1993). Toward an interactive analogy model of reading development: Decoding vowel graphemes in beginning reading. *Journal of Experimental Child Psychology, 80*, 443–475.

Goswami, U., & Bryant, P. (1992). Rhyme, analogy, and children's reading. In L. C. Ehri and R. Treiman (Eds)., *Reading acquisition* (pp. 49–63). Mahwah, NJ: Erlbaum.

Graves, D. (1979). Let children show us how to help them write. *Visible Language, 13*, 16–28.

Groff, P. (2001). Teaching phonics: Letter-to-phoneme, phoneme-to-letter, or both. *Reading & Writing Quarterly, 17*, 291–306.

Hall, M. A. (1980). *Teaching reading as a language experience.* Columbus, OH: Merrill.

Hart, B., & Risley, T. (1995). *Meaningful differences.* Baltimore, MD: Brooks.

Hayes, D. P., & Ahrems, M. G. (1988). Vocabulary simplification for children: A special case of motherese. *Journal of Child Language, 15*, 395–410.

Hiebert, E. (1994). Invented spelling. In A. C. Purves (Ed.), *Encyclopedia of English studies and language arts* (pp. 666–668). New York: Scholastic.

Hirsch, E. D., Jr. (2000). You can always look it up! Or can you? *American Educator, 24*, 4–9.

Hunsberger, M. (1994). Language fluency. In A. C. Purves (Ed.), *Encyclopedia of English studies and language arts* (pp. 705–707). New York: Scholastic.

Johnson, D. D., & Pearson, P. D. (1984). *Teaching reading vocabulary* (2nd ed.). New York: Holt, Rinehart & Winston.

Johnston, F. (1999). The timing and teaching of word families. *The Reading Teacher, 53*, 64–75.

Juel, C. (1994). Reading fluency. In A. C. Purves (Ed.), *Encyclopedia of English studies and language arts* (pp. 1278–1279.) New York: Scholastic.

Kamberelis, G. (1999). Genre development and learning: Children writing stories, science reports, and poems. *Research in Teaching of English, 33*, 403–460.

Kameenui, E., & Carnine, D. (1998). *Effective teaching strategies that accommodate diverse learners.* Upper Saddle River, NJ: Merrill.

Kucera, H., & Francis, W. N. (1967). *A computational analysis of present day American English.* Providence, RI: Brown University Press.

Kuhn, M., & Stahl, S. (1998). Teaching children to learn word meanings from context: A synthesis and some questions. *Journal of Literacy Research, 30*, 119–138.

Laminack, L. (2000). Supporting emergent readers and writers. *Teaching K–8, 3*, 62–63.

Lancy, D. (1994). The conditions that support emergent literacy. In D. Lancy (Ed.), *Children's emergent literacy: From research to practice* (pp. 1-19). Westport, CT: Praeger.

Leslie, L., & Caldwell, J. A. (2001). *Qualitative reading inventory-II* (3rd ed.). New York: HarperCollins.

Leu, D., Jr., & Kinzer, C. (1999). *Effective literacy instruction* (4th ed.). Upper Saddle River, NJ: Merrill.

May, F. (1998). *Reading as communication: To help children write and read* (5th ed.). Upper Saddle River, NJ: Merrill.

McIntyre, E., & Pressley, M. (1996). *Balanced instruction: Strategies and skills in whole language.* Norwood, MA: Christopher-Gordon.

McKee, P. (1948). *The teaching of reading in the elementary school.* New York: Houghton Mifflin.

McNeil, J. D. (1987). *Reading comprehension: New directions for classroom practice.* Glenview, IL: Scott, Foresman.

Mesmer, H. A. (2001). Decodable text: A review of what we know. *Reading Research and Instruction, 40*, 121–141.

Moats, L. (1998). Teaching decoding. *American Educator, 22*, 42–49, 95.

Moffett, J. (1994). Foreword. In D. Lancy (Ed.), *Children's emergent literacy: From research to practice* (pp. xv–xix). Westport, CT: Praeger.

Moffett, J. (1998). *The universal schoolhouse: Spiritual awakening through education.* Herndon, VA: Calender Islands.

Moffett, J., & Wagner, J. (1992). *Student-centered language Arts, K–12* (4th ed.). Portsmouth, NH: Boyton/Cook.

Monson, R. J., & Pahl, M. M. (1991). Charting a new course with whole language. *Educational Leadership, 48,* 51–53.

Moustafa, M., & Maldonado-Colon, E. (1999). Whole-to-parts phonics instruction: Building on what children know to help them know more. *The Reading Teacher, 52,* 448–456.

National Reading Panel. (2000). *Teaching children to read: An evidence-based assessment of the scientific literature on reading and its implications for reading.* Bethesda, MD: National Institute of Child Health and Human Development.

Office of Juvenile Justice and Delinquency Prevention (1999). *Juvenile mentoring program: 1998 report to congress.* Washington, DC: Author.

Pearson, P. D., & Johnson, D. D. (1978). *Teaching reading comprehension.* New York: Holt, Rinehart and Winston.

Pearson, P. D. & Raphael, T. E. (1999). Toward a more complex view of balance in the literacy curriculum. In W. D. Hammond & T. E. Raphael (Eds.), *Early literacy instruction for the new millennium* (pp. 1–21). Newark, DE: International Reading Association.

Piaget, J. (1963). *The origin of intelligence in children.* New York: Norton.

Pinnell, G. S. (1994). Reading recovery. In A. C. Purves (Ed.), *Encyclopedia of English studies and language arts* (pp. 1012–1014*).* New York: Scholastic.

Pinnell, G. S., Lyons, C., & Jones, N. L. (1996). Response to Hiebert: What difference does reading recovery make? *Educational Researcher, 25,* 23–25.

Rasinski, T., & Padak, N. (2000). *Effective reading strategies: Teaching children who find reading difficult* (2nd ed.). Upper Saddle River, NJ: Merrill.

Rayner, K. & Pollatsek, A. (1994). *The psychology of reading.* Mahwah, NJ: Erlbaum.

Reutzel, D. R., & Cooter, Robert, Jr. (1999). *Balanced reading strategies and practices.*Upper Saddle River, NJ: Merrill.

Robinson, R., & McKenna, M. (1994). Controlled vocabulary. In A. C. Purves (Ed.), *Encyclopedia of English studies and language arts* (pp. 297–298). New York: Scholastic.

Ross, E. (1996). *The workshop approach: A framework for literacy.* Norwood, MA: Christopher-Gordon.

Routman, R. (2000). *Conversations: Strategies for teaching, learning, and evaluating.* Portsmouth, NH: Heinemann.

Ruggiero, V. R. (2000). Bad attitude: Confronting the views that hinder students' learning. *American Educator, 24,* 10–15, 44–48.

Sakiey, E., & Fry, E. (1984). *3000 instant words* (rev. ed.), Providence, RI: Jamestown Press.

Schwartz, R. M., & Raphael, T. E. (1985). Concept of definition: A key to improving students' vocabulary. *The Reading Teacher, 39,* 198–205.

Seefeldt, C. (2001). A room rich in words. *Scholastic Early Childhood Today, 16,* 34–41.

Sinatra, R. (1981). Using visuals to help the second language learner. *The Reading Teacher, 34,* 539–546.

Sinatra, R. (1988). Styles of thinking and literacy proficiency for males disabled in print acquisition. *Reading Psychology, 9,* 33–50.

Sinatra, R. (1989). Verbal/visual processing for males disabled in print acquisition. *Journal of Learning Disabilities, 22,* 69–71.

Sinatra, R. (1991). Integrating whole language with the learning of text structure. *Journal of Reading, 34*, 424–433.

Sinatra, R. (2000). Teaching learners to think, read, and write more effectively in content subjects. *The Clearing House, 73*, 266–273.

Sinatra, R., & Dowd, C. (1991). Using syntactic and semantic clues to learn vocabulary. *Journal of Reading, 35*, 224–229.

Smith, F. (1994). *Understanding reading; A psycholinguistic analysis of reading and learning to read* (5th ed.). Mahwah, NJ: Erlbaum.

Smith, F. (1997). *Reading without nonsense* (3rd ed.). New York: Teachers College Press.

Smith, F. (1999). Why systematic phonics and phonemic awareness instruction constitute an educational hazard. *Language Arts, 77*, 150–155.

Smith, P. (1998). Coming to know one's world: Development as social construction of meaning. In R. Cambell (Ed.), *Facilitating pre-school literacy* (pp. 12–28). Newark, DE: International Reading Association.

Snow, C., Burns, M. S., & Griffin, P (1998). *Preventing reading difficulties in young children.* Washington, DC: National Academy Press.

Spencer, A. (1996). *Morphological theory: An introduction to word structure in generative grammar.* Malden, MA: Blackwell.

Spivey, N. (1994). Constructivism. In A. C. Purves (Ed.), *Encyclopedia of English studies and language arts* (pp. 284–286). New York: Scholastic.

Sprenger, M. (1999). *Learning and memory: The brain in action.* Alexandria, VA: Association for Supervision and Curriculum Development.

Stahl, S. A. (1999). Why innovations come & go: The case of whole language. *Educational Researcher, 28*, 13–22.

Stahl, S. A., Heubach, K., & Cramond, B. (1997). *Fluency-oriented reading instruction: Reading research report no. 79.* Athens, GA: University of Georgia National Reading Research Center.

Stahl, S. A., & Stahl, K. (1998). Everything you wanted to know about phonics (but were afraid to ask). *Reading Research Quarterly, 33*, 338–358.

Stahl, S. C. (1986). The principles of effective vocabulary instruction. *Journal of Reading, 29*, 662–668.

Stauffer, R. G. (1970). *The language-experience approach to the teaching of reading.* New York: Harper & Row.

Strickland, D. (1998). What's basic in beginning reading? Finding common ground. *Educational Leadership, 55*, 6–10.

Swanborn, M.S.L., & deGlopper, K. (1999). Incidental word learning while reading: A meta-analysis. *Review of Educational Research, 69*, 261–285.

Teale, W. (1994). Emergent literacy. In A. C. Purves (Ed.), *Encyclopedia of English studies and language arts* (pp. 424–426). New York: Scholastic.

Teale, W. H. & Sulzby, E. (1986). *Emergent literacy: Writing and reading.* Norwood, NJ: Ablex.

Thorndike, E., & Lorge, I. (1944). *The teacher's word book of 30,000 words.* New York: Teachers College Press.

Tompkins, G. E. (1998). *Language arts: Content and teaching strategies* (4th ed.). Upper Saddle River, NJ: Merrill.

Tompkins, G. E. (2002). Struggling readers and struggling writers, too. *Reading & Writing Quarterly, 18*, 175–193.

Treiman, R. (1983). The structure of spoken syllables: Evidence from novel word games. *Cognition, 15*, 49–74.

Treiman, R. (1985). Onsets and rimes as units of spoken syllables: Evidence from children. *Journal of Experimental Psychology, 39,* 161–181.

Van Allen, R. (1976). *Language experiences in communication.* Boston: Houghton Mifflin.

Vanderuelden, M., & Siegel, L. (1995). Phonological recoding and phoneme awareness in early literacy: A developmental approach. *Reading Research Quarterly, 30,* 854–875.

Verriour, P. (1994). Nonverbal learning. In A. C. Purves, (Ed.), *Encyclopedia of English studies and language arts* (pp. 880–882). New York: Scholastic.

Vygotsky, L. (1978). *Mind in society: The development of higher psychological processes.* Cambridge, MA: Harvard University Press.

Vygotsky, L. (1986). *Thought and language.* Cambridge, MA: MIT Press.

Walker, B. (2000). *Diagnostic teaching of reading* (4th ed.). Upper Saddle River, NJ: Merrill.

Weinberger, N. (1998). The music in our minds. *Educational Leadership, 50,* 36–40.

Wishon, P., Crabtree, K., & Jones, M. (1998). *Curriculum for the primary years: An integrative approach.* Upper Saddle River, NJ: Prentice Hall.

Wylie, R., & Durrell, D. (1970). Teaching vowels through phonograms. *Elementary English, 47,* 787–791.

Yopp, H. K., & Yopp, R. H. (2000). Supporting phonemic awareness development in the classroom. *The Reading Teacher, 54,* 130–143.

Zakaluk, B., & Samuels, S. J. (Eds.). (1988). *Readability: Its past, present, and future.* Newark, DE: International Reading Association.

About the Author

Richard Sinatra is Professor, Director of the Reading Clinic, and Chairman of the Department of Human Services and Counseling at St. John's University, Queens, New York. He has been an educator for over 40 years, serving as an English teacher in the junior-high grades, a third- and fourth-grade teacher, a reading specialist, a district reading coordinator, and university literacy professor. He has authored numerous book chapters and journal articles which have appeared in such publications as *The Reading Teacher, The Journal of Reading, Reading Psychology, The Reading and Writing Quarterly, The Elementary School Journal, Educational Leadership, The Executive Educator, The Journal of Learning Disabilities, The Clearing House*, and *Remedial and Special Education*. His two earlier books were *Using the Right Brain the Language Arts* (co-authored) and *Visual Literacy Connections to Thinking, Reading, and Writing*. He has been a literary consultant to many school districts and has helped them achieve higher performance standards in reading and writing for mainstreamed and special students through all the grade levels. For the past seven years, he has been the Project Director of the Inner City Games CAMP-US Project which provides literacy, computer, cultural, and athletic programs to thousands of housing development children from the five boroughs of New York City. In 1987, he received the College Reading Educator Award given annually by NYS Reading Association, and in the spring of 2000 he received the prestigious St. Vincent DePaul Teacher-Scholar award at St. John's University. In 1972, he received his Ph.D. in Reading Education from Hofstra University.

Index

Boldface page numbers indicate the boldface occurrence of concept words and terms in the text.

ABC center, 121
Abstract representation, **157**
Academy of Orton-Gillingham Practitioners and Educators, 57
Activities of action, **157**
Affix, 14, 15, 16
Ahrems, Margaret, 109, 110
Allington, Richard, 49
Alphabetic principle, **30**-31, 34, 35, 49, 66, 68, 83, 96
  approaches to, 70-78
Alphabetic understanding, 22
Analogy, **66**
  approach, 65-70, 78, 82
Analytic phonics, **60**-61, 83
Arnoff, Mark, 172
Art, 121-122, 142-143
Ashton-Warner, Sylvia, 125
Atwell, Nancy, 48
Authentic, **58**
Automatic word reading, importance of, 101-104

Balanced literacy instruction, **44**-49
Barry, Anita, 12
Basal reader, **39**-40, 43, 45, 101
Benchmark Word Identification Program, 69-70
Blend, 32, 75
Blending, **54**, 65, 66, 67
Bound morpheme, **15**
Breaking the code, 21; *see also* Decoding
"Bridge books," 40

Calkins, Lucy, 88
Capitalization, **95**
Carroll, B., 18, 104, 109, 171
Casual word learning, **180**
Chall, Jeanne, 19, 42, 171
  stage model of, 113-117
Chard, David, 33
Clause, 24

Clay, Marie, 40, 45-46, 117
Cloze, **132**
Cluster story, **133**
Coady, James, 14, 37
Compounding, **16**
Concept-Level Relations Taxonomy, 157, 162, 165-166, 200-213
Concept map, **162**-165
Concept word, **23**
Cone of Experience, **157**
Configuration, **94**, 95, 96
Construction, 116-117
Constructivism, **40**-44, 89
Content word, **20**,
Context clues, 24, 176-178
Context cues, 24
Contraction, 56
Control, issues of, 58
Controlled vocabulary, **39**, 40
Convention, **168**
Core vocabulary, **19**, 37
Cramer, Ronald, 125, 140
Creative spelling, **30**, 41, 76-77, 121; *see also* Invented spelling
Cue, **93**-101
Cue system, **93**-101
Cunningham, Anne, 181
Cursive writing, **136**

Dale, Edgar, 19, 157, 171
Dahl, Karin, 59
Davies, P., 18
Decodable text, **49**
Decoding, 21, 35, 37, 53, 56, 69, 70, 71-72, 81-82, 83, 114
Deep processing, **177**
Deep structure, **6**, 97
Derivation, **16**
Dickson, Shirley, 33
Dipthong, **75**
Discourse, **91**-92
Dolch, Edward, 19
Dowd, Cornelia, 177

Editing, **168**
Elkind, David, 10
Elley, Warwick, 111

Embedded, **93**
Embedded phonics, **58**, 61
Emergent literacy, 11, 40, 41, 43, 76, 77, 78, 113, 117-121
Encoding, **80**, 81
English language learners, 20
Experience language, **154**-158
Explicit phonics, **56**-57, 59

Fabb, Nigel, 16
Familiar word, **18**
Fernald, Grace, 134
Fixate, **102**
Fixation, **102**
Flash cards, 128, 129-130, 137-139
Fluency, 11, 99, 100, 101, 114-115, 123
Fluent, **92**, 99, 102
Fowler, Dorothy, 44
Francis, W. Nelson, 18
Franzen, A. M., 113
Free morpheme, **15**
Fromkin, Victoria, 16
Fry, Edward, 19, 66
Function word, **19**-20, 21

Gallagher, Tanya, 9
Glass-Analysis System for Decoding Only, 71-72
Goodman, Ken, 40
Goodman, Yetta, 40, 119
Grammatical rule, **96**
Grapheme, **29**, 37, 55, 57, 59
Grapheme-phoneme correspondence, **31**, 44, 49, 55, 57, 60, 62, 67, 76, 78, 83
Graphophonic cue system, 53, 56, 58, 93, 96
Graves, Donald, 122
Groff, Patrick, 80

Hall, Mary Ann, 125
Hayes, Donald, 109, 110
High-frequency word, **18**, 20, 21, 22, 37-39, 109, 123-124
Hunsberger, Margaret, 11

Implicit phonics, **57**-58, 60
Incidental phonics, **58**
Incidental word learning, **180**
Inflection, **15**,
Inflectional ending, 14, 15
Instant word, **19**
Instantaneous word recognition, 22,
Intelligent guess strategy, **178**-179
International Reading Association, 38

Invented spelling, 41, **76**-77, 78, 121; *see also* Creative spelling
Irving, Washington, 100

Johnson, Dale, 165
Journal writing, 48-49

Keywords, 69-70
Kinesthetic, 78, **80**
Kinesthetic movement, **135**
Kucera, Henry, 18

Laminack, Lester, 118
Language experience approach, 47, 123, **125**-134, 140
Lindbergh, R., 65
Literature anthology, **43**-44
Literature-based instruction, 40, 41, 42
Lorge, Irving, 18, 38

Macrostructure, **167**
Maldonado-Colon, Elba, 68
Martin, Bill, 57
May, Frank, 152
McIntyre, Ellen, 44
McNeil, John, 177
Mental lexicon, **13**
Mental schema, **3**, 9
Mesmer, Heidi Anne, 49
Metacognitive, **124**
Microstructure, **168**
Milne, A. A., 43, 159
Minilessons, 48
Miscue, **46**, 94
Miscued text, **46**
Moffett, James, 40, 41, 90, 117
Morpheme, **14**-15, 16, 87, 154, 170-172
Morphology, **14**, 170-171
Moustafa, Margaret, 68
Multiple viewpoints, 116

Narrative, **10**
development of, 9-12
National Council of Teachers of English, 40
National Reading Panel, 35, 61, 65, 81, 151
Neural connection, **2**,
New reading word, **22**,

Observation, **157**
Onset, **33**, 67, 68, 69, 70, 71, 72
Open Court Publishing Company, 49
Oral language, 121
vs. book language, 108-110

Orthographic representation, **14**, 29

Paragraph indentation, **95**
Pattern book, **57**
Pattern box, 67-68, 74
Pearson, P. David, 165
Peer conferencing, 41
Perceptual conditioning, **71**
Peripheral vision, **102**
Phoneme, **14**, 31-33, 35, 54, 55, 57, 78, 87
Phonemic awareness, 22, **32**-33, 34-35, 57, 59, 77, 88, 120-121; *see also* Phonological awareness
Phonetic analysis, 21
Phonic element, 49, 55, **57**, 60
Phonics, 21, 22, **34**-35, 37, 44, 53, 73, 78, 82, 88, 94
   advocates of, 42
   appeal of, 54-56
   approaches to, 56-65
   goal of, 56
Phonogram, 49, **65**-70, 74
Phonological awareness, **32**, 65, 75; *see also* Phonemic awareness
Phrase, 24
Piaget, Jean, 3, 4, 40
Pollatsek, Alexander, 102
Practice books, 43
Pragmatic cue system, **93**, 98
Prefix, 14, 44, 56, 70, 172, **173**-176, 215
Prereading, 113-114
Pressley, Michael, 44
Pretend play, **9**
Pretend reading, 120
Print experience extensions, 131-134
Print-rich environment, **120**, 124, 144
Prior knowledge, **90**, 108
Process writing, 41
Punctuation, 91, **95**

Rayner, Keith, 102
Readability, **38**
Readability formula, **38**
Readers-writers workshop, 41
Reading aloud, **110**-112, 120
Reading Clinic, 103
Reading comprehension, 88
Reading readiness, 42, **113**
Reading Recovery, **45**-47
Reading to learn, 115-116
Reading volume, **180**-181
Reading workshop, **47**-49
Representational play, **9**
Representational thought, **4**, 121

Retelling strategy, 123, **141**-146, 157, 159-161
Retold book, **144**, 191-199
Revising, **168**
Rhyme, 33, 57, 60, 65
Richman, Barry, 18
Rime, **34**, 67, 68, 69, 70, 71, 72
Rodman, Robert, 16
Root, 14, 15-16, 44, 56, 70, 172, **173**-176, 216
Ross, Elinor, 48
Routman, Regie, 48
Ruggiero, Vincent, 109
Running record, **46**

Scaffolding, **8**-9, 40, 41
Scharer, Patricia, 59
Seefeldt, Carol, 119
Segment, 32
Semantic cue system, **93**, 97-98
Sentence dissection, 41
Service words, 72
Seuss, Dr., 57, 65
Sight word, **21**, 22, 39
Sight word list, **19**, 21, 37
Situation-dependent spoken language, **5**
Smith, Frank, 5, 6, 10, 31, 40, 42, 54, 90
Social interaction,
   effect on language growth, 8-9, 41, 88-89, 103
Sound-symbol relationship, 21, 49, 53, 68, 70, 76, 77, 83, 94, 95, 96, 101, 123, 124
Sounding out, **21**-22, 93
   visual and auditory components of, 31-37
Spelling pattern, **65**-70, 75, 83
Spelling process, 78-82
Spencer, Andrew, 14
Stage model, **113**
Stahl, Steven, 125, 177
Stanovich, Keith, 181
Stauffer, Russell, 125
Story chart, 128-129
Story map, 142
Strickland, Dorothy, 44
Structural element, 14
Substitution, **54**, 65
Substructure, **92**,
Suffix, 14, 16, 44, 56, 70, 172, **173**-176, 217-218
Surface level, **97**
Surface structure, **7**
Syllable, 56, 70, 171

Syntactic category, **13**
Syntactic class, **13**, 16
Syntactic cue system, **93**, 96-97
Synthetic phonics, **59**-60, 61, 83

Talk,
   forming the foundation of, 5-8
Taxonomy, **165**, 177
Taxonomy of Concept-Level Compre-
   hension, 154
Teachable moment, **58**
Teale, William, 118
Thematic units, 41, 43, 161-165
Thorndike, Edward, 18, 38
Tompkins, Gail, 81
Transaction model, 89
Transfer, 54, 55
Transformation, 97
Transmission model, **89**-90
Treiman, Rebecca, 33
Typographical feature, **96**

Unknown word, **18**
Using the context, **24**, 176-178

VAKT approach, **134**-139
Van Allen, Roach, 125
Venezky, Richard, 31
Verbal symbol, **157**
Visual cue system, **93**, 94-96, 103
Visual information, 90
Visual symbol, **157**
Vocabulary development, 151-184
Vocabulary knowledge, **98**
Vocabulary word, **22**
Vowel pattern, **72**-76
Vygotsky, Lev, 8, 9, 40, 122

Wagner, Betty Jane, 90
Whole language, 40, 41, 42-43, 44, 76,
   117, 140
   advocates of, 58
   phonics in, 58-59
Whole-part-whole instruction, **44**-45,
   60, 89, 101
Whole-word approach, **101**
Word analysis, 21, 53
Word attack skills, 21, 22, 53, 56-59, 82,
   88, 93, 124
Word bank, 132, 139-141
Word challenge exercises, 26-27, 51-52,
   85-86, 105-106, 148-149, 184-185
Word chunk, 100, 102
Word family, 22, **65**-70, 74, 78, 82
Word identification, **53**-83

auditory factors of, 32-34
   visual factors of, 34, 80, 82
Word lists, 18
Word mediation, 21
Word recognition, **56**, 59, 91, 101
   visual, 55
Word structure map, **147**
Word wall, **68**, 120, 123
Words,
   coining new, 13
   controlling those children learn, 37-40
   connection to environment, 2-12
   language of, 17-25
   meaning of, 12
   properties of, 12-17
   use of, 1-2
Writing activities and assignments,
   166-170
Writing workshop, **47**-49
Written language, 87-105
   and fluency, 92-93
   versus oral language, 91-93

Yopp, Hallie Kay, 33
Yopp, Ruth Helen, 33

Zone of proximal development, 8, 9